BATTLE

OF

BRITAIN

COMBAT ARCHIVE

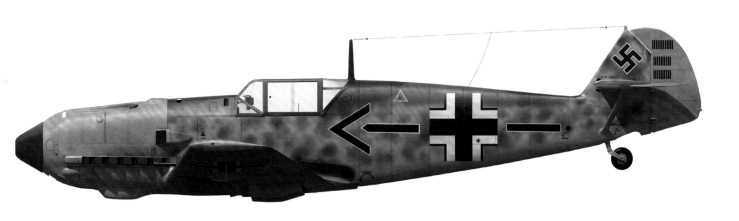

VOLUME
9 SEPTEMBER – 11 SEPTEMBER 1940

Simon W Parry

THE BATTLE OF BRITAIN COMBAT ARCHIVE SERIES

Author: Simon W Parry   simon@wingleader.co.uk

Design/Profiles: Mark Postlethwaite mark@wingleader.co.uk

Illustrator/Profiles: Piotr Forkasiewicz info@peterfor.com

Specialist contributors:
Dave Brocklehurst MBE (RAF pilots)
John Foreman (RAF and Luftwaffe Claims)
Nigel Parker and Milan Krajči (Luftwaffe)
John Vasco (Luftwaffe)
Chris Goss (Luftwaffe)
Andy Saunders
Andy Thomas (RAF)
Johnny Wheeler (601 Squadron)
Andy Long (RAF)
Steve Vizard
Peter Tookey
James Barnes
David Smith
Robin Hill
Peter Nash
Peter Cook
Mark Kirby
Mariusz Łożyński

Photo Credits:
Kent Battle of Britain Museum
ww2images.com
BofB Memorial Trust
Geoff Simpson
Andy Thomas
Chris Goss Archive
Johnny Wheeler
Andy Saunders
Dennis Knight
Ian Simpson
Philippa Wheeler
Ashley Lamb

First Edition
ISBN 978 1 906592813
First published 2022 by
Red Kite
PO Box 223, Walton-on-Thames,
Surrey, KT12 3YQ.
England
Tel. 0116 340 1085
www.wingleader.co.uk

Printed in the UK by SBS Leicester.

The Battle of Britain Combat Archive Series is a totally unique project that sets out to cover every aerial combat that was fought by RAF Fighter Command during the Battle of Britain. The series will run to approximately 15 volumes and will cover the period from 10 July 1940 - 31 October 1940.
The publishers hope to feature as many of The Few as possible during the course of the series so if any readers have photos or information on any airmen involved in the Battle, please do get in touch with the author.

All volumes available directly from the publishers at www.wingleader.co.uk

9 SEPTEMBER

466 RAF fighters fly 68 patrols.   Luftwaffe - 94 bomber and approximately 550 fighter sorties

Weather: Cloudy with some showers at first, clearing in the afternoon.

COMBAT A: Bill Watling of 92 Squadron bales out over Rye

Night operations 8/9 September

The main Luftwaffe effort was targeted on Beckton to the east of London and Battersea Park to the west.

Take off times for the bombers was from 20.00 to 05.10 hrs. 206 tonnes of bombs and 327 BSK incendiary bomb containers, each holding 36 1 kg incendiaries, were dropped.

Luftflotte 2 - 51 bombers and Luftflotte 3 - 132 bombers, 119 of which reported bombing London successfully.

Other targets attacked:

I/KG27;
2 He111s - Liverpool
2 He111s - Bristol
2 He111s - Bournemouth
1 He111 - Swansea
1 He111 - Plymouth
1 He111 - Exmouth
1 He111 - Weymouth

KGr 606;
1 Do17 - Poole
2 Do17s - Thames Estuary
KGr 806;
1 Ju88 - Bournemouth.
III/KG55
1 He111 - Bognor Regis.
Other units;
Waddington, Scampton, Edinburgh

A heavily laden Heinkel 111 heads for England at dusk

Luftwaffe Casualties

5/KG27 **He111P Wn.2839 1G+NN** Crashed on take-off from Brest-Süd for night sortie to Liverpool after colliding with an He111 of Wekusta 2. Ff: Fw Heinz Klempien and Bo: Gefr Kurt Bengeser badly injured and died in Brest Hospital. Gefr Willi Hey slightly injured.

2/KG54 **Ju88A-1** **Wn.4032** **B3+BK** Crashed near Serans, France, during night sortie to London. Ff: Hptm Matthias Briesch, Bf: Ofw Rudolf Zingel, Bo: Fw Günther Ofschonka and Bs: Flg Helmut Kubina all killed.

I/KG54 **Ju88A-1 Wn.7086** Landed near Paris 40% damaged. Crew safe.

Stab LG1 **Ju88A-1 Wn.5093 L1+DA** Crashed and burned out on take-off from Orléans-Bricy. Ff: Ofw Hans Gutt, Bo: Ogefr Werner Mothes, Bf: Fw Herbert Offhaus and Bs: Fw Willi Standtke all killed.

4/LG1 **Ju88A-1 Wn.5106 L1+BM** Landed at Orléans-Bricy 40% damaged. Crew safe.

6/LG1 **Ju88A-1 Wn7078 L1+JP** Crashed and burned out on take-off at Orléans-Bricy for night sortie to London. Ff: Uffz Walter Hetmank, Bo: Uffz Siegfried Bergmann, Bf: Uffz Hans Reissner and Bs: Uffz Alexander Gurski all killed.

RAF Casualty

600 Sqn Blenheim L1111 BQ-N P/O H B L Hough, Sgt E C Barnard, Sgt J Smith - all safe. Lost following R/T failure during night patrol 21.30 hrs. Abandoned at 6,000 feet over Basingstoke after fuel was exhausted. Crashed near Odiham, Hampshire.

COMBAT A

16.40 - 18.00 hrs... attack on London

FROM RAF DUXFORD
11 HURRICANES | 242 SQN

FROM RAF DUXFORD
9 SPITFIRES | 19 SQN

FROM RAF DUXFORD
12 HURRICANES | 310 SQN

FROM RAF NORTHOLT
12 HURRICANES | 229 SQN

FROM RAF HORNCHURCH
12 SPITFIRES | 603 SQN

FROM RAF MIDDLE WALLOP
13 SPITFIRES | 609 SQN

FROM RAF NORTHOLT
12 HURRICANES | 303 SQN

FROM RAF NORTHOLT
12 HURRICANES | 1(RCAF)SQN

FROM RAF CROYDON
12 SPITFIRES | 72 SQN

FROM RAF MIDDLE WALLOP
3 SPITFIRES | 234 SQN

FROM RAF BIGGIN HILL
12 SPITFIRES | 92 SQN

FROM RAF CROYDON
12 HURRICANES | 605 SQN

FROM RAF KENLEY
12 SPITFIRES | 66 SQN

FROM RAF KENLEY
9 HURRICANES | 253 SQN

FROM RAF WESTHAMPNETT
11 SPITFIRES | 602 SQN

FROM RAF TANGMERE
12 HURRICANES | 607 SQN

FROM RAF TANGMERE
11 HURRICANES | 17 SQN

RAF and Luftwaffe forces

358

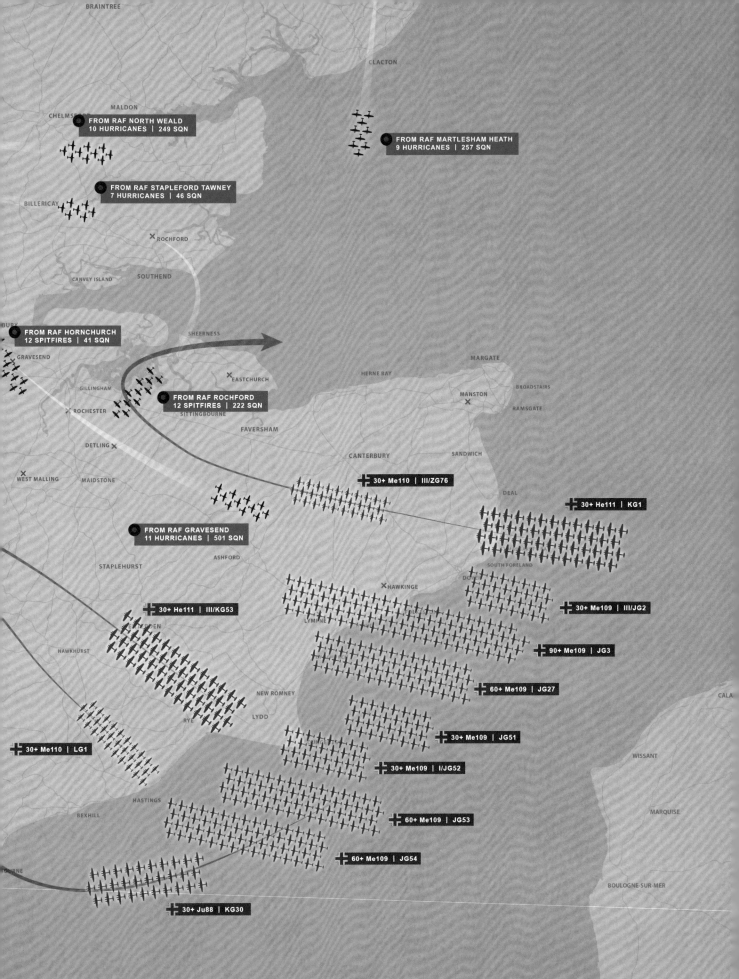

FROM RAF NORTH WEALD
10 HURRICANES | 249 SQN

FROM RAF MARTLESHAM HEATH
9 HURRICANES | 257 SQN

FROM RAF STAPLEFORD TAWNEY
7 HURRICANES | 46 SQN

FROM RAF HORNCHURCH
12 SPITFIRES | 41 SQN

FROM RAF ROCHFORD
12 SPITFIRES | 222 SQN

FROM RAF GRAVESEND
11 HURRICANES | 501 SQN

30+ Me110 | III/ZG76

30+ He111 | KG1

30+ He111 | III/KG53

30+ Me109 | III/JG2

90+ Me109 | JG3

60+ Me109 | JG27

30+ Me110 | LG1

30+ Me109 | JG51

30+ Me109 | I/JG52

60+ Me109 | JG53

60+ Me109 | JG54

30+ Ju88 | KG30

BRAINTREE
CLACTON
MALDON
CHELMSFORD
BILLERICAY
ROCHFORD
CANVEY ISLAND
SOUTHEND
SHEERNESS
MARGATE
BURY
GRAVESEND
EASTCHURCH
HERNE BAY
BROADSTAIRS
MANSTON
GILLINGHAM
RAMSGATE
ROCHESTER
SITTINGBOURNE
FAVERSHAM
DETLING
CANTERBURY
SANDWICH
WEST MALLING
MAIDSTONE
DEAL
SOUTH FORELAND
STAPLEHURST
HAWKINGE
DOVER
ASHFORD
LYMPNE
HAWKHURST
NEW ROMNEY
LYDD
RYE
WISSANT
HASTINGS
BEXHILL
MARQUISE
CALA
BOURNE
BOULOGNE-SUR-MER
ETAPLES

359

A scattering of cloud and bombers

16.40 - 18.00 hrs 9th September 1940

This day's attack did not develop until late afternoon, when the cloud that covered south-eastern England began to clear slightly. Signs that an attack was building were noticed at 16.00 hours when several groups of aircraft were detected over the Channel. Four groups of aircraft each estimated as '30+' were plotted from RDF reports at 16.55 hours crossing the coast on a broad front between North Foreland and Beachy Head. The cloud, which was reported at 7/10ths at 7,000 feet, prevented the Observer Corps identifying and tracking the raids inland over north and east Kent.

Fighter Command reacted early and 11 Group scrambled nine squadrons:

41 Squadron 12 Spitfires up from Hornchurch to patrol Maidstone - TO 16.44 hours.
46 Squadron 7 Hurricanes up from Stapleford Tawney to patrol Rochford - TO 16.45 hours.*
249 Squadron 10 Hurricanes up from North Weald to patrol Maidstone - TO 16.45 hours.*
222 Squadron 12 Spitfires up from Rochford to patrol Maidstone - TO 16.45 hours.
501 Squadron 11 Hurricanes up from Gravesend to patrol Canterbury - TO 16.49 hours.
92 Squadron 12 Spitfires up from Biggin Hill to patrol Canterbury - TO 16.50 hours.
605 Squadron 12 Hurricanes up from Croydon to patrol Maidstone - TO 16.53 hours.
66 Squadron 12 Spitfires up from Kenley to patrol Maidstone - TO 16.55 hours.
257 Squadron 9 Hurricanes up from Martlesham Heath to patrol West Mersea - TO 16.55 hours.*
* Did not engage the enemy.

Another large force was seen on the plotting tables making its way west, along the Channel to Sussex. This raid included the Ju88s of KG30 that had been moved from Luftflotte 5 in Scandinavia to Luftflotte 2. Anticipating an attack designed to outflank 11 Group, the controller requested the support of 10 Group to his west. Support was also requested from 12 Group from the north to help fend off another major attack on London.

Combat was joined between Canterbury and Maidstone by 41 Squadron, then 92 Squadron and 501 Squadron. Cloud not only hindered the Observer Corps, but also the fighter pilots who simply stumbled upon scattered groups of bombers and fighters. 605 Squadron first headed east towards Maidstone, then followed a raid west, past Croydon, to Weybridge and on to Alton in Hampshire. Some sections of 605 Squadron met with the 'Duxford Wing' squadrons. 222 and 66 Squadrons found the enemy over mid Kent. Bombs were scattered randomly over east Kent, centred on Canterbury, and the raid dissipated over the north Kent coast.

Just as the Kent raid ended, the attack from the west developed. At 17.20 hours the main phalanx crossed the coast between Hastings and Beachy Head, heading for an area identified by the RAF as 'Mayfield', which is a picturesque village between the coast and Tunbridge Wells of no military importance.

By now nine more squadrons were in the air and five about to take off:

603 Squadron 12 Spitfires up from Hornchurch to patrol base - TO 16.55 hours.
607 Squadron 12 Hurricanes up from Tangmere to patrol Mayfield - TO 16.55 hours.
602 Squadron 11 Spitfires up from Westhampnett to patrol Mayfield - TO 17.04 hours.
17 Squadron 11 Hurricanes up from Tangmere to patrol base - TO 17.05 hours.*
253 Squadron 9 Hurricanes up from Kenley to patrol Biggin Hill - TO 17.12 hours.
1 (RCAF) Squadron 12 Hurricanes up from Northolt to patrol Guildford - TO 17.29 hours.
303 Squadron 12 Hurricanes up from Northolt to patrol Guildford - TO 17.35 hours.
72 Squadron 12 Spitfires up from Croydon to patrol Biggin Hill - TO 17.35-18.15 hours.
229 Squadron 12 Hurricanes up from Northolt to patrol base - TO 17.40 hours.*

Below: This raid saw the first appearance in the south of the Ju88s of KG30 which had recently moved down from Scandinavia to bolster the attacks on London.

A scattering of cloud and bombers

12 Group 'Duxford Wing':
242 Squadron 11 Hurricanes up from Duxford to patrol North Weald - TO 17.00 hours.
19 Squadron 9 Spitfires up from Fowlmere to patrol North Weald - TO 17.00 hours.
310 Squadron 12 Hurricanes up from Duxford to patrol North Weald - TO 17.05 hours.

10 Group:
609 Squadron 13 Spitfires up from Middle Wallop to patrol Guildford - TO 17.00 hours.*
234 Squadron 3 Spitfires up from Middle Wallop to patrol Brooklands - TO 17.50 hours.*
* Did not engage the enemy.

607 and 602 Squadrons were first to engage in the 'Mayfield area', then the raid swung north west in the general direction of Brooklands and dispersed over Hampshire.
253 Squadron clashed with a formation of Ju88s from KG30 and their Me109 escort as they approached Kenley from the south.

12 Group's 'Duxford Wing' had by now formed up and were near Croydon when they ran into a group of Me110s. A wild and confused combat took place as the eager 'Duxford Wing' hurled itself at the enemy, which was identified as 120 strong. This was the largest force seen this day, and it was only seen by the 'Duxford Wing'. 19 Squadron attempted to execute the plan of holding the Me109s at bay while the Hurricanes attacked the bombers, but were completely overwhelmed. The raid broke up and one element headed south east, the other north east.
The final combats were reported by 72, 303 and 1 (RCAF) Squadrons as they chased after the last of the retiring raiders.
Scattered bombing was reported from all over the southern outskirts of London and from Fulham, Chelsea and Lambeth, closer to the City. The British Wireless Interception 'Y Service' intercepted Luftwaffe radio traffic, which was passed on to Fighter Command later in the evening of September 9th, instructing the leaders of the formations to break off their attacks if strong opposition was met.
The RAF concluded that this large-scale attack on London had been a failure, frustrated by heavy cloud and strong fighter opposition.

Luftwaffe Summary
104 tonnes of bombs dropped

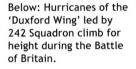

Below: Hurricanes of the 'Duxford Wing' led by 242 Squadron climb for height during the Battle of Britain.

RAF Victory Claims

16.40 - 18.00 hrs 9th September 1940

RAF Victory Claims		Combat A	16.40 - 18.00 hrs
41 Sqn	F/Lt E N Ryder	Me109 destroyed	Maidstone - South London
41 Sqn	P/O G H Bennions	Me109 destroyed	Maidstone - South London
41 Sqn	P/O J G Boyle	He111 destroyed	Maidstone - South London
41 Sqn	P/O E S Lock	Me109 destroyed	Maidstone - South London
41 Sqn	P/O E S Lock	Me109 destroyed	Maidstone - South London
41 Sqn	Sgt E V Darling	Me109 destroyed	Maidstone - South London
41 Sqn	Sgt E V Darling	Me109 destroyed	Maidstone - South London
41 Sqn	Unknown pilot	Me109 damaged	Maidstone - South London
222 Sqn	F/O T A Vigors	Me109 destroyed	Maidstone - South London
222 Sqn	P/O H L Whitbread	Me109 destroyed	Ashford
222 Sqn	P/O J W Broadhurst	Me109 damaged	Maidstone - South London
222 Sqn	Sgt E Scott	Me109 damaged	Maidstone - South London
92 Sqn	S/Ldr P J Sanders	He111 destroyed	south - south east of Biggin Hill
92 Sqn	S/Ldr P J Sanders	Me109 probable	south - south east of Biggin Hill
92 Sqn	F/Lt C B F Kingcombe	Me109 probable	north east of Biggin Hill
66 Sqn	S/Ldr R H A Leigh	He111 destroyed	20 miles north of Brighton
66 Sqn	P/O G H Corbett	Me109 probable	Rye
66 Sqn	P/O A B Watkinson	Me109 damaged	east of the Sussex coast
66 Sqn	P/O A B Watkinson	Me109 damaged	east of the Sussex coast
66 Sqn	P/O H R Allen	He111 destroyed	north of Brighton
66 Sqn	P/O R W Oxspring	Do215 destroyed	Seaford
66 Sqn	P/O I J A Cruickshanks	He111 destroyed	north of Brighton
66 Sqn	Sgt M Cameron	Me109 probable	Dungeness
66 Sqn	Sgt M Cameron	Me109 damaged	Dungeness
607 Sqn	Sgt P A Burnell-Phillips	Do17 destroyed	Mayfield
603 Sqn	P/O J S Morton	He111 damaged	10 miles north of Ford
603 Sqn	P/O McPhail	He111 damaged	

Below: 66 Squadron C/O Rupert Leigh claimed a Heinkel destroyed in this Spitfire R6800 during this combat.

Above: Archie McKellar of 605 Squadron was the top scorer in this encounter with four enemy aircraft claimed as destroyed.

RAF Victory Claims		Combat A	16.40 - 18.00 hrs
602 Sqn	S/Ldr A V R Johnstone	Do17 destroyed	20 miles north of Mayfield
602 Sqn	P/O A McL Lyall	- shared -	
602 Sqn	F/Lt P C Webb	Ju88 destroyed	Mayfield
602 Sqn	F/Lt P C Webb	Ju88 damaged	Mayfield
602 Sqn	P/O A McL Lyall	Me109 destroyed	20 miles north of Mayfield
602 Sqn	Sgt B E P Whall	Do17 destroyed	south of Mayfield
602 Sqn	Sgt J Proctor	Do17 probable	20 miles north of Mayfield
602 Sqn	Sgt A McDowall	Me109 destroyed	south of Mayfield
253 Squadron		4 Ju88s destroyed	Brooklands - Leatherhead
605 Sqn	F/Lt A A McKellar	Me109 destroyed	Brooklands area
605 Sqn	F/Lt A A McKellar	He111 destroyed	Brooklands area
605 Sqn	F/Lt A A McKellar	He111 destroyed	Brooklands area
605 Sqn	F/Lt A A McKellar	He111 destroyed	Brooklands area
605 Sqn	P/O C F Currant	Me109 destroyed	Brooklands area
Hurricane LE-F 242 Sqn		- shared -	
605 Sqn	P/O J Humphreys	He111 probable	Farnborough
605 Sqn	Sgt E W Wright	Me110 destroyed	Brooklands
605 Sqn	P/O C F Currant	- shared -	
19 Sqn	S/Lt A G Blake	He111 destroyed	London
19 Sqn	F/Lt W G Clouston	Me109 destroyed	London
19 Sqn	F/Lt W G Clouston	Me109 damaged	London
19 Sqn	F/O F N Brinsden	He111 probable	south of The Thames estuary
unknown fighter		- shared -	
19 Sqn	F/O F N Brinsden	He111 probable	south of The Thames estuary
19 Sqn	P/O A F Vokes	Do215 damaged	north of London
19 Sqn	P/O W Cunningham	Me109 destroyed	London
19 Sqn	P/O W J Lawson	Me110 destroyed	south of The Thames estuary
19 Sqn	F/Sgt H Steere	Me110 probable	south east London
19 Sqn	Sgt D S G R Cox	Me109 destroyed	south east London
242 Sqn	S/Ldr D R S Bader	Do17 destroyed	London, south of The Thames
242 Sqn	F/Lt G S ff Powell-Shedden	Do215 destroyed	south west of London
242 Sqn	F/Lt G E Ball	Me109 destroyed	south of The Thames
242 Sqn	P/O W L McKnight	Me109 destroyed	London, south of The Thames
242 Sqn	P/O W L McKnight	Me109 destroyed	London, south of The Thames
242 Sqn	P/O J B Latta	Me109 destroyed	London, south of The Thames
242 Sqn	P/O C R Bush	Me110 destroyed	London, south of The Thames
242 Sqn	P/O H N Tamblyn	Me110 destroyed	London, south of The Thames
242 Sqn	P/O H N Tamblyn	Me110 destroyed	London, south of The Thames
242 Sqn	Sgt R H Lonsdale	Do215 destroyed	south west suburbs of London
242 Sqn	Sgt E Richardson	Do215 destroyed	south of The Thames
310 Sqn	F/Lt G L Sinclair	Do17 destroyed	south west London
310 Sqn	P/O S Fejfar	Me110 destroyed	south west London
310 Sqn	P/O V Bergman	Me110 destroyed	south west London
310 Sqn	P/O S Zimprich	Me110 damaged	south west London
310 Sqn	P/O S Zimprich	Do17 destroyed	south west London
310 Sqn	A-F/Lt F Rypl	Me109 probable	south west London
310 Sqn	Sgt J Rechka	Me110 probable	south west London
310 Sqn	Sgt J Hubacek	Me110 probable	south west London
72 Sqn	P/O R D Elliott	Me110 destroyed	Lewis
303 Sqn	F/Lt J A Kent	Me110 destroyed	south of Beachy Head
303 Sqn	F/Lt J A Kent	Ju88 damaged	Channel
303 Sqn	P/O J Zumbach	Me109 destroyed	Beachy Head
303 Sqn	P/O J Zumbach	Me109 probable	Beachy Head
303 Sqn	Sgt J Frantisek	He111 destroyed	Beachy Head
303 Sqn	Sgt J Frantisek	Me109 destroyed	Horsham
1(RCAF) Sqn	S/Ldr E A McNab	Me109 damaged	south east of Guildford
1(RCAF) Sqn	F/O O J Peterson	Me109 destroyed	south east of Guildford
1(RCAF) Sqn	F/O P W Lochnan	Me109 damaged	south east of Guildford

Luftwaffe Victory Claims

16.40 - 18.00 hrs 9th September 1940

Luftwaffe Victory Claims	Combat A	16.40 - 18.00 hrs	
Stab III/JG2	Maj Dr Erich Mix	Hurricane	
St JG3	Hptm Günther Lützow	Hurricane	
3/JG3	Lt Eberhard Bock	Morane	
3/JG3	Lt Eberhard Bock	Morane	
4/JG3	Ofw August-Wilhelm Otto Müller	Hurricane	
4/JG3	Oblt Werner Voigt	Hurricane u/c	
6/JG3	Oblt Erich Woitke	Spitfire	Staplehurst
6/JG3	Oblt Erich Woitke	Spitfire	Staplehurst
8/JG3	Oblt Wilhelm Stange	Hurricane	
Stab III/JG26	Oblt Gerhard Schöpfel	Spitfire	Thames Estuary
Stab III/JG26	Oblt Gerhard Schöpfel	Spitfire	Thames Estuary
Stab III/JG26	Oblt Gerhard Schöpfel	Spitfire	Thames Estuary
8/JG26	Lt Hermann Ripke	Spitfire	Thames Estuary
1/JG27	Oblt Werner Ahrens	Hurricane	London
1/JG27	Oblt Karl-Wolfgang Redlich	Hurricane	London
8/JG27	Oblt Erbo Graf v Kageneck	Spitfire	Rochford
Stab/JG51	Maj Werner Mölders	Spitfire	London
1/JG51	Fw Oskar-Heinz Bär	Hurricane	
1/JG51	Oblt Hermann-Friedrich Joppien	Hurricane	
1/JG51	Oblt Hermann-Friedrich Joppien	Hurricane	
2/JG51	Oblt Viktor Mölders	Spitfire u/c	
2/JG51	Hptm Ernst Wiggers	Spitfire u/c	
1/JG52	Ofw Oskar Strack	Spitfire	eastern suburbs of London
Stab I/JG53	Hptm Hans-Karl Mayer	Hurricane	
1/JG53	Fw Herbert Tzschoppe	Hurricane	London
9/JG53	Oblt Jakob Stoll	Spitfire	north west of Calais
9/JG53	Uffz Kurt Sauer	Spitfire	
9/JG53	Lt Erich Schmidt	Spitfire	London
9/JG53	Oblt Jakob Stoll	Spitfire	
4/JG54	Ofw Karl Hier	Spitfire u/c	
5/JG54	Oblt Joachim Schypek	Spitfire	10k south east of Ramsgate
9/JG54	Uffz Karl-Heinz Kempf	Spitfire	
9/JG54	Lt Hans-Ekkehard Bob	Spitfire u/c	Tunbridge Wells

Below left: Joachim Schypek of 5/JG54 takes a nap in the summer sunshine between operational sorties.

Below: Erich Woitke in the cockpit of hs 6/JG3 Me109 in September 1940. Note how the yellow nose extends all the way back to the windshield. Woitke claimed two Spitfires in this combat.

222 SQUADRON OPERATIONS RECORD BOOK

13.45 hrs. Squadron left for forward base at Rochford.

16.45 hrs. During the afternoon the squadron were ordered off on patrol and at 27,000 feet encountered a formation of fighter aircraft. P/O Whitbread destroyed one Me109 and the pilot was seen to bale out. A further Me109 was shot down by P/O Vigors, who himself force landed at Dartford. P/O Broadhurst and Sgt Scott damaged two more Me109s and the former, having a large portion of the tail of his aircraft shot away, successfully landed at Rochford.

Weather overcast - cloudy towards evening.

COMBAT REPORT:
F/O T A Vigors - A Flight, 222 Squadron

The squadron dived to attack a large formation of bombers and fighters. On seeing a formation of Me109s above the rest, I climbed and dived on them from the rear. I opened fire at 150 yards and fired a six-seconds burst, breaking away at 30 yards. Just before I broke away, I saw smoke and flames coming from the enemy aircraft's engine. As I broke away, an Me109 dived out of the sun at me and put my machine out of action.

COMBAT REPORT:
Sgt E Scott - A Flight, 222 Squadron

I was flying line astern with my section which dived on a formation of 15 bombers, the type of which I am unable to state for certain. On the tail of the bombers were 2 Me109s, one slightly to port and one slightly to starboard. I commenced a beam to astern attack, opening fire at 300 yards approximately. He went into a steep dive and I followed him down, still firing at him. I saw my fire entering the fuselage of the Me109. The enemy aircraft appeared to quiver for a second or two, then rolled on its back and disappeared through the clouds. I followed him, but lost him because my windscreen frosted up and for at least a couple of minutes I was unable to see ahead or behind.

On finding my position, I estimate this engagement to have taken place south-west of Kenley.

 I was returning to base after my aircraft had been damaged by a cannon shell, when I saw an Me110 travelling very fast in a south-east direction. I chased it and fired a number of short bursts at it. The port engine was emitting clouds of brownish smoke and the speed of the enemy aircraft dropped considerably, when my ammunition ran out. When landed, I found that only four guns had been firing.

P/O J W Broadhurst - B Flight, 222 Squadron **"**

COMBAT REPORT:
P/O H L Whitbread - B Flight, 222 Squadron

While on patrol over Kent with 222 Squadron, we sighted a formation of enemy bombers flying west at 20,000 feet above cloud. It had an escort of Me109 fighters flying behind and above at 26,000 feet, and also another formation of fighters flying to one side, at the same height as the bomber formation. The fighters were engaged. I had a combat with an Me109. A burst of fire of roughly 4 seconds from my guns appeared to shoot off the starboard aileron, when the Me109 went into a spin. It continued to spin downwards through cloud layer, when it disappeared from view. My flight leader states that he observed the Me109 spinning downwards and also the baling-out of the pilot.

Contemporary Accounts various squadrons

16.40 - 18.00 hrs 9th September 1940

41 SQUADRON OPERATIONS RECORD BOOK

16.44 hrs. Twelve A/C ordered to patrol Maidstone and south of London. Sighted large formation of enemy A/C and engaged them. Enemy casualties, 1 He111 destroyed and 1 damaged. 7 Me109s destroyed and 1 damaged. Our casualties NIL.

Author's Note: No detailed reports from 41 Squadron of this combat have been found.

46 SQUADRON OPERATIONS RECORD BOOK

A single patrol was carried out by the squadron, working with 249 Squadron over Rochford. No enemy aircraft were seen.

501 SQUADRON OPERATIONS RECORD BOOK

The squadron (11 aircraft) took off at 16.45 hours to patrol Canterbury at 25,000 feet. Red 1 who had lost the rest of the squadron saw a formation of enemy bombers near Canterbury. Flight Lieutenant Gibson attacked one of the enemy aircraft in formation without result. The squadron landed at 18.08 hrs. Ten aircraft were again sent off to patrol Hawkinge at 19.20 hours in company with 72 Squadron but landed at 20.00 hours without making interception. The squadron was released at 20.00 hours.

257 SQUADRON OPERATIONS RECORD BOOK

'A' Flight patrolled Felixstowe at 15,000 ft from 14.21 for nearly an hour. At 16.55 the whole squadron patrolled West Mersea for an hour and a half.

Below: A 41 Squadron Spitfire returns from a combat at the height of the Battle. With the dogfights sometimes literally taking place above the ground crews' heads, they all wear steel helmets as they prepare to refuel and rearm the aircraft as quickly as possible.

92 SQUADRON INTELLIGENCE REPORT

Twelve aircraft of 92 Squadron at Biggin Hill were ordered to patrol Canterbury at 16.50 hours at 26,000 feet.

The squadron got split up and the first to attack seems to be F/Lt Kingcombe who first saw a large formation of enemy bombers being attacked by a squadron of Spitfires. See pilot's Combat Report.

The bomber formation was now out of sight of the fighter formation, S/Ldr Sanders saw Green Section behind him being attacked by Me109s. See pilot's Combat Report.

Weather - clouds from 3 to 10,000 feet. No cine gun carried. R/T was OK.

Take off Biggin Hill 16.30 hours. Landed Biggin Hill 18.15 hours. 10 aircraft landed Biggin Hill.

1 aircraft crashed at Rye - P/O Saunders baled out wounded in leg by shrapnel.

1 aircraft destroyed - P/O Watling baled out burned in face and hands.

Left: 92 Squadron was badly bounced in this encounter. This is the damaged windscreen of Alan Wright's Spitfire after the combat.

COMBAT REPORT:
F/Lt C B F Kingcombe - Red 1, A Flight, 92 Squadron

I lost the squadron while proceeding to our objective, but by following the vectors I heard, I saw a large formation of enemy bombers. They were already being attacked by a squadron of Spitfires, so I climbed up to 12 yellow-nosed 109s which were circling in line astern above and to the left of the bomber formation. I joined in on the open formation and gave the last machine a short burst with slight deflection using normal sighting.

He dived away from the formation with smoke coming back. The remainder turned on me and I dived away, climbed back and gave another a very short burst with no apparent effect. They all attacked me again, so I dived into a cloud and returned to base as my oxygen supply was exhausted. By the time I dived into the cloud, the bomber formation was out of sight of the fighter formation.

COMBAT REPORT:
S/Ldr P J Sanders - Ganic Leader, 92 Squadron

While patrolling over Dungeness at 26,000 feet I heard a warning of snappers and turned sharply to the left. I saw that Green Section behind me had been attacked and I got a short burst at one Me109 as it broke away from them in a left-hand turn. I could not observe the effect of my fire as my turn was too tight and I spun out of it.

Blue 2 rejoined me and on instructions from Rastus we returned to base. I was told there were bandits at 15,000 feet. At about 13,000 feet I encountered a formation of He111s in close vic about 10 miles south-south-east of Biggin Hill heading north. I attacked the left-hand aircraft from dead ahead firing about a 4 second burst closing to about 100 yards. I broke away upwards and turned right and saw my target had slid out of the formation and appeared to be going down on left hand turn.

Immediately afterwards I saw an aircraft with a yellow nose and a yellow patch on the front of the fuselage. This turned out to be an Me109. We circled around each other a few times, and I got in a deflection shot by turning inside it. Immediately after I fired, it half-rolled and dived for cloud, black smoke only came out behind it. I followed and I fired several short bursts at about 200 yards diving very fast. It entered cloud at about 8,000 feet and I never saw it again.

66 SQUADRON INTELLIGENCE REPORT

12 a/c (Spitfires) of 66 Squadron left Kenley at 16.55 hours, having been ordered to patrol Maidstone. Orbiting above cloud at about 22,000 feet they sighted a formation of enemy bombers proceeding north-west about 4,000 feet below. At first they saw no trace of enemy fighters, above and gave the warning. The squadron dived in pairs as prearranged for thick cloud at about 6,000 feet.

Sgt M Cameron (Blue 4) lost contact with the formation during these manoeuvres, and suddenly saw three Me109s right in front of him about 30 yards away. He had three short bursts at the nearest at extremely short range and saw a considerable amount of black smoke come back. He broke away and dived almost vertically onto another Me109 into which he fired two bursts, and saw pieces of the e/a breaking off. Hearing a sudden explosion behind him he dived steeply through the cloud, and having used up his ammunition he returned to base landing at 17.55 hours.

On arriving below cloud the C.O. called up on the R.T. for the squadron to reform, but not everyone succeeded in making contact.

F/Lt Gillies (Green 1) could not find the squadron. He saw a British pilot bale out, and he circled round him till he was down to 1,000 feet and saw him land west of Tunbridge Wells. He then climbed to 15,000 feet in an endeavour to find a friendly fighter formation, when an Me109 passed him in a dive, he turned on its tail and chased it, but its speed was too great for him to catch up. He climbed again but could not locate anyone and hearing the order to pancake he returned to base.

P/O Mather (Red 1) also failed to re-contact the squadron. On one occasion he saw fighting overhead but it was too high to take action.

P/O Bodie (Red 2) saw no one when the C.O. called up from beneath the cloud. Runik told him of bandits from 15,000 feet upwards so he climbed to 23,000 feet and saw enemy fighters 3,000 feet below. He attacked and on pulling out ½ mile away at 15,000 feet he saw one crash in a field. He has no idea of the exact position and on looking round he saw another fight going on; uncertain whether or not he was responsible he makes no claim. Having exhausted his ammunition, he returned to base.

P/O G H Corbett (Blue 3) broke from line astern in a steep left-hand turn when the danger signal was given, and he saw an e/a coming up in a climbing turn in front and below him. For an account of his further actions see Pilot's Combat Report attached. He attacked an Me109, and broke off only when it seemed extremely likely to crash, but later he was himself shot up and baled out landing near Cowden.

P/O A B Watkinson (Green 3) also got separated, but in subsequent actions succeeded in damaging two Me109s. For story see Combat Report.

P/O R W Oxspring (Green 4), another who was left on his own, cruised around looking for suitable e/a to attack. He saw several other bomber formations each with fighter escort, all too large to risk attack with a single aircraft. But in the neighbourhood of Seaford he saw a Do215 returning home on its own. He delivered three attacks; after the last both engines took fire, and the e/a which had hitherto been diving slowly, went into a steep dive into the clouds at 8,000 feet. As he then saw an Me109 trying to get on his tail, and as he had no ammunition left he broke off and dived into cloud and returned to base.

Four pilots, **P/O H R Allen** (Blue 2), **P/O I J A Cruickshanks** (Red 3), **Sgt Forrest** (Green 2) and **Sgt Hunt** (Red 4) succeeded in contacting the C.O. They started to climb again and on getting up to 8,000 feet they saw another large formation of e/a flying south with one He111 well away on the port side just above the clouds at approximately 6,000 feet. The C.O. (**Squadron Leader R H A Leigh**, Blue 1) delivered three attacks on this solitary plane, before breaking off as it entered the cloud. Blue 2 took the attack up and was followed by Red 3. The plane crashed in a ploughed field near the east Sussex coast; three men climbed out and were arrested by soldiers who ran up. Meanwhile Sgt Forrest (Green 2) had noticed another He111 straggler at 7,000 feet which he attacked on his own. He gave it two bursts of 3 seconds each at 300 yards and observed his tracer entering the port engine. But no effect on e/a was apparent and he lost it in cloud. He was then unable to re-contact the others and he landed at Tangmere Satellite to re-fuel and obtain his bearings. Sgt Hunt followed the others into the attack, but had no need to attack himself. They then received the order to pancake and returned to base. 10 a/c landed at Kenley between 17.55 - 18.35, and Sgt Forrest landed there at 18.45 after refuelling.

Our casualties: One aircraft Category 3. P/O G H Corbett slightly injured - seven days sick leave.

COMBAT REPORT:
P/O R W Oxspring - Green 4, B Flight, 66 Squadron

One Dornier 215 sighted 18.00 hours. Black or dark green upper wing surfaces with usual black crosses and swastika. No evasive action taken before attack. Three astern attacks delivered, one being from well above and following into the astern position using deflection. In the third attack which consisted of a very long burst I must have been almost exactly 250 yds as my tracer bullets could be seen converging into the E/A. The first attack resulted in the port engine smoking, on the second I hoped to hit the pilot in my attack from above but there was no apparent result. The third attack resulted in both engines taking fire.

No return fire was experienced by me at any time i.e. I did not see any.

The latter end of the first attack resulted in the E/A diving shallowly on his original course of south, but fast toward cloud, and continuing until practically the end of the third attack when engines fired and it dived almost vertically into cloud.

Throughout I had a feeling that E/A was a decoy but before and between attacks I could see no sign of other aircraft until after the third attack when I found an Me109 trying to get behind my tail. Having no ammunition left I dived into cloud.

Eight/tenths large cumulous cloud of which the top was approx 8,000 ft and bottom about 4,500 to 5,000 ft spreading to the ground further east. I commenced each attack with the sun behind me. Sun was apparently due west.

COMBAT REPORT:
P/O H R Allen - Blue 2, B Flight, 66 Squadron

He111 sighted 17.45, 9-9-40, 5,000 ft flying east. Fibus Leader attacked and I followed (Blue 2). Enemy had dark camouflage. I opened with an astern attack slightly from above. Enemy then made for cloud, but I intercepted using emergency boost. My tracer indicated direct hits on the engines. After the second attack (from abeam) I noticed one engine stopped and after further attacks, one from very close range, both engines were stopped. I then flew across enemy's path indicating that he should pancake immediately and, as he seemed to take an unnecessarily long while for this, I gave him another burst. He glided down and crashed in a ploughed field surrounded by woods and 3 men got out. I circled to make sure they did not escape and waited until the Army arrived. This took about 10 minutes. When I saw the crew was apprehended I flew away making derisive signs as I went.

2/10 cloud at 5,000 ft Hazy. Sun behind me - I attacked from out of sun. Took-off 16.55. Landed 18.25.

Below: 'Dizzy' Allen's Heinkel was actually a Junkers Ju88, probably this one, 4D+AA of Stab/KG30 which force landed amongst the trees at Nuthurst in Sussex.

9 SEPTEMBER

Below: 66 Squadron C/O Rupert Leigh climbs aboard his Spitfire LZ-N R6800, which is widely reported to have had a red spinner. He was flying this aircraft during the combat written about on the opposite page. Note the chocks have been bolted together to make removal quicker.

COMBAT REPORT:
S/Ldr R H A Leigh - Blue 1, B Flight, 66 Squadron

I was leading 66 Squadron which was ordered up at 16.55 hours from Kenley to intercept an enemy raid. We were first ordered to orbit Maidstone district. Orbiting above cloud at about 22,000 feet it was impossible to give an exact position when about 17.30 we sighted a formation of enemy bombers proceeding north-west about 4,000 feet below. At first we saw no trace of enemy fighters and were getting into position to attack when enemy fighters attacked us. We broke formation in pairs as prearranged. Eventually I tried to reform the squadron below cloud and called up on the R/T ordering the squadron to reform. Only four were able to contact me. We started to climb again and on getting up to 8,000 feet we saw another large formation of enemy a/c flying south with one He111 well away on the port side just above the clouds at approximately 6,000 feet. I was flying as Blue 1 and led the formation into attack and myself delivered 2 - 3 deflection attacks from both port and starboard, flying across the tail of e/a. I broke off as the e/a dived into cloud and did not actually see it crash. But Blue 2 and 3 followed it through, continued the attack and saw it crash. I then returned to base and landed at 18.25 hours.

Contemporary Accounts 66 Sqn

16.40 - 18.00 hrs 9th September 1940

COMBAT REPORT:

P/O A B Watkinson - Green 3, B Flight, 66 Squadron

When E/A was sighted the squadron went into line astern for attack on bombers when several E/A fighters dived from above which made me turn away and take evasive action with three Me109s on my tail. After circling around a bit one fighter and then another was lost. The third dived vertically towards the cloud layer. At that time I was able to give two bursts of one second each with no effect. The E/A then pulled out of his dive and I was able to do a head-on attack with one two second burst which made black smoke pour out of the E/As engine. He then dived below cloud level and headed out to sea and I broke off engagement. I climbed up through the cloud layers again and just as I got above a large formation of enemy bombers were passing about 100 feet above me going towards the coast so I pulled the nose up and gave a two second burst into one of the E/A which did not have any visible effect. Then I saw one Me109 pass under me about 200 feet below so I dived on him and gave one long burst until ammunition was finished and I observed black smoke coming from E/A engine and he dived into the cloud heading towards the coast behind the bombers and below them. I then requested homing and returned to base.

COMBAT REPORT:

Sgt M Cameron - Blue 4, B Flight, 66 Squadron

At 16.55 hrs 66 Squadron were ordered to patrol Maidstone at 15,000 ft. When airborne we were vectored onto enemy and climbed to 25,000 ft. We intercepted the enemy bombers and manoeuvred into position for attack. I as Blue 4 of our formation. Before we could carry out our attack on the enemy bombers the danger signal was given and I observed a considerable number of Me109s in our close vicinity. During the violent manoeuvres which followed I lost touch with our formation but saw 3 Me109s about 30 yds in front to me. I had 3 bursts on one E/A and saw a considerable amount of black smoke come back. I broke away and dived almost vertically onto another Me109 giving him 2 bursts and allowing considerable deflection. I saw pieces of the E/A flying off and then heard an explosion in my vicinity and thinking that someone was firing at me I dived away steeply turning all the time to about 1,000 ft and returned to base. I landed at 17.55 hrs.

Weather: above 6,000 ft cloudless vis. VG.   A layer of broken strato cu. from 4,000-6,000 ft. 7/10 Vis. underneath cloud layer about 4 miles.

COMBAT REPORT:

P/O G H Corbett - Blue 3, B Flight, 66 Squadron

Took off from Kenley 16.55 hours. When the squadron received the 'danger' signal I broke from line astern in a steep left-hand turn and saw an e/a coming up in a climbing turn in front and below me. I dived and delivered a quarter attack with one two-second burst. He immediately flick-rolled and went down in a steep dive towards the coast with white vapour issuing from fuselage. I followed him down and delivered two more short bursts from astern and slightly to port. He made no further evasive tactics but continued his dive. I broke off the attack at 6,000 feet thinking I was getting too low. I climbed back to approximately 18,000 feet heading towards London in an endeavour to contact my squadron. As I was climbing I sighted a very large formation of enemy bombers and fighters above and to the west of me proceeding towards London. I endeavoured to get into a position to attack the rear bombers but was myself attacked by three enemy fighters. I turned towards them and a tail-chase resulted. Suddenly while in a steep turn I felt an explosion under the seat and the cockpit filled with smoke. At the same time the control column jumped out of my hand and jammed in the far left-hand corner of the cockpit. My machine went into a tight spiral dive to the left and I abandoned aircraft at about 12,000 feet and landed near Cowden, Kent at 18.05 hours.

COMBAT REPORT:

P/O I J A Cruickshanks - Red 3, A Flight, 66 Squadron

I was flying No. 3 in line astern in a formation of 6 aircraft of my squadron which had reformed below a large enemy formation which we had just attacked.

We started to climb up again, on no particular course when we sighted one enemy bomber flying well to the port side of a larger formation. This E/A was just above the clouds approximately 6,000 ft when the first A/C in our formation attacked. E/A dived through the clouds as No. 2 attacked it and I waited for it to reappear below cloud.

As it came below the cloud I saw that its engines had stopped so I only gave a short burst, but it then began to turn to port and as there was no sign of fire I suspected 'foxing' so as it turned I turned inside it, and fired off the rest of my rounds into the engines and fore parts of E/A.

It made a crash landing in a ploughed field and I observed three men get out apparently uninjured. During my attacks I noticed no return fire from E/A.

Took off 16.55 Landed 18.25. Cloud 3/10 at 5,000 ft misty. Sun had no effect as my attack was made below cloud and in thick mist.

Right: Ian Cruickshanks's bomber was probably this one, another KG30 Ju88, 4D+KK which came down at Barcombe in East Sussex. The crew set fire to the aircraft before surrendering.

Contemporary Accounts 253 Sqn

16.40 - 18.00 hrs 9th September 1940

253 SQUADRON INTELLIGENCE REPORT

9 Hurricanes left Kenley 17.12 hours to patrol base and Biggin Hill below cloud. At 17.40 hours one Hurricane landed owing to the panel on side of cockpit breaking open. The squadron patrolled line at 6,000 feet and raiders approaching from the east at 15,000 consisting of approximately 17 bombers and heavy fighter escort, were sighted by squadron through gap in the clouds. The squadron, which was then ordered to engage the enemy, turned west climbing to 14,000 feet and when nearly in position were told to vector 150° and intercept a bigger raid coming in from the east, and a formation of 34 Ju88s at 15,000 feet escorted by a large number of fighters were sighted 5 miles on the starboard bow. Squadron turned west and climbing to 16,000 feet then turning towards bombers delivered a diving beam attack on to the bombers starboard bow in sections line astern opening fire at about 450 yards closing to 50 yards. The attack was apparently successful as the bombers broke formation and turned south jettisoning their bombs. It was observed that as the squadron were about to attack, the bombers signalled to their fighters by firing a red star cartridge and the second attack was prevented by enemy fighters engaging the squadron until the bombers were out of range. No individual claims are made but several pilots agree that 5 Ju88s broke off and dived away as though destroyed.

Observer Corps confirm that five enemy aircraft crashed at the time of the battle in the vicinity of the combat.

Visibility was good with no cloud above 7,000 feet.

7 Hurricanes landed Kenley 18.30 hours.

Our casualties -	1 Hurricane	Cat.1.
	1 Hurricane	Cat.2.
Enemy casualties -	5 Ju88s destroyed overland.	

G Henry P/O
Squadron Intelligence Officer,
No.253 Squadron, Kenley.

Note:
With reference to the above enemy losses, no individual claims are made but the number destroyed is claimed on behalf of the squadron.

(signed)

Squadron Leader, Commanding,
No.253 Squadron, R.A.F. Kenley

Below: 253 Squadron was one of the few that correctly identified Ju88s being involved and may well have helped bring this one down which force landed in the shallow waters of Pagham Harbour. It is 4D+AD of Stab III/KG30. The A was in blue with a white outline (staffel colour) and the diving eagle emblem had a yellow background (gruppe colour).

603 SQUADRON INTELLIGENCE REPORT

16.55-18.30 hours.

12 aircraft of 603 Squadron, when 10 miles north of Ford at 26,000 feet, saw about 25 Me109s in vics of 3 at 25,000 feet and below them about 15 He111s in vics of 3, line astern, heading north. Some of the Me109s had yellow noses, others white noses. The squadron attacked the bombers out of the sun and turned them round.

Right: The Germans thoughtfully placed the Ju88's swastika on an easily removable panel, ideal for souvenir hunters!

Contemporary Accounts 607 Sqn

16.40 - 18.00 hrs 9th September 1940

607 SQUADRON INTELLIGENCE REPORT

16.55 - 18.10 hrs. Combat took place in Mayfield area at about 17.00 hrs (S/Ldr Vick leading). When squadron were at 17,000 ft 60/70 E/A possibly Ju88s and Do17s were seen flying north in several formations of 5 in Vic. Squadron turned towards formation of bombers when escorting fighters, about 40/50 Me109s, were seen to both sides and astern of bombers at about 19,000 ft. Blue section attacked bombers from underneath with Green Section doing rear-guard action, and bombers being now too far ahead, S/Ldr Vick ordered Red and Yellow Sections to attack fighters.

Own losses: Personnel - P/O Parnall, P/O Lenahan, P/O Drake missing. Sgt Burnell-Phillips, Sgt Spyer slightly wounded.

1 Hurricane Cat 3 - 3 Hurricanes missing.

COMBAT REPORT:
Sgt P A Burnell-Phillips - Yellow 2, A Flight, 607 Squadron

As Yellow 2 accompanying Yellow 1 (F/O Foster) I made a quarter attack from below. 1st attack unsuccessful, I made a 2nd attack from approx 5,000 ft above, diving under fighter escort from out of sun. This time attack was successful. The e/a a Dornier broke away with both motors on fire. I continued to attack firing approx 1,500 rounds. At this point I was myself attacked by 3 Me109s. A burst in my oil tank forced me to land near Northolt* with a seized engine. The e/a also landed approx 4 miles away. This was confirmed by local Police.

Author's note: Actually near Sevenoaks.

Below: 607 Squadron had five Hurricanes shot down in this encounter leading to the deaths of three of the pilots. George Drake was one of the pilots killed, flying this Hurricane P2728, seen here probably at Gosport before receiving its 607 Squadron AF codes.

602 SQUADRON INTELLIGENCE REPORT

Combat took place 20 miles north of Mayfield, 17.40 hours 9.9.40. 602 Squadron, 11 Spitfires took off from Westhampnett 17.04 hours, ordered to patrol Mayfield at 15,000 feet. When orbiting Mayfield at 18,000 feet squadron sighted 30/40 Do17s (some He111s believed also present) in Vic formation, with stragglers forming box at 16,000 feet, 10 miles north-east on north-west course. Many Me109s were seen beyond and above the bombers and more high above the Spitfires; not possible to state that these were Me109s, were escorting bomber formation. Squadron of Hurricanes dived on bomber formation before Spitfires could intercept and 3 Do17s were seen to break away as result. Squadron attacked Do17s dispersed by Hurricane attack.

Red 1 (S/Ldr Johnstone) and Red 2 (P/O Lyall) did four attacks, all beam, on one Do17 which had altered course to south, and destroyed it. Red 2 attacked an Me109 which had attacked Red 1, from behind in a turn and again dead astern and saw it crash in sea. Red 3 (S/P Phillips) does not report damage to e/a. Yellow 1 (F/Lt Webb) crash landed near Tangmere, report not yet available. Yellow 2 (F/O Mount) attacked He111 and saw four Hurricanes subsequently attack, does not claim damage. Yellow 3 (P/O Payne) reports nil. Blue 1 (F/O Jack) reports attack on Do17 without result. Blue 2 (S/P Babbage) reports nil. Blue 3 (S/P Proctor) attacked Do17, quarter astern and claims probable.

Green Section when brought to readiness were being taxied by non-operational pilots for practice flying, with the result that Green Section took off too late to contact remainder of squadron, and proceeded to Mayfield alone, and orbited 15,000 feet, where they saw 15/20 Do215s at 10,000 feet on south course, escorted by 50 Me109s, in tiers up to 15,000 feet. Top tiers, 15 in number went into defensive circle at 15,000 feet. Green 1 (S/P McDowall) turned outside circle in opposite direction and was attacked by two leading Me109s; he dived, and one Me109 passed behind from right to left. Green 1 turned left and fired at 150 yards, 2 seconds. Pilot of Me109 baled out. Green 2 (S/P Whall) destroyed 1 Do17, full report not yet available as S/P Whall has ricked his neck and was not able to furnish details on landing. Green 3 (S/P Whipps) nil report.

Attacks used …

Red 1 - Full beam, opening 400 yards, closing to 100 yards, 5 seconds burst.

Red 2 - Three full beam attacks, 3 seconds. One astern in a turn opening 250 yards, closing to 100 yards. One full astern, opening 100 yards, closing 30 yards, 3 seconds.

Blue 3 - Squadron astern, opening 250 yards, closing to 100 yards, 8 seconds.

Green 1 - Behind in turn, 150 yards, 2 seconds.

Total ammunition: 10,800 rounds (excluding F/Lt Webb's a/c). No stoppages.

Enemy's return fire. Cannon fire from Me109s. Believed cannon fire from top rear position of Do17.

Enemy camouflage. Yellow paint on upper surface of Me109.

Weather. 10/10ths cloud, 3/7,000 feet, clear above.

Enemy fighter tactics. Not clear whether Me109s encountered near bombers by Red, Yellow and Blue Sections were escorting bombers or maintaining standing patrol or dispersed by previous action.

Own losses. 1 Spitfire Cat.3. F/Lt Webb slightly injured. S/P Whall slightly injured.

Enemy losses. 2 Do17s destroyed. 2 Me109s destroyed. 1 Do17 probable.

COMBAT REPORT:
Sgt J Proctor - Blue 3, B Flight, 602 Squadron

I was Blue 3 and took off from Westhampnett 17.04 hrs. I saw Do17s on NW course in straggling formation and attacked one of the rear three quarter astern on same level. E/A fell out of formation turning to left with large quantities of black smoke streaming from fuselage. I followed E/A down to 5,000 ft when it was still diving into cloud. I pulled up and began to climb when what appeared to be 3 Hurricanes got on my tail and I had to go down to ground level over Shoreham aerodrome to shake them off. I then returned to Westhampnett.

Contemporary Accounts 602 Sqn

16.40 - 18.00 hrs 9th September 1940

COMBAT REPORT:

S/Ldr A V R Johnstone and P/O A McL Lyall – Villa Leader, Red 1 and Red 2, A Flight, 602 Squadron

I was Villa Leader (Red 1) and took off from Westhampnett 17.04 hrs, I saw a formation of 30/40 Do17s and He111s flying NW and many Me109s above and all around. A Hurricane squadron attacked the close formation of bombers and dispersed it. I attacked a Do17 separated from the other bombers nearly full beam from 1,500 ft above. White smoke developing into black began to stream from starboard engine which stopped. Red 2 (P/O Lyall) did three attacks on this Do17 full beam slightly above (3 seconds each) and saw a Me109 close in to attack Red 1. Red 2 closed on Me109 when in a turn opening 250 yds closing to 100 yds and white smoke appeared from underneath. At this time Red 2 saw Do17 first attacked crash into sea 1/2 mile out from coast not far from Bognor. The Me109 Red 2 attacked dived down to sea level and Red 2 attacked dead astern opening 100 yds closing to 30 yds 3 seconds and overtook E/A. Red 2 then turned across nose of Me109 an saw it crash in sea.

Red flashes resembling cannon fire were seen coming from top rear gun position by Red 1 and Red 2.

COMBAT REPORT:

Sgt A McDowall – Green 1, B Flight, 602 Squadron

I was Green 1 and my section was delayed in the take-off by practice flying so that I was unable to keep contact with the remainder of Squadron. I flew to Mayfield and orbited 15,000 ft and saw 15/20 Do215s at 10,000 ft on south course escorted by 50 Me109s in tiers up to 15,000 ft. The top tier, 15 in number, of Me109s (at one level) went into defensive circle. I did opposite circuit into sun and made to attack rear of the circle. The two leading Me109s of that circle broke and attacked me. I dived, blacking out on pulling out (maybe due to lack of oxygen) and saw one Me109 firing at me; I was then about 12,000 ft. He passed behind me, going to left; I went into left hand turn and got on his tail as he straightened out. My attack was 20 degrees out of dead astern. I saw pilot of enemy aircraft bale out. I last saw E/A 8,000 ft over large wood due east of Seaford (Beachy Head).

COMBAT REPORT:

Sgt B E P Whall – Green 2, B Flight, 602 Squadron

I was Green 2 and took off from Westhampnett 17.04 hrs. Green Section was unable to keep contact with remainder of Squadron. At 15,000 ft when orbiting Mayfield I saw about 50 Do215s on southerly course in straggling formation at 16,000 ft and climbed to attack one Do17 at tail of formation, doing beam attack from underneath wing hoping he wouldn't see me. I flew straight on past E/A below, circled and did full beam from starboard above. E/A turned away showing me his tail and dived. As E/A dived I followed and delivered two more full beam attacks, and E/A slowed up and levelled out. As E/A levelled out I climbed above and dived nearly vertically delivering fifth attack, as I did this E/A hit the water and before leaving him I saw the E/A lying on water with wings awash practically undamaged 1 mile south of east end of Brighton. No sign of life in E/A.

605 SQUADRON INTELLIGENCE REPORT

12 Hurricanes of No.605 Squadron left Croydon 16.53 hours, on 9th September, 1940, with orders to scramble Maidstone 'Angels' 15,000 feet. No.605 Squadron was led by 'A' Flight (Red Section) at 15,000 feet followed by 'B' Flight in echelon stepped up to act as fighter escort to 'A' Flight. Near Farnborough, Kent, and approaching from the south-east a large enemy formation was observed heading west consisting of 17 He111s flying in three vics of five sections line astern, and two stragglers at 20,000 feet, with about 20 Me110s slightly above and behind them and a large formation of about 50 Me109s and He113s weaving at 25,000 feet to 30,000 feet some four to six miles south of the bombers. As No.605 Squadron were climbing to attack the bombers the rear He111 released two streams of red vapour, presumably as a signal for the fighter escort to attack, for two Me109s followed by another 6 Me109s dived down to attack Yellow Section, which forced them to make evasive action and lose sight of the bombers; and some more Me109s dived down on 'B' Flight, which attack they evaded and carried on parallel to the bombers, preparing for a beam attack. Then three more Me109s dived upon 'B' Flight. Blue 1 destroyed the leader with a two second burst with a quarter head-on attack, the leader diving down in flames a bit south of Croydon.

'B' Flight then recovered their parallel course to the bombers trying to get into position for a beam attack. As the flight were in a position to attack, the He111s turned into them so Blue 1 ordered head-on attacks. Blue 1, with Blue 2 protecting him from Me109s who were diving down to attack, then opened fire from a slight dive at about 700 yards on the leader of the formation and smoke and flames issued from each wing. Blue 1, then fired on the leader's left-hand machine and almost at the same moment the leading machine exploded, a wing flew off the left-hand machine, and the right-hand machine rolled over on to its back and dived down in flames - all three destroyed. Blue 1 thinks the explosion of the leading machine (which was near to the right-hand machine) must have caused the destruction of the right-hand machine as he had not fired at it. The destruction of all 3 He111s was witnessed by Red 1. Blue 1 expended only 1200 rounds of ammunition. The attack took place in the neighbourhood of Farnborough, Hants, Green 1 baling out and landing near Bordon slightly wounded, and Blue 3 still missing - both their machines presumably Cat.III., the bombers returned in a south-easterly direction.

Meanwhile Yellow 1 and Yellow 3 had joined up together again at 16,000 feet, Yellow 2 having landed at Croydon to re-arm, and near Weybridge observed a scattered formation of Me109s flying south-east at 20,000 feet, hotly pursued by A.A. fire. Yellow 1 saw one Me109 spiralling, into which he fired a two seconds burst from 250 yards. It spun down in flames followed by a Hurricane (markings LE/F) who probably had a share in its destruction. Yellow1 and Yellow 3 then turned from Croydon, where they saw an Me110 above clouds above base.

Yellow 1 and Yellow 3 both attacked head-on from 300 yards, each with a two seconds burst, the enemy aircraft then turned left and Yellow 1 and Yellow 3 both attacked full beam (1 ring deflection) each with two to three seconds burst from about 200 yards. The enemy aircraft then dived and climbed in a right-handed turn, so Yellow 1 and Yellow 3 turned inside it and each tried a 3 seconds burst full beam from 200 yards. By now Yellow 1's ammunition had run out and bits were falling off the Me110 as it dived towards the clouds. Yellow 3 followed it giving a 4 seconds burst from the beam. The enemy aircraft was observed to crash in flames near the south-west corner of Croydon aerodrome.

Remaining 10 aircraft 605 Squadron returned Croydon 18.10 - 18.35 hours. R.2's machine being Cat.2.

Red 1	S/Ldr	Churchill
Red 2	P/O	Ingle
Red 3	P/O	Cooper-Slipper
Yellow 1	P/O	Currant - 1 Me110 destroyed, but shared with Yellow 3.
		1 Me109 destroyed, but shot at by LE/F.
Yellow 2	P/O	Glowacki
Yellow 3	Sgt	Wright
Blue 1	F/Lt	McKellar - 3 He111s and 1 Me109 destroyed.
Blue 2	Sgt	Budzinski
Blue 3	P/O	Forrester
Green 1	P/O	Humphreys
Green 2	F/O	Passy
Green 3	P/O	Watson

COMBAT REPORT:

F/Lt A A McKellar - Blue 1, B Flight, 605 Squadron

16.55 hours 605 squadron ordered to patrol Maidstone at 15,000 feet. After various vectors, and while orbiting, I, who was leading 'B' Flight, stepped up and echeloned to act as fighter protection for 'A' Flight, reported bomber bandits east of us heading west and 3,000 feet above, plus 5 formations of Me109s or He113s much higher still. The last machine of the bomber formation released two streams of red vapour when I reported 'Bandits', I presume as some indication to his fighter escort. Turkey Leader with 'A' Flight started to climb on a parallel course as e/a. I however found myself unable to keep up. Turkey Leader went in to do a beam attack with 'A' Flight and I lost sight of them. At the same time I saw several e/a fighters, diving down on my rear section (Green), I warned them of this by R/T and carried on parallel and climbing to the course of the bombers, shortly after this I noticed 3 Me109s coming in as if to do a quarter attack on my section, I at once turned in to them and did a quarter head-on to beam shot on the leader (giving about 3 second burst). He burst into flames and went down somewhere south of Croydon I think.

I then resumed my parallel course to the bombers trying to get into a position for a beam attack, the whole flight still being with me. Now I was in position and ordered Blue Section to attack with me, Green to cover us against fighters, as I started my attack the bombers turned into me I therefore ordered head-on attack. I opened fire from a slight dive at about 700 yards range on the leader of the formation, and noticed smoke and flames coming from each wing. I then fired at his left machine, and almost at the same instant the leading machine exploded and a wing flew off the left-hand machine, the right-hand machine at the same time rolled over onto its back and dived down with smoke and flames coming from each wings, destroyed I think by the explosion of the leader as I had not fired at this right-hand machine. The destruction of the 3 He111s was confirmed by Turkey Leader. Rounds fired 1,200.

COMBAT REPORT:

P/O J Humphreys - Green 1, B Flight, 605 Squadron

I sighted enemy aircraft stepped up in vics of 5 astern at 20,000 feet. Proceeded with Blue Section on parallel course with intention of delivering beam attacks. Enemy aircraft turned 90 degrees towards us, so delivered head-on attack. I saw Blue 3 do a half barrel roll and strike the outside aircraft of the leading vic on its port main plane which broke off at the engine nacelle. I delivered approximately a 4 second burst at the leading enemy aircraft of the 3rd vic. Return cannon fire ceased at once. Perceived Perspex and portions of forward fuselage break off. Broke downwards, just missing enemy aircraft, and was struck by cross fire, which shot away left-hand side of my cockpit and badly damaged other parts of my machine. Enemy aircraft left formation in steady left-hand spiral. Lost sight of enemy aircraft shortly after breaking away, I had to bale out and landed near Bordon Camp.

Left: This was the Heinkel that Blue 3 (P/O Forrester) collided with, ripping off its port wing. Coded A1+ZD it was in the lead formation as part of Stab III/KG53.

COMBAT REPORT:
Sgt E W Wright - Yellow 3, A Flight, 605 Squadron

Shared with Yellow 1 P/O C F Currant

Yellow Section airborne at 16.53. The squadron led by Red Section vectored 105° and climbed through cloud to 15,000 feet. At 15,000 feet 20 to 30 Me109s observed 10,000 feet above us circling and weaving. Bomber formation of 16 to 18 He 111s (with escort of Me110s in vic formation behind bombers 1,000 feet above) observed at 20,000 feet 6 miles to starboard with 20 to 30 more Me109s behind at 25,000 feet. I followed Yellow 1 with Red Section flying parallel to bombers. We got within 1,000 yards of bombers and 1,000 feet above when two Me109s dived down on us. I did a steep climbing turn right, just as they came within range. One Me109 went straight down past me as I turned, and I gave him a 1 to 2 second burst with no apparent effect. I had now lost touch with Yellow 1 so I dived down on another single aircraft but this turned out to be friendly. Yellow 1 now flew alongside me so I joined up again with him at 16,000 feet over Weybridge. We orbited base Angels 15 and observed a bomber formation flying east hotly pursued by A.A. fire. I followed Yellow 1 down on to an Me109 and saw him fire a burst into it. It burst into flames on hitting the ground. We next saw an Me110 over base above clouds. I followed Yellow 1 into attack, and fired a 2 second burst head-on. Aircraft turned left and I got a full deflection shot (one wing) firing for 2 seconds. Aircraft headed off flying straight and level and then went into another left-hand turn. I turned inside him and fired a 4 second burst on the beam, pieces were now falling off him.

Yellow 1 had now finished his ammunition so I fired the rest of mine from astern as he headed for clouds. His starboard engine was now on fire and pieces were now falling off. Three Spitfires were in the vicinity during engagement. I landed base 18.15 hours. My crew observed Me110 crash after emerging in flames from clouds.

Yellow 1, P/O Currant. Yellow 2, P/O Glowacki. Yellow 3, Sgt Wright.

COMBAT REPORT:
P/O C F Currant - Yellow 1, A Flight, 605 Squadron

The squadron led by Red Section vectored 105° and climbed through cloud. Yellow 2 lost during this climb and returned to base. After vectors and when at 15,000 feet, 20 - 30 Me109s observed 5,000 feet above us, circling and weaving. Bomber formation of 17 He111s with rear escort of Me110s observed at 20,000 feet, 6 miles to the east, with a further formation of 20 - 30 Me109s behind at 25,000 to 30,000 feet. I followed Red Section as we climbed and flew parallel to the bomber formation. We got within a half mile to west of bombers and 1,000 feet above, with 'B' Flight well back to our left rear and below. At this point the Me109s dived down on us from above and we were forced to turn in a defensive circle. These dived past and then a further 6 Me109s dived down on us from above, and again we had to turn, and after this evasive action, the bombers and fighters had disappeared from view. I saw Yellow 3 below me and he joined up. We were now at 16,000 feet over Weybridge and Control told me to orbit base, Angels 15. I observed a scattered formation east of Weybridge at 20,000 feet, flying south-east with heavy A.A. gun fire bursts amongst them. Whilst climbing to intercept this formation I saw what appeared to be a Hurricane diving away, followed closely by an Me109. I dived towards them and when close, I saw an Me109 spiralling, I fired a 2 seconds burst at 250 yards. The Me109 dived into a field and burst into flames and I noticed a Hurricane (markings LE-F)* circling the crash. I flew back to base with Yellow 3, and saw an Me110 over base just above the clouds. I engaged, firing a 2 second burst head-on at 300 yards. Enemy aircraft turned left and I turned inside and fired a three second burst at 200 yards on a full beam (1 ring deflection).

Enemy aircraft dived and then climbed in a right-hand turn. I turned inside and fired a 3 second burst full beam at 200 yards. I noticed bits of metal flying off the enemy aircraft. The enemy aircraft then did a tight left-hand turn, diving slightly, and I gave a quarter deflection 4 second burst at 200 yards and again saw bits flying off. Enemy aircraft disappeared in a shallow dive into the clouds and appeared to be on fire. Yellow 3 was following it, and also 3 Spitfires were in the vicinity during the whole engagement. I landed base 18.15 hours.

Author's Note 242 Squadron. Although P/O Currant reports the enemy aircraft as an Me109, the location and circumstances fit with the destruction of the Me110 of 15(Z)/LG1 that fell near Worcester Park, Surrey.

The 'Big Wing' goes into action

16.40 - 18.00 hrs 9th September 1940

Air Vice-Marshal Trafford Leigh-Mallory, (below right) AOC 12 Group, submitted a report on the Big Wing's second action to Dowding:

Second Wing Patrol

The Wing, consisting of three squadrons with 32 aircraft, left Duxford at 17.00 hours on the 9th September to patrol North Weald and Hornchurch. When they were at 20,000 feet they saw two large rectangular formations of enemy aircraft, which each consisted of at least 60-60 Do215s with a large number of escorting fighters. The upper formation, which appeared to consist of Messerschmitts and He113 fighters, was 500 feet above the lower one, which also had fighters in the formation. In all there must have been between 150-200 E/A. The enemy, which were at 22,000 feet, were flying north about 15 miles to the south west of the Wing. The Spitfire squadron (19) climbed to 23,000 feet to attack the fighters whilst the Hurricanes climbed to attack the bombers. The number of escorting fighters was large enough to enable some of them to dive on our fighters as they attacked the bombers whose formation had then been broken up. In the result, therefore, more enemy fighters were destroyed than bombers, although the proportion of bombers destroyed was increased when compared with the first action. Bombs were dropped by the enemy during this engagement, which took place over the south west suburbs of London, but the enemy were driven off to the south east. The leader of the Wing considered that at least 20 further bombers could have been shot down if additional fighters had been available to renew the attack after the bomber formation had been broken up.

Enemy Casualties

Destroyed: 21 Fighters 8 Bombers
Probable: 5 Fighters 0 Bombers
Damaged: 2 Fighters 1 Bomber

Fighter Casualties

4 Aircraft lost, 3 damaged, 2 pilots killed

Dowding replied, in part:
'I read a great many combat reports and I think I am beginning to pick out those which can be relied on and those which throw in claims at the end for good measure.'

Editor's Note: With the luxury of hindsight, the enemy aircraft definitely attributable to the Duxford Wing's squadrons are; two Me110s (one as a result of a fatal collision) and possibly one Me109 and an He111. It is also possible that one or more of the Me109s that force landed, or eventually fell into the sea, were damaged by the 'Duxford Wing' pilots, but not the 29 destroyed and 5 more probable as claimed. Although Dowding did not have the detail of the Luftwaffe losses available to him as we do today, he did have the daily reports from RAF Intelligence, giving accurate numbers of enemy aircraft that fell on land. These figures doubtless helped form his opinion of the accuracy of Fighter Command's claims for aircraft destroyed.

19 SQUADRON INTELLIGENCE REPORT

9 a/c of 19 Squadron whilst patrolling North Weald at 20,000 feet with two other squadrons, sighted a large formation of enemy bombers and fighters flying north-west. The bombers were in vic formation, the vics being line astern. The fighters were above weaving and searching.

It had been arranged that 19 Squadron should attack the fighters, so Blue 1, who was leading them, put them into line astern and climbed to 23,000 feet preparatory to an attack on six or seven Me110s who were also climbing in line astern. As they were about to attack, two Me109s cut across in front and Blue Leader opened fire on them. The first burst into flames and the second glided down in apparent distress.

The squadron, still in line astern, went on to attack the Me110s, Blue Leader had used all his ammunition so took no further part in the action. Blue 2 cut across in front of Blue Leader and Blue 3 attacked with full deflection shot closing to within 50 yards and breaking away underneath. The e/a was then slipping inwards and was seen by Blue Leader to go into a left-hand spiral apparently out of control. Blue 2 then chased another Me110 out over the Channel but was unable to get within range.

Blue 3 stayed with Blue Leader and so did not take part in the main attack. He only fired a short burst at an Me109.

Red Leader dived on the tail of an Me110, opened fire at 300 yards, stopped his starboard engine and blew pieces off his starboard wing. The e/a finally crashed about 5 miles east of Biggin Hill.

Red 2 did not open fire in the first dog-fight but followed the main formation out to sea, and attacked an He111 which was straggling slightly. He saw bits of the e/a fly off and left it sinking in flames towards the sea. Red 2's windscreen was pierced by a bullet which ended in his petrol tank.

Red 3, after breaking formation to chase the Me110s, got on the tail of an Me109. Some parts of the engine flew out and he left it enveloped in flames. The spinner of his e/a was painted yellow. Red 3's aircraft was hit by a bullet in the mainspar.

Yellow Leader attacked one of the Me109s with a 150° deflection burst, but observed no result. He then saw a Hurricane attacking an He111 and joined in, making several attacks from dead astern until his ammunition was exhausted. By that time Red 3 had landed at Detling and the He111 was down to 1,000 feet with both engines stopped and his flaps and undercarriage down. He was gliding in an easterly direction with the apparent intention of making a forced landing a little south of Detling.

Yellow 2 dived to attack one of six Do215s which was straggling and had his wheels down. He saw bits come off the e/a during his attack and having fired all his ammunition he left it to another Spitfire which was about to attack.

Yellow 3, after dog-fighting with the Me109s, got onto the tail of one and gave it two bursts which resulted in the e/a diving vertically in flames. Yellow 3's machine was hit in the mainplane and airscrew.

No cine camera guns were carried.

R/T receipt was poor from ground to air owing to interference by other stations. Air to air was good. Weather was fine with haze up to 8,000 feet and 4 to 4/10ths cumulo-stratus cloud at about 7,000 feet.

Pilots and rounds fired.   Stoppages

			Stoppages
Blue 1 F/Lt W G Clouston, DFC	rounds fired	2,542	cross feed in starboard 2.
Blue 2 F/Sgt H Steere, DFM	' '	1,466	starboard 1 did not fire detonated ammunition.
Blue 3 F/Lt E Burgoyne	' '	600	No stoppages.
Red 1 P/O W J Lawson	' '	2,600	' '
Red 2 Sub/Lt A G Blake	' '	825	separated case in starboard 3.
Red 3 P/O W Cunningham	' '	1,710	No stoppages.
Yellow 1 F/O F N Brinsden	' '	2,712	' '
Yellow 2 P/O A F Vokes	' '	2,264	Port 1 cross feed Port 2 breakage
Yellow 3 Sgt D G S R Cox	' '	2,445	Port 2 bullet through tank.

19 SQUADRON OPERATIONS RECORD BOOK

Squadron on patrol over North Weald along with Wing. Squadron led by F/Lt Clouston. Initial attack broke up enemy formation and individual dog-fighting ensued. P/O Lawson got a Do215, Sub Lt Blake got an He111, and almost got it himself, a bullet entering the sliding roof and ricocheting from the windscreen passed into the top of the petrol tank. F/O Brinsden got a probable He111, P/O Cunningham an Me109. Station total 29 today.

COMBAT REPORT:
F/Lt W G Clouston - Blue 1, B Flight, 19 Squadron

While on patrol leading 19 Squadron at 20,000 feet we encountered a large formation of E/A. We had been detailed by Wing Leader to attack fighters so I climbed and put squadron into position to attack 7 Me109s, Just as I was about to attack two Me109s crossed my sights so I turned on to them. The rear one emitted glycol fumes after a short burst and then burst into flames. I then attacked second 109 and finished rest of ammunition. I could see my shots hitting the a/c and when my ammo had finished I saw him go down in a left hand gliding turn looking rather the worse for wear. F/O Brinsden saw this machine go down apparently out of control.

COMBAT REPORT:
F/Sgt H Steere - Blue 2 B Flight, 19 Squadron

I was line astern and cut across in front of Blue Leader and Blue 3 and closed with a '110' which was line astern with 5 others and closed giving a full deflection shot and saw my tracers going home, I closed to within 50 yards and was forced to break underneath him - he was slipping inwards in a very peculiar attitude. I then came round again and chased another 110 half way across the Channel but was unable to close with him. I turned round when the guns on the French coast looked uncomfortably close.

I saw this first Me110 of F/Sgt Steere turn down in a left-hand spin, which appeared to be completely out of control. W G Clouston F/Lt.

COMBAT REPORT:
F/O F N Brinsden - Yellow 1, A Flight, 19 Squadron

While on patrol with Blue and Red Sections of 19 Squadron we encountered a countless number of E/A. We formed line astern and attacked the E/A fighter escort. In the first attack I saw F/Lt Clouston destroy an Me109 which disappeared out of control. We all broke the engagement still in line astern and after climbing again attacked 5 Me110s which had formed a circle. Our own formation was then broken up and I joined up in line astern with 2 Me109s. I fired a long burst at about 15 degrees deflection with no apparent result. They turned quickly and I lost them in the sun. After watching the general action for some minutes I joined with a Hurricane in destroying an He111, then I left. All my attacks being carried out from dead astern. After firing all my rounds I passed quite close to the E/A and noticed that his flaps and undercarriage were 'out' and both the engines had stopped. I last saw the E/A gliding on an easterly course a little south of Detling at about 1,000 ft. No rear fire was experienced.

COMBAT REPORT:
P/O A F Vokes - Yellow 2, A Flight, 19 Squadron

I was No. 2 in Yellow Section, climbing to attack Me109s. I saw 6 Do215s below and dived down on the nearest one. He was flying south and by the time I attacked was separated from the others and had his wheels down. I fired all my ammunition into him and saw bits coming off. Just before breaking away experienced a heavy bump from beneath which I think was AA fire. Subsequently saw another Spitfire attack the Do215, so returned home as my ammunition had run out.

COMBAT REPORT:
P/O W J Lawson – Red 1, A Flight, 19 Squadron

I was leading Red Section (3 aircraft) on patrol with 242 and 310 Squadrons. Enemy aircraft were sighted to port heading approx NW and about 2,000 ft below. I sighted an Me110 to my starboard and approx. 2,000 ft below me. I turned to starboard and dived onto his tail and got in a short burst at 300 yds. Then ensued a really enjoyable dog-fight which ended by my hitting his starboard engine causing it to stop, he then started losing height and pieces fell away from his starboard wing, he continued to go down in a slow spiral turn and when at about 5,000 ft two Hurricanes and a Spitfire followed him down, he finally crashed in a field approx 5 miles east of Biggin Hill.

Type of attack No 1. from astern.

Took off 17.00 hrs Landed 18.40 hrs Enemy fire Front guns only.

COMBAT REPORT:
Sub Lt A G Blake – Red 2, A Flight, 19 Squadron

Flying as Red 2 in formation, on patrol with 242 and 310 Squadrons. E/A were sighted on port side heading approx NW. In the ensuing dog-fight that followed I didn't fire a round, so having turned myself inside out, I straightened up and followed the main formation out to sea climbing all the while. Picked out an He111 on the port side and behind the formation. Made a shallow dive out of the setting sun and carried out an astern attack. Saw bits flying off and as I broke off observed him to be smoking and on fire.

COMBAT REPORT:
P/O W Cunningham – Red 3, A Flight, 19 Squadron

Flying as Red 3 in formation along with 242, 310 Squadrons. Sighted large formation of E/A approx 60 bombers and remainder fighters. They were proceeding in a NW direction at a height of approx 2,000 ft below us. Attack was delivered to front starboard quarter. No results from this attack. Afterwards broke formation from leader to chase off Me110s on tail. Found a stray Me109 (yellow nose) passing to the right in front of me. Took up position on his tail and fired two very long bursts until he was flaming and some parts of his engine flew out. I left off attack as it was quite evident the a/c was destroyed. As long as I had him under observation he made no attempt to jump.

Layer of cloud about 6/10ths at 7,000 ft. One bullet hole in main spar of port wing.

COMBAT REPORT:
Sgt D S G R Cox – Yellow 3, A Flight, 19 Squadron

I was Yellow 3 when the Squadron attacked some Me110s in line astern. I was the end machine and spotted some Me109s away to the south above us. I attacked an Me109 which dived on me but without any result. I was then attacked by three Me109s. After a dog-fight for a while I got on an Me109's tail and after two bursts it burst into flames and dived straight down.

Me109s all white underneath.

I took off from G.1. (Fowlmere) 17.00 hours, landed 18.30 hours

Contemporary Accounts 242 Sqn

16.40 - 18.00 hrs 9th September 1940

242 SQUADRON INTELLIGENCE REPORT

Squadron 242 were ordered to patrol North Weald - Hornchurch at 20,000 feet. They climbed to 22,000 feet and patrolled. At about 17.40 hours saw a large enemy formation coming in from south-east about 15 miles south-west of 242 Squadron at 22,000 feet. The squadron turned and climbed to get above.

Enemy were in two large rectangular formations, one of approximately 60, then a space of a quarter of a mile and another 60 with a 500 feet step-up between them.

S/Ldr Bader ordered his squadron to attack in loose sections in line astern and to try and break up formations. Immediately some Me109s attacked his squadron and in turn he had to attack them. S/Ldr, Red 1, attacked the leader and saw him turning away with white smoke pouring from both wings and was told afterwards that the e/a went down in flames. The e/a was a Do215. He attacked several other e/a but could not see results.

A salvo of bombs was seen to drop from the bombers who were still in formation, but there were plenty of stragglers. It was obvious that bombing was indiscriminate.

Red 2, **P/O W L McKnight**, followed in with his leader and was immediately attacked by an Me109 but succeeded in getting behind e/a, giving one short burst and seeing e/a burst into flames. He was again attacked by two more but got in between them opening fire and saw bit of e/a break off and dive to ground. He was still being attacked and his left aileron was blown off. He broke off engagement and in doing so saw his second Me109 crash to ground.

Yellow 1, **F/Lt G E Ball**, took his and another section into attack. He dived through the formation and made a frontal attack on the leading section. He saw no effect of his fire but saw an Me109 and managed to get on e/a's tail. He gave him a burst of about 5 seconds and saw e/a blow up in the sky.

Blue 1, **F/Lt G Powell-Shedden**, went in with Yellow Section and dived to attack leader of bomber group. He overshot and did not open fire but went into steep turn, attacking this time the second leader. He opened fire at about 50 yards at port engine of e/a and noticed bullets strike engine and wing. Looking back he saw e/a's port engine on fire. He then himself got out of control for a short time, his starboard aileron control cable having been shot through, but managed to return to base.

Blue 2, **P/O R Bush**, dived in with his section and found an Me109 attacking him. He evaded e/a, climbed and saw an Me110 which he attacked. He gave it two short bursts and e/a burst into flames.

Blue 3, **P/O F Tamblyn**, saw 5 Me110s detach themselves from the e/a formation, make a right-hand circle and attack our fighters. He saw an Me110 on the tail of a Hurricane and attacked, giving it two short bursts. E/A straightened up and both engines caught fire. He then went to the far side of the formation and saw an Me110 cross his path, so gave it a burst, E/A caught fire and crashed in front of cricket club house where he saw another e/a burning.

Green 1, **Sgt G Richardson** saw Do215 which attempted to evade by turning steeply to the right. He got in a burst of six seconds and saw smoke coming from e/a starboard engine. He regained position, made another attack from astern and port engine started to smoke. After the third attack e/a burst into flames.

Green 2, **P/O J B Latta**, went in to attack the bombers, but found he was being attacked by e/a, Me109. He evaded and managed to get in a dead astern attack for 6 - 8 seconds on an Me109 which burst into flames. He was then attacked receiving a bullet in his port aileron but dived steeply and found no one on his tail so returned to base.

Weather was hazy up to 9,000 feet and clear above that height. Reflector sights were used by the whole squadron and generally satisfactory.

242 Squadron took off from Duxford 17.00 hours and 10 a/c landed at Duxford between 18.00 and 18.30 hours.

242 SQUADRON OPERATIONS RECORD BOOK

Squadron operating Duxford; Squadron Leader Bader leading Wing consisting of Nos 242, 310 and 19 Squadrons. Patrolling over London encountered large formation of Enemy Aircraft. Bombers and Fighters. S/Ldr and 242 Squadron led the attack and shot down 10. No 310 (Czech) Squadron shot down 7 and No 19 Squadron 2. One pilot 242 killed (P/O Sclanders). One pilot (Sgt Lonsdale) baled out and returned to squadron next day unhurt.

Congratulations received from Air Officer Command and Chief of the Air Staff.

COMBAT REPORT:

S/Ldr D R S Bader - Leader - Red 1, A Flight, 242 Squadron

Squadrons 242, 310, 19 ordered to patrol N. Weald-Hornchurch at 20,000. Climbed to 22,000 and patrolled. At about 17.40 saw large enemy formation coming in from S-N about 15 miles SW of us at 22,000 feet. I turned to head them off and climbed to get above. Enemy was in two large rectangular formations one of approx 60 then a space of 1/4 mile and another 60 with 500 feet step up between them. I radioed Duxford to tell 19 Squadron to climb up and protect our tails and turned 242 and 310 in from S-N above the front bomber formation, nearly down sun and 1,000 feet above. 242 had been instructed by me to attack in loose line astern (sections) and try to break up the formations. I was to get the Leader, who was slightly in front of leading section. I noticed as I turned the squadron to directly above the bombers some single-seater fighters diving out of the sun between the two enemy bomber formations but dismissed them as friendly fighters. Actually, they were Me109s and attacked my formation on the turn. However, some of my formation turned and attacked them so that I was not worried by them. I dived on the leader and gave him a point-blank 2 secs burst, continuing the dive past him and through and under the formation. I pulled up underneath intending to give him another squirt from below, but saw him turning away with white smoke pouring from both wings and roll over on his back in a dive. I did not bother to watch him further but Sgt Brimble and P/O Bush confirm seeing the aeroplane go down in flames and at least 1 person bale out. The E/A was a Dornier 215 or 17. I find it hard to tell the difference. I remained under the formation (about 300 feet below) pulling up and squirting various aeroplanes at very close range but although definitely damaging them I saw no definite results. I did see another Dornier in the front

dive slowly down in a left-hand turn obviously out of action and smoking and I am certain it was about to catch fire. This I understand was the 2nd leader which F/Lt Powell-Shedden shot down. I suddenly discerned salvoes of bombs falling all about me and so decided to get away to the fight, which I did. The bomber formation turned right-handed and went off SE. They were still in formation about 20 of them, but there were a lot of stragglers all over the sky, some damaged and others going fairly slowly. I could not see a single other British fighter in the sky, and these aeroplanes going home could have been broken up and shot down if two fresh squadrons had arrived. I continued chasing stragglers and firing short close-range bursts until I ran out of ammunition. When I turned for home I saw a very large bomber with single rudder flying home quite slowly so I attacked by flying very close and turning across it etc, but it took no notice and did not even fire at me. It was obvious that the bombing was absolutely indiscriminate. London was covered by a 5,000 feet layer of broken cloud, thick haze up to 9,000 ft and clear above that height. They were bombing from 20,000 feet, and so far as I could see, south of the Thames around London Bridge and Battersea areas but from 20,000 feet it might have been several miles away. It must be emphasised that the Germans adopted identical tactics with a previous interception 242 made. The Germans approaching from the south flying due north over the west side of London and then turned SE for home. 12 Group Wing was instructed to patrol N. Weald and Hornchurch, a useless procedure because we could see 50-80 miles to the east but no distance to the west - up sun. We should have been patrolling many miles SW where we would have been up sun from the enemy and could have attacked him before he got to the Thames and shot down at least twice the number.

If Sector Controllers could confine themselves to telling formation leaders where the enemy are supposed to be and leave it to the formation leaders to choose height and place to patrol much better results could be achieved. If aerodromes like N Weald and Hornchurch want protecting, the patrol line should be somewhere south west of the Thames in the evening and south east in the morning because the Hun usually approached from a point where his fighters can be in the sun.

The effectiveness of de Wilde ammunition is noticed by all pilots.

COMBAT REPORT:
Sgt R H Lonsdale - Yellow 3, A Flight, 242 Squadron

We were ordered to patrol N Weald when approx 150 E/A were sighted over London; we approached them and as the C/O went into attack I sighted three Me109s coming towards the rear of our formation at approximately a thousand feet below our squadron.

I did a quick turn and made to attack them but could not get into range so I broke away and found myself on the tails of a formation of Do215s slightly apart from the main formation. I attacked the rearmost machine and gave it a burst of about six seconds and it swung across the formation and I found I was almost on the tail of another and slightly to one side. I immediately attacked this one and although my a/c had been hit several times by heavy cross fire from the rear gunners I managed to fire all my remaining rounds into him from approximately 200 yds.

I was being repeatedly hit in the engine and controls while carrying out this second attack and smoke was coming into my cockpit as well as streams of glycol mixture and oil, also my controls were practically useless except for the elevator. As I broke away from the attack the E/A had smoke coming from the fuselage and one engine was smoking badly. I jumped out at about 19,000 ft and finished up in a pine tree in Caterham; my machine landed at Kenley Gardens about 200 yds from the Main Guard Room.

The Inspector of Police at Caterham and several soldiers confirmed my report and stated that the machine I was attacking came down some distance away and started to come down at the same time as I jumped out. There were also other witnesses at Kenley Aerodrome. While dropping slowly to earth a Spitfire pilot flew around me and stayed with me until I had nearly reached the ground.

> " *Sighted E/A over Thames near London Bridge. Line astern attack from sun on bombers. Had to evade fire of Me109. Climbed and found Me110 and shot it down with my second burst and E/A broke up in air. Fire from behind by 2nd Me110 did half roll and could not find any E/A on coming out of dive.*
> *P/O C R Bush - Blue 2, B Flight, 242 Squadron* "

COMBAT REPORT:
F/Lt G Ff Powell-Shedden - Blue 1, B Flight, 242 Squadron

At about 17.35 we sighted the enemy flying in a northerly direction, we were about 10 to 15 miles away and they were between us and the sun. We climbed up as we approached them and got two thousand feet above them. I was flying as leader of the third section in No. 242 Squadron. Before the attack the sections became open and irregular with the CO in front. We dived immediately the CO dropped his nose and attacked the first group of bombers which numbered about 30. These bombers were protected by an escort of fighters. I made a mess of my attack, tried to get the leader but overshot him and did not fire (attack was from starboard side of bombers), I went up into a steep climb, turned rapidly, attacked the bomber group again aiming this time at the second leader of the formation and opened fire at about 50 yards at his port engine, a three-second burst, I saw the bullets strike the engine and wing, I passed about 20 feet over the E/A and broke away to the left in a steep climb, looking back I saw the port engine on fire with a stream of smoke pouring from it, the bomber lagged behind and fell out of formation with smoke still coming from the engine. I then lost sight of it, as I became out of control owing to, as I found out on landing, my starboard aileron control cable having been shot clean through and broken. By the time I regained control I had lost the E/A in the haze and cloud.

COMBAT REPORT:

P/O W L McKnight - Red 2, A Flight, 242 Squadron

We attacked enemy from 1,000 ft above and on his left beam and I broke to the left to attack protecting enemy fighter a/c. I succeeded in getting behind one e/a and after one short burst he went up in flames. I then was attacked by two more e/a and succeeded in getting between them. I again opened fire and e/a shed bits and dived steeply to ground. E/A behind me then opened fire and blew my left aileron off. Going down out of control I saw my second Me109 crash and then burn.

Right and below: Willie McKnight's Hurricane P2961 LE-A carried this striking piece of nose art on both sides of the cockpit.

Contemporary Accounts 242 Sqn

16.40 - 18.00 hrs 9th September 1940

COMBAT REPORT:
Sgt E Richardson – Green 1, B Flight, 242 Squadron

Observed a E/A slightly east of main formation of E/A. Climbed to 1,000 ft above and commenced rear quarter attack from above and from out of sun. E/A attempted evading by turning steeply to the right. Commenced firing burst of 6 secs duration and observed smoke pouring from the aircraft's starboard engine and mainplane. Broke away after closing to 200 yds, down to the left of the E/A. Regained position 300 yds behind E/A and delivered another attack, closing to 100 yds, burst of further 6 secs. Broke away underneath E/A after seeing smoke coming from port engine. Experienced long burst of fire from E/A apparently tracer, with no apparent effect on own aircraft.

Regained position 100 yds astern of E/A and gave it further 6 secs burst. Observed flames coming from starboard main plane and broke off attack, satisfied that E/A was destroyed returned to base.

Weather very clear at commencement of combat, but hazy from 15,000 ft to ground level.

Took off 17.00 hrs and landed 18.15 hrs. Reflector sight span 60 ft ranged 250 yds.

COMBAT REPORT:
P/O H N Tamblyn – Blue 3, B Flight, 242 Squadron

Ordered off 17.00 hrs E/A sighted 17.35. As we approached E/A from the east I saw 5 Me110s detach themselves from the formation and turn in a right-hand circle towards mass of formation at 22,000 ft. I turned into an astern attack and noticed that a Hurricane was on the tail of an Me110 which it set on fire. On the tail of the Hurricane was an Me110 which fired a long burst at the Hurricane. I opened fire on the Me110 whereupon it straightened up and after another burst both engines caught fire. I noticed one Hurricane with its port wing folding up and another machine which I took to be a Hurricane also with its port wing folding up.*

I went to the far side of the formation and climbed again. I saw an Me110 making across me in a steep turn. I gave a short burst and went into dead astern when after a burst of about 7 seconds the port engine caught fire. The machine went into a fairly steep dive and I followed him down and watched him crash in front of a cricket clubhouse** within one hundred yards of another crash near a burning house. There were many star-like spots on the ground which were perhaps incendiary bombs.

I climbed to 18,000 ft but as I could see no aircraft and heard some squadrons being ordered to land I landed at base.

Author's Note: These would have been the Hurricanes of Boulton and Sinclair, 310 Squadron.

*** An Me110 of 15(Z)/LG1 did crash in front of a cricket clubhouse, but he was mistaken about a second crash.*

COMBAT REPORT:
P/O J B Latta – Green 2, B Flight, 242 Squadron

Squadron attacked from 1,000 ft above. Enemy bomber's formation sections vic line astern. Fighters above but holding no definite formation. Before making contact with enemy bombers Green section was attacked by 8 or 10 Me109s who broke away from the main body of fighters. I was able to engage one and get a burst of 6 to 8 secs from dead astern. His only evasive tactic was a steep climbing turn left. He burst into flames apparently in the cockpit, and spun off the climb and continued spinning. I was then myself attacked and received a bullet in my port aileron, jamming it. I dived steeply and was not followed.

General combat very confused but saw two other machines either Do215s or Me110s go down in flames. Cloud 3/10 at 10,000 ft but clear above. Visibility good. Attack carried out with sun at our back.

Reflector sight used, span 60 ft. Range 300 yds. One burst 6 to 8 secs. R/T OK.

Contemporary Accounts 310 Sqn

310 SQUADRON INTELLIGENCE REPORT

12 a/c of 310 Squadron took off from Duxford at 17.05 hours to patrol North Weald at 20,000 feet. The squadron joined up with 19 and 242 to form a Wing, 242 Squadron taking the lead. A formation of 75 Do215s escorted by about 150 Me109s, 110s and He112s were sighted south of the estuary heading north-west. The main formation consisted of bombers and fighters flying in close herring bone formation with alternate lines of Do215s and Me110s, this formation being protected by further Me110s, 109s and He112s.

S/Ldr Blackwood ordered his squadron into line astern in preparation for an attack on main formation from the rear. An Me110 was sighted breaking away from formation possibly due to previous attack by other fighters as one engine was smoking. He dived after it but lost sight of the Me110 in the haze. At this time a collision occurred between 2 Hurricanes and was seen by the other pilots of 310 Squadron, who, on a signal, broke formation to avoid further collisions and then engaged in a series of dog-fights.

Pilots of 19 Squadron - part of the wing - state they saw 1 Hurricane and 1 Me110 collide but cannot give squadron letter.

Lt G D Cooper, Irish Guards, Caterham, saw a Hurricane (most probably piloted by F/O Boulton) collide in the air with F/Lt Sinclair's Hurricane. He saw F/Lt Sinclair bale out and met him when he landed. He also saw the other Hurricane collide with a Do215 and both these aircraft crash in flames. This confirms reports of pilots of 310 Squadron that they saw 2 Hurricanes collide and also report of F/Lt Clouston of 19 Squadron that he saw a Hurricane collide with a twin engine e/a. This makes an extra Do215 destroyed.

Acting F/Lt Rypl as a result of being chased by about 10 Me109s ran short of petrol and landed in a large field near Oxted which had been obstructed, crashed and aircraft probably a write off, cine camera gun not carried, R/T satisfactory.

Weather: haze up to 8,000 feet, cloud 4/10 at 7,000 feet.

Below: 310 (Czech) Squadron had a few English pilots to help them become operational. Johnny Boulton (left) was a flying instructor and Jerrard Jefferies (centre) and Gordon Sinclair (right) flew as flight commanders. On 9 September, Boulton, who had been given permission to fly combat sorties with the Czechs, was seen to collide with Sinclair's Hurricane whilst attacking an Me110 which was also caught up in the collision. Sinclair survived but Boulton was killed when his Hurricane crashed near Croydon.

Contemporary Accounts 310 Sqn

16.40 - 18.00 hrs 9th September 1940

COMBAT REPORT:

F/Lt G L Sinclair - Red 1, A Flight, 310 Squadron

I was Red Leader of 310 Squadron in a wing attack on bombers. As we turned into attack in sections line astern I saw Me109s coming down on us from port; the squadron was turning starboard and I myself turned very slightly port to see what the Me109s were doing, when, without warning I received a hard blow across the shoulders accompanied by a loud noise, followed by three distant bangs, quickly. I then found myself in an inverted spin, thrown hard against the roof, and apparently without any starboard plane, but it was very hard to see anything in that position. I then decided to get out. I had considerable difficulty in opening the roof and undoing the straps, owing to the pressure in the cockpit; having done this I just shot out into space without any effort on my part. The parachute descent took almost exactly 13 minutes, and I finally landed in a wood just off the Purley Way in Coulsdon. I was picked up by Lieutenant G D Cooper (Irish Guards) who told me that I had collided in mid-air with another Hurricane and that one of the Hurricanes had then hit a twin-engined e/a, which crashed in flames. He saw the whole action through glasses.

COMBAT REPORT:

P/O S Zimprich - Blue 3, B Flight, 310 Squadron

I wanted to make an attack on a formation of Do 215s with the leader of my section, but I lost him in a sharp turn. Then I tried to attack the formation myself. I sighted an Me110. I attacked him from the starboard side at 300 - 50 yards. I saw black smoke pouring from his port engine. I wanted to make another attack on him, but I sighted an Me110 in my rear, and I could not find any details about the result of my first attack. I broke away, lost sight of the other Me110 as well, and then I climbed to attack the e/a formation. I picked up a Do 215 which was a certain distance from his formation and delivered an attack on him from above, and from starboard at 300 - 50 yards, and saw him go down in a steep dive. I attacked him again from the front and port at about 50 yards and noticed that the gunner did not fire at me anymore. I repeated the attack from the starboard and fired a long burst. I saw the engines stopped and the Do 215 gliding. Then I saw something fall out of the e/a, probably bombs. Then this e/a landed without undercarriage down near Westerham. I circled above him, and as I saw the army approaching his crew, I landed at the Biggin Hill aerodrome.

COMBAT REPORT:

P/O V Bergman - Yellow 3, A Flight, 310 Squadron

I was No.3 in the Yellow Section with F/Lt Maly as leader. After the two Hurricanes collided in front of us I made a sharp right turn, and the leader of our section dived. I saw an Me110 attacking a Hurricane from the rear, so increased the boost, and followed him. The Hurricane broke away in a dive and I opened fire. Me110 suddenly made a right climbing turn and in this moment I gave him a long burst. The gunner ceased fire and the e/a went into a steep dive. I saw heavy black smoke pouring from both engines, and it was apparent that they caught fire, as I saw a red glow. The e/a disappeared in smoke and I returned to the fighting section.

Right: Stanislav Zimprich and Vaclav Bergman photographed in September 1940 at Duxford.

COMBAT REPORT:
P/O S Fejfar - Red 3, A Flight, 310 Squadron

I was No.3 in the section led by F/Lt Sinclair. We approached the formation of enemy bombers from the starboard side, when enemy fighters made a counter attack and tried to get in rear of us. I made a sharp left turn and came in rear of the formation of 8 Me110s. These aircraft parted when attacked. I followed an Me110, which by turns, steep climbing and diving tried to escape. I delivered three attacks on him and the e/a went into a steep dive. I saw smoke pouring from his port engine. I dived at him and fired one more burst and the port side of e/a caught fire. In this moment I noticed that starboard leading edge fairings were loosened and my aircraft began to vibrate and went to the ground. I slowly pulled the aeroplane's nose up, and by then I had lost the Me110 from my sight. In the last moment I saw that this burning e/a was followed by another Hurricane. I thought that my a/c was hit by splinter from AA shell, and I left the battle.

COMBAT REPORT:
Acting F/Lt F Rypl - Blue 2, B Flight, 310 Squadron

I took off as No.2 in the first section. At about 20,000 feet above east part of London we made several turns, and I saw two of our aircraft crashing to the ground. Above our heads I sighted a number of enemy fighters, none of them already in action. When I noticed that some of them were attacking our section, which flew below me, I attacked one of the e/a immediately and fired a burst at the distance of about 150 yards. It was an Me109, and after I fired at him I saw grey smoke pouring out of his engine, so that the e/a was evidently put out of action. It dived, and I climbed with my aircraft to attack a formation of enemy bombers. When I was a little above one of them, I sighted several enemy fighters on my tail. Immediately I dived to escape, and I was long chased by them. I used various manoeuvres and at about 3,000 feet I noticed I was over hilly, partly wooded country. As I was flying with the reserve petrol tank open, and had therefore not much time for orientation, and as I could find no aerodrome, I decided to make an emergency landing to save the aircraft. I landed in a long field with undercarriage down, but it was obstructed with wire fixed on wooden bars, which I could not see from above, and this is the reason for the damage to my aircraft. I point out that the visibility was very poor towards the evening.

COMBAT REPORT:
Sgt J Hubacek - Green 2, B Flight, 310 Squadron

I was No.2 of the Green Section when I approached a formation of enemy bombers, the enemy fighters lined up to attack our squadron. The leader of our section made a turn to the left and in this moment two of our Hurricanes collided. I made a right turn and attacked immediately an Me110, which made an attack on a Hurricane together with another Me110. This broke away and escaped at great speed in eastward direction. Then I attacked once more jointly with the attacked Hurricane. Then I broke away and attacked 4 Me's from the side out of the sun, and the last one of them made a counter attack. I attacked him several times from turns at the distance of 100 to 200 yards. The fuselage and rudder were damaged and I saw several splinters fall away from it. Then it dived into a cloud and I lost sight of it. The fighting finished at about 8,000 feet from 20,000 feet.

72 SQUADRON INTELLIGENCE REPORT

The squadron was ordered to patrol Biggin Hill below cloud base. 12 a/c from 72 Squadron left Croydon between 17.35 and 18.15 hours. When they had climbed to Angels 5 they were ordered to patrol at Angels 15. When climbing to intercept the enemy, which consisted of about 80+ aircraft, comprising Do17s, Me110s and Me109s, a single Me110 was seen coming down. The Squadron Leader ordered line astern, but owing to bad R/T his order was not heard and four or five pilots dived after it.

They failed, however, to contact, but P/O Elliot flying in the rear guard section attacked it and brought it down in flames near Lewes. The pilot reports the enemy aircraft had the upper part of fuselage painted grey green and markings of a white cross in a white circle. Two bursts of six seconds were delivered into the fuselage, but no return fire experienced after the first burst.

COMBAT REPORT:
P/O R D Elliott - Yellow 1, A Flight, 72 Squadron

I was Yellow 1 in my section acting as 'rear guard' to the squadron. We were climbing up to 15,000 ft to engage E/A, when at 8,000 ft I saw an Me110 about 2,000 ft below and flying on a SE course, I turned and was then astern E/A and with the aid of Max Boost (12 lbs) I gradually closed with enemy and after giving two 6 sec bursts the port engine caught fire and E/A started to lose height, I followed up and fired all remaining rounds into the E/A fuselage - the E/A continued its downward course and crashed near Lewes (approx.) about 12 miles in from the South Coast - the whole E/A was in flames and completely destroyed.

The upper fuselage was of a greenish grey camouflage with white crosses with a white circle around. I did not notice crew jump and think this highly improbable.

Return fire was experienced at first but not after second 6 secs. burst.

229 SQUADRON OPERATIONS RECORD BOOK

Following instructions received from Headquarters Fighter Command. All aircraft and pilots departed Wittering for Northolt at 13.40 hours on detachment estimated to last for two weeks. At the same time, all pilots and machines of No.1 Squadron departed Northolt, to remain at Wittering also for two weeks, the idea being to give No.1 Squadron a 'rest'.

At 17.40 hours twelve aircraft took off on a Base Patrol below cloud: enemy aircraft were seen, but these were too distant and no contact resulted, all our machines returning at 18.30 hours.

1 (RCAF) SQUADRON INTELLIGENCE REPORT

12 Hurricanes No.1 Canadian Squadron left Northolt 17.29 hours 9.9.40, nine landed Northolt 18.15 - 18.35 hours, and two at 20.00 hours.

The squadron was led by S/Ldr McNab and accompanied by 303 Squadron in rear, was proceeding in Guildford area to intercept enemy raids, when a large formation of bandits were seen about ten miles away going north and about 4,000 feet higher. To close with e/a, a climbing turn to port was made but in doing so bandits were lost sight of. Suddenly they found themselves in amongst eight or ten Me109s who were a protection screen for bombers below.

The squadron were in line astern when the engagement started and when attacked by e/a most pilots found e/a on their tails and broke away before being able to fire.

F/O Millar was in rear section acting as rear guard and at some stage in the attack was shot down, baled out and is now in hospital at Horsham with burns and a wound in the leg. No report has been received from this pilot in regard to his part in this sortie.

Some of the pilots were able to fire at the enemy but with no conclusive results, while others were unable to find a target due to the suddenness of the attack and having to break away on finding themselves the object of attack. The squadron as a whole were at a disadvantage throughout as they were too low and too late to intercept the original raid of enemy bombers sighted. This combat developed south-east of Guildford and proceeded south.

Contemporary Accounts 1 (RCAF) Sqn

1 (RCAF) SQUADRON OPERATIONS RECORD BOOK

There was a threat of welcome rain early in the morning which, however, cleared up about noon. The squadron spent most of the day at dispersal point and came to readiness from 16.00 hours.

Enemy raids started on London about 17.00 hours and we were dispatched to intercept. We had bad luck as the original raid sighted was above and in climbing to make attack, suddenly ran into a protective screen of Me109s who were above and proceeding south. The squadron was attacked and fortunately only one pilot was forced to bale out, F/O Millar, who is reported wounded in the leg and burned, at Horsham Hospital. We managed to add an Me109 to the list of destroyed, F/O Peterson blowing one to bits, and three Me109s were severely damaged, two by F/O Lochnan and one by S/Ldr McNab. The former visited most of the seashore resorts on his way back to base where he arrived at dusk after a long conversation with the controller over the R/T. The night was quiet around the station, a few bombs being heard dropping in London, and the e/a droned overhead as usual.

24 hours leaves are not being spent in London as frequently as heretofore for some reason.

COMBAT REPORT:
S/Ldr E A McNab - Blue 1, B Flight, 1 (RCAF) Squadron

I was Blue 1 and leading the squadron, with 303 Squadron following below. While proceeding vector 170° and over Guildford / Redhill area a large number of bandits were seen 10 miles east flying north 4,000 feet above. I turned north climbing at full throttle with aircraft in line astern. We ran directly into a large number of enemy bombers with the Me109 escort going south for the Channel. In the engagement I got a deflection shot on an Me109 at 200 yards range and followed him to line astern, smoke began coming from the starboard side and he dove away. I continued to attack from 18,000 feet to 4,000 feet, when he disappeared in a cloud 5 miles south of Brighton over the Channel.

COMBAT REPORT:
F/O P W Lochnan - Blue 2, B Flight, 1 (RCAF) Squadron

I was Blue 2 of the leading section. We were broken up when Me109s came out of the sun. After evasive action I climbed up after main body of enemy and on the way tried to join up with two aircraft. As they turned I saw the yellow noses and dived at one. I fired two bursts and saw bits flying off. As I turned to follow him, saw a third Me109 firing at me from rear quarter. Did tight climbing turn and came out diving on him. Had him in sights from 250 yards closing fast to 50 yards and fired one burst of three seconds following him in a tight climbing turn. No smoke but damaged badly. Lost them all after that in heavy clouds. Came up again and was quite alone so returned.

COMBAT REPORT:
F/O O J Peterson - Green 2, B Flight, 1 (RCAF) Squadron

I was Green 2 and was the second section in line astern and climbing. Suddenly the squadron leader did a sharp break away to the left, Green Section followed. I saw two Me109s apparently diving on the squadron leader. Green 1 attacked one of them and I immediately swung on the other's tail and opened fire at about 250 yards closing to about 75 yards. Suddenly I saw bits flying off the e/a and then it began to smoke, flames pouring out the belly, the aircraft just disintegrated. I immediately began my break away but ran into some loose part of the e/a, breaking my windscreen the pieces of glass and Perspex cutting my face and obscuring my vision. My propeller was also hit by pieces of e/a and broke 8 inches off the end. I came down from about 15,000 to 4,000 before even being able to see my instruments. I still lost height due to my obscured vision. At 1,500 my vision improved and I was able to proceed to base at that level.

Contemporary Accounts 303 (Polish) Sqn
16.40 - 18.00 hrs 9th September 1940

303 SQUADRON INTELLIGENCE REPORT

Combat at 18.00 hours on 9.9.40 near Beachy Head.

Squadron of 12 Hurricanes up 17.35 hours. Ten Hurricanes landed at Northolt at 18.25 - 19.00 hours.

F/Lt Kent reports:

I took off from Northolt to join up with No.1 Canadian Squadron at 2,000 feet. I was leading the squadron - 12 Hurricanes. We were vectored in a southerly direction, climbing all the time. When we got not far from the coast at 11,000 feet, I saw many aircraft - Me's and Spitfires probably at 20,000 feet. We turned north-west. I saw some aircraft cross below the Canadians. Suddenly out of the sun came about 40 bombers going south. We were at 13,000 feet. I watched No.1 Canadian to see what they were going to do. They seemed to be sending off a section or two, and I lost them in the sun. I turned off after the bombers, but we were too late to make good contact, and only the leading section did so. I caught up with one straggler, and he started to dive into cloud, just south of the coast. I followed and opened fire at 500 yards. Meanwhile I was being chased by two or three Me109s which were kept off my tail by Red 3 (F/O Henneberg) who was doing crossovers behind me. After my third burst at about 400 yards - his tracer had been going under me - the rear gunner stopped firing. I gave another short burst and saw a lot of pieces come off his starboard engine, and it began to pour out dense clouds of smoke. He turned slightly to the right as he went into cloud. I followed him down into the clouds, and came out over the Channel. It was very dark and hazy under the clouds. I could see no sign of the e/a. As I was circling around I saw another a/c at about 1,000 feet flying towards France. I approached to investigate, and was surprised to find that it was coloured with our camouflage, and had a yellow mark on the side of the fuselage. At this juncture I think the rear gunner fired. I decided to attack. I think it was an Me110, but it might have been a Dornier. He immediately dived low over the sea at about 500 feet, doing gentle turns in order to evade me, and heading for France. I had no difficulty in following him. His rear gunner appeared to be firing at me until after my second burst. He did a swift turn to the left, right across my bows, and at this angle looked very like a Do17. I got a very good burst in now at about 150 yards and saw large pieces of stuff flying off his starboard engine, and a lot of smoke began to pour out of it. Immediately afterwards it started to burn. He continued his turn and made back towards England. I did not waste any ammunition, as he was rapidly losing height, so I flew along parallel, and a little above to see whether he crashed.

At this point an Me109 came out of the cloud, and started a quarter attack on me, so I turned to meet him, where upon he made off very fast towards France. I was unable to catch him, so I turned back to follow my victim. I caught up with him just as he hit the water about ten miles south of Beachy Head. Immediately there was a large flash of flame. I saw the tail sticking out of the water and as I watched, it disappeared, leaving only a large smear of oil, and I think I saw a rubber boat. I decided not to attack it as I wanted to conserve my remaining ammunition in case I had need of it. I flew around Newhaven, and rocked my wings, but I saw no boats going out, so as I was getting short of petrol I returned to base.

In general I would say that we were too low and too late for a successful interception, and we did not see the enemy bombers soon enough, as they were in the sun. They must have been coming from a higher altitude as they were going at a great speed when I saw them, and it was very difficult to catch up with them.

Johnny Kent 303 Sqn

P/O Zumbach reports:

When we saw the bombers and the Me's which were fighting with the Hurricanes and Spitfires, I saw a bomber being attacked by a Hurricane (Sgt Frantisek). This Hurricane was being attacked by two Me's, and escaped into cloud. I looked and saw one fighter in front of me. Thinking it was F/Lt Kent I went up to it and at 50 yards I saw it was an Me with yellow strips on wings and nose to make it look like a Hurricane. I only recognised it by the struts on its tail. I gave it a two seconds burst, and from the starboard wing root many pieces fell off, and the e/a burst into flames. At this moment I was attacked by an Me on my port side 800 yards away which missed me from 800/600 yards. I began dog-fighting with him. After a few minutes four more Me109s appeared 3 from below and one from above, and attacked me. Two gained height as I made tight circles and dived on me giving long burst. I should not like to have that happen to me again. I continued doing tight circles. One of the Me's came up towards me, and I gave him about 60 rounds from 150 yards. He turned over on his back smoking and fell into cloud.

I was now very tired and I also got into cloud and came out on the French side of the Channel. At first I thought it was England, but the AA fire woke me up. I made for England and on my way I met an Me109 but I was too tired to attack it. I decided to go down at the first aerodrome I saw and landed at White Waltham. Men ran to me and I got out and rested for 10 minutes, and came home.

Jan Zumbach 303 Sqn

Contemporary Accounts 303 (Polish) Sqn

Sgt Frantisek reports:

The enemy was escaping southwards at great speed losing height; when we arrived in sight of the Germans, swarms of Me109s dived from a great height to attack us. I saw one Me109 going in to attack a Hurricane in front of me. I attacked it, starboard beam, firing at 150/100 yards at the engine, which began to burn. He tried to escape by climbing, and I saw him open the cockpit preparatory to jumping. I shot at the cockpit and the pilot collapsed. The e/a fell in flames to the ground (Horsham area). I then saw a Hurricane in flames and the pilot jumped. A Spitfire came down to circle round the pilot. I went for an He111, and two Me109s attacked me. I hid in a cloud at about 17,000 feet for seven minutes - I played hide and seek with them in the clouds. During a right turn I came out of the cloud, and saw in front of me, 10 yards away, also coming out of cloud, an He111. I very nearly collided with it, and fired at the front of the fuselage at an angle of 40 degrees from above and behind. The front of the e/a fell to pieces with the cockpit and both engines in flames. I do not know if this e/a fell on the ground or in sea, owing to the clouds.

As I broke away one Me109 attacked me from above, and another from below. I hid again in the clouds and flew towards France to keep under cover. Over the Channel I climbed out of cloud and was hit by four Me shells, one in the port wing, one through the left tank which did not catch fire, and one through the radiator. It is only due to the armour plating behind me that the fourth shell did not kill me. Two Spitfires came to my rescue, and shot down the Me109 which was apparently the one which had hit me. I saw the damage which had been done, and was obliged to find a landing place as the engine temperature was mounting dangerously.

On a little hill north-east of Brighton, I found a field of cabbages and made an excellent landing. The police came immediately - not only did they not make any difficulty, but they were very kind to me. They anchored the Hurricane, shut off the petrol and oxygen, and left the plane guarded by policemen. They took me by car to Brighton, and I returned to Northolt by train. Sgt Wunsche's parachute was at the police station; I brought mine home.

At the railway station the people were very kind to me, and girls gave me some chocolate, and people photographed me. I am very grateful for the kindness which was shown me by everybody.

The rest of the squadron failed to make contact with the enemy, and there is nothing to comment upon except perhaps the difficulty which P/O Zumbach had in distinguishing the Me109 with its yellow camouflage in the poor light, from a Hurricane. The enemy tactics appeared simply to be to lose height and escape over France as quickly as possible.

From telephone conversations with the hospital at Hove, it appears Sgt Wunsche was shot down by cannon fire near Hove without damaging any of the enemy. He was seriously wounded in the back and arm, but is believed to be doing well.

Right: Kazimierz Wunsche was shot down in flames during this combat but managed to bale out albeit with injuries. He returned to the squadron on 23 October 1940.

Me110
15(Z)/LG1

Hurricane
310 Squadron
F/O Boulton

Hurricane
310 Squadron
F/Lt Sinclair

Hurricane
253 Squadron
F/O Watts

Me110
9/ZG76

Me109
1/JG53

Hurricane
607 S...
Sgt P...

Hurricane
242 Squadron
Sgt Lonsdale

Hurricane
242 Squadron
P/O Sclanders

He111
3/KG1

Hurricane
310 Squadron
P/O Rypl

Hurricane
605 Squadron
P/O Forrester

Hurricane
605 Squadron
P/O Humphreys

Spitfire
66 Squadron
P/O Corbett

He111
Stab III/KG53

Me109
7/JG27

Hurricane
1(RCAF)Squadron
F/O Millar

Ju88
Stab/KG30

Me109
8/JG53

Me109
5/JG27

Ju88
Stab II/KG30

Hurricane
303 Squadron
Sgt Wunsche

Spitfire
602 Squadron
F/Lt Webb

Spitfire
602 Squadron
Sgt Whall

Hurricane
303 Squadron
Sgt Frantisek

Ju88
Stab III/KG30

Ju88
8/KG30

Ju88
Stab II/KG30

Me109
4/JG3

Me1
9/Z...

RAF and Luftwaffe crash locations

Hurricane
249 Squadron
Sgt Davidson

Spitfire
222 Squadron
P/O Vigors

Me110
7/ZG76

Hurricane
607 Squadron
Sgt Spyer

Hurricane
607 Squadron
P/O Drake

Hurricane
7 Squadron
P/O Parnall

Hurricane
607 Squadron
P/O Lenahan

Me109
6/JG27

Me109
7/JG3

Me109
Stab I/JG27

Spitfire
92 Squadron
P/O Saunders

Spitfire
92 Squadron
P/O Watling

Me109
7/JG3

Me109
I/JG54

Me109
4/JG53

Me109
3/JG54

ROCHFORD

SOUTHEND

CANVEY ISLAND

MARGATE

HERNE BAY

BROADSTAIRS

SHEERNESS

MANSTON

RAMSGATE

LBURY

EASTCHURCH

GILLINGHAM

ROCHESTER

OURNE

FAVERSHAM

CANTERBURY

SANDWICH

DEAL

DETLING

WEST MALLING

MAIDSTONE

ST MARGARET'S BAY

SOUTH FORELAND

ASHFORD

DOVER

LEHURST

HAWKINGE

FOLKESTONE

RDEN

LYMPNE

HYTHE

HAWKHURST

DYMCHURCH

LYDD

BATTLE

DUNGENESS

WISSANT

HASTINGS

BEXHILL

MARQUISE

BOURNE

BOULOGNE-SUR-MER

ETAPLES

BERCK

RAF Casualties

16.40 - 18.00 hrs 9th September 1940

RAF Casualties	Combat A	16.40 - 18.00 hrs

1 (RCAF) Sqn Hurricane P3081   F/O W B M Millar - wounded. Shot down by Me109s and fell at Loxwood, West Sussex. 25-year-old William Millar baled out wounded and burned, and was treated in Bramshott Hospital, Surrey, before returning to Canada.

1 (RCAF) Sqn Hurricane   F/O O J Peterson – slightly injured. Damaged - struck by pieces of enemy aircraft destroyed near Horsham.

19 Sqn Spitfire P9431   Sub-Lt A G Blake - safe. Damaged by bullets through windscreen and gravity tank.

19 Sqn Spitfire P9546   P/O W Cunningham - safe. Damaged by bullets through port main spar.

66 Sqn Spitfire N3049   P/O G H Corbett - injured. Shot down by Me109s and fell at Skinners Farm, Edenbridge, Kent. 20-year-old Canadian George Corbett baled out with abrasions and sprained an ankle on landing at Furnace Farm, Cowden, he was sent on seven day's sick leave.

92 Sqn Spitfire L1077   P/O C H Saunders - wounded. Crash-landed at Midley near Rye. 29-year-old Cecil Saunders was admitted to RAMC Brookland with shrapnel in one leg and re-joined his squadron in October.

92 Sqn Spitfire P9372   P/O W C Watling - wounded. Crashed near Rye. 20-year-old William Watling baled out with burns to his face and hands. He was admitted to Rye Hospital and re-joined his squadron in November.

Below: 20 year old Bill Watling of 92 Squadron who was shot down and burned in P9372 (below left) during this combat. He returned to the squadron in November but was killed in February 1941 when his Spitfire crashed in bad weather.

92 Sqn Spitfire R6596   P/O A R Wright - safe. Damaged by Me109s.

222 Sqn Spitfire X4058   P/O T A Vigors - safe. Crash-landed at Southfleet with three 20mm cannon shells in the engine.

222 Sqn Spitfire P9469   P/O J W Broadhurst - safe. Damaged by Me109s and landed with a large section of tailplane shot away.

242 Sqn Hurricane P3087 LE-Q   P/O K M Sclanders - killed. Shot down near Kenley. Crashed at Birchwood House Farm, Woldingham, Surrey.

Kirkpatrick Maclure Sclanders (24)
Born: Saskatoon, Canada.
Joined the RAF in 1935, but left due to illness.
He re-joined the RAF in July 1940 having escaped from France.
Joined 242 Squadron on 26th August from 6 OTU.
Combat claims - none.

242 Sqn Hurricane P2831 LE-K   Sgt R H Lonsdale - safe. Hit by return fire from Do17s over Kenley. Crashed at Ninehams Road, Kenley, Surrey. Canadian Robert Lonsdale baled out landing at Caterham. He did not fly again operationally with 242 Squadron and was posted to 501 Squadron in October.

249 Sqn Hurricane P3667 GN-O   Sgt H J Davidson - safe. Force-landed at Cooling, Kent.

253 Sqn Hurricane V6639   F/O R F Watts - safe. Damaged; cockpit side panel broken open. Force-landed at Cobham Park Farm, Surrey.

303 Sqn Hurricane P3700 RF-E   Sgt K Wunsche - wounded. Shot down by Me109s over Beachy Head. Crashed and burned out at Saddlescombe Farm, Poynings, West Sussex. 21-year-old Pole Kazimierz Wunsche baled out with slight burns to his face and left foot, landing near Devils Dyke, and admitted to Hove Hospital. He re-joined his squadron on 23rd October.

303 Sqn Hurricane P3975 RF-U   Sgt J Frantisek - safe. Shot down in action with Me109s over Beachy Head and force-landed at Cambridgeshire Farm, Falmer, West Sussex, with machine gun damage to radiator, fuselage and port wing.

310 Sqn Hurricane V7412 NN-P   F/O J E Boulton - killed. Lost control following collision with F/Lt Sinclair and then hit an Me110. Aircraft fell off Woodmansterne Lane, Woodmansterne, Surrey.

John Eric Boulton (20)
Born: Bosham, West Sussex.
Joined the RAF in October 1937.
Joined 2 Flying Training School in December 1938 as an instructor.
Attached to 310 Squadron on 14 July 1940 as an instructor to convert Czechs to Hurricanes and given permission to fly operationally.
Combat claim -1:
7/9/40 He111 shared.

Below: 303 Squadron's Kazimierz Wunsche was shot down in this Hurricane P3700 RF-E on 9 September 1940.

RAF Casualties

16.40 - 18.00 hrs 9th September 1940

17 September 1940
To, Air Ministry
London

Dear Sirs,

So far I have received no further information about my son, Flying Officer John E Boulton. I have received a letter from the Section Chaplain, also one from his Squadron Leader J D Blackwood. They seem convinced that my son has lost his life.

There is no statement as to where it happened, or if any trace of him or his aeroplane has been found.

We were astounded to receive a letter from my boy after he had crashed? Telling us of his brave deeds on the Saturday over London. He also informed me in this letter that he is still under the Training Command.

His Squadron Leader tells me my boy asked to take part in the operations with his squadron of Czechs, and that he was given permission to allow my son to do so. I also understand he was flying a Hurricane.

Was he properly equipped as a fighter? Had he his life saving jacket if he should come down in the sea? Had he enough ammunition? I am asking all these questions as my son told me in his engagement with a Heinkel 111 on Saturday, he ran out of ammunition after he had hit the two gunners and put the port engine out of action of the Heinkel. Could this have happened a second time?

His Squadron Leader tells me my son crashed into another Hurricane and then into a German bomber and they came down together, but the pilot of the Hurricane baled out.

Do you realize my son, like many others, was a very experienced pilot and had completed his 1,000 hours flying and should have continued to have been most helpful to the Air Ministry in training good pilots and it seems to me that this war is going to be won by Good pilots.

I am a widow and my dear son was my only support. I live here with two young daughters who have a struggle to carry on.

The loss of my son is going to make a tremendous difference to us.

My late husband was Captain and 2 Lt of distinguished service, but when he died in 1929 his pension finished and I have nothing whatsoever.

Please do not imagine that I cannot realize the chaos there must be in the air when these tremendous battles are going on. I do, but I am still concerned that something must have gone radically wrong for my son to have crashed into a German bomber. Can I have an explanation please and is it possible for me dear boy to have a decent burial?

I am proud of him and I am glad he had the pluck and spirit to ask to have a transfer to a fighter squadron. I am proud of his achievements in these short years and not yet twenty-one.

But was he properly equipped and had he enough ammunition?

If he was with the squadron, why was he fighting alone? His Section Chaplain's letter was the first line of sympathy we received.

I am

Yours faithfully

Anne E Boulton

Below: Johnny Boulton was only 20 when he was killed. He was a non-operational flying instructor helping the Czech pilots of 310 become familiar with flying RAF aircraft. He's seen here in the instructor's seat of a Miles Master.

Although the incident had been witnessed, John Boulton's body was not immediately identified. His mother was officially told that his death had been confirmed in a letter dated 24th September. An investigation was subsequently launched by the Imperial War Graves Commission and Captain Houden enquired of the cemetery authorities at Bandon Hill, Wallington, where he had been buried as an unidentified airman.

2nd October, 1940.
Dear Capt Houden,

I have to acknowledge your letter of the 30th September but I regret that I am unable to help you in your enquiry. The particulars as far as I can tell you are as follows.

The airman was the pilot of a fighter aircraft which crashed on September 9th or 10th during a dog fight over this area.

He came down with his machine which burnt out in Woodmansterne Lane, Wallington.

The body was removed and taken to the A.R.P. Mortuary in Wallington the R.A.F. at Croydon were informed and as no evidence of his identity was forthcoming the Medical Officer of Health for this district gave an order to a local undertaker to provide a coffin. The body was then removed to Bandon Hill Mortuary and finally buried on the 13th September; the R.A.F. Chaplain from Croydon aerodrome officiated and my grave diggers acted as bearers, the Town Clerk, Medical Officer, British Legion etc being in attendance.

I overheard the R.A.F. Chaplain say that he had had the engine dug out and had obtained the engine number and probably that would help to identify the machine number and finally the pilot. This I am afraid is all I can tell you. Our Town Clerk I believe suggested a photograph but that was impossible.

310 Sqn Hurricane R4084   F/Lt G L Sinclair - safe. Collided with the Hurricane of F/O Boulton and crashed off Purley Way, Wallington, Surrey. 24-year-old Gordon Sinclair baled out and landed after a 13 minute descent in a wood just off the Purley Way in Coulsdon.

310 Sqn Hurricane P3142 NN-M   Acting F/Lt F Rypl - safe. Landed at Limpsfield, Surrey, having run out of fuel and hit anti-invasion obstacles.

310 Sqn Hurricane V7436 NN-H   Sgt J Hubacek - safe. Damaged in a heavy landing at Duxford.

602 Sqn Spitfire K9910   F/Lt P C Webb - injured. Crash-landed in a wood at Crocker Hill, Boxgrove, West Sussex. 22-year-old Scotsman Paul Webb from Greenock suffered a broken wrist and facial injuries, and did not fly again during the Battle.

602 Sqn Spitfire N3282   Sgt B E P Whall - injured. Landed near Arundel, West Sussex. 22-year-old Basil Whall slightly injured his neck, but was operational again by the end of the month.

605 Sqn Hurricane P2765 UP-N   P/O J S Humphreys - wounded. Hit by crossfire from He111s of KG53 over Hampshire 5.30. The cockpit side was shot away and the pilot wounded in the left thigh, arm and hand by a cannon shell that exploded. Abandoned over Bordon near Petersfield. Aircraft fell at The Straits, Kingsley, Hampshire. 21-year-old New Zealander James Humphreys landed near the Canadian Army Camp at Bordon after being shot by the soldiers. Fortunately their aim was poor and he got away with a graze to his body, but the troops then took the buttons off his tunic, his boots and maps. He was admitted to Aldershot Military Hospital where his badly injured left little finger had to be amputated. He returned to his squadron on 28th November.

605 Sqn Hurricane L2059 UP-P   P/O G M Forrester - killed. Collided with He111 A1+ZD of Stab III/KG53. Fell minus starboard wing at Southwood Farm, Shalden, Hampshire.

George Mathwin Forrester (26)
Born: Newcastle.
Joined the RAF in 1938.
Joined 605 Squadron from 6 OTU on 5th August 1940.
Combat claims - none.

RAF Casualties

16.40 - 18.00 hrs 9th September 1940

FLYING ACCIDENT - P/O G M FORRESTER (S1369) HURRICANE AIRCRAFT L.2059.

12 Hurricanes of No.605 Squadron left Croydon at 16.53 hours on 9.9.40., and encountered 17 He111s at 20,000 feet near Farnborough, Kent, with some Me110s behind them and about 50 Me109s some miles to port of the bombers. The formation were proceeding towards the west. 605 Squadron were flying in echelon port, 'A' Flight leading. The squadron were jumped by Me109s when about to attack the bombers. 'B' Flight recovered formation and followed the enemy formation on parallel course westwards, until enemy aircraft turned 90° towards them, allowing head-on attacks by 'B' Flight. P/O G M Forrester was Blue 3, and was seen by Green 1 (P/O J S Humphreys) to attack the leading aircraft of the second vic of He 111s, do a half-barrel roll on to the left-hand machine of that vic, colliding with that machine and breaking off its port main plane. P/O Forrester crashed with his machine near Alton.

Total Flying Times …….………… 364.30 hours.
Flying Times in Hurricanes …….. 74.30 hours.

Below: An artist's impression of Forrester's Hurricane L2059

607 Sqn Hurricane P3574   P/O S B Parnall - killed. Flying with Blue Section from Tangmere and attacked bombers from beneath, but was not seen to go down. Crashed at Lime Tree Farm, Goudhurst, Kent. (Casualty File records Parnall flying P3117).

Stuart Boyd Parnall (30)
Born: Esher, Surrey.
Joined the RAF and 607 Squadron in 1939.
Served with 263 Squadron in Norway.
Re-joined 607 Squadron on 24th June 1940.
Combat claims - 2:
26/5/40 He111 in Norway.
15/8/40 Me110 probable.

His brother, S/Ldr James Boyd Parnall was the CO of 504 Squadron and was lost on 14th May 1940 over Belgium.

607 Sqn Hurricane P3117   P/O J D Lenahan - killed. Flying with Green Section as rear guard when the squadron attacked 60 - 70 He111s, but he was not seen to go down. Crashed Mount Ephraim, Cranbrook, Kent. (Casualty File records Lenahan flying P3574).

John Desmond Lenahan (20)
Born: Tayport, Fife.
Joined the RAF in 1938.
Joined 607 Squadron on 1st June 1940.
Combat claims - none.

607 Sqn Hurricane P2728   P/O G J Drake - killed. Shot down at Bockingfold Farm. Goudhurst, Kent. He was posted as missing and the location of the crash not known until his body was recovered with the wreckage of his Hurricane in 1972.

George James Drake (20)
Born: Kroonstad, Orange Free State, South Africa.
Joined the RAF in 1939.
Joined 607 Squadron on 13th June 1940 from 263 Squadron.
Combat claims - none.

Below: The AF coded Hurricanes of 607 Squadron were hit hard in this encounter with five aircraft being shot down and one damaged. Three pilots were killed and three injured.

607 Sqn Hurricane P2912   Sgt P A Burnell-Phillips - wounded. Force-landed at Curry Farm, Halstead, Kent. Engine seized after being damaged by Me109s. Peter Burnell-Phillips was slightly wounded in one ankle, but returned to his squadron.

607 Sqn Hurricane P2680   Sgt R A Spyer - wounded. Shot down and aircraft fell at Stilstead Farm, East Peckham, Kent. 22-year-old Richard Spyer baled out slightly wounded.

607 Sqn Hurricane   Sgt J Lansdell - injured. Returned damaged.

Luftwaffe Casualties

16.40 - 18.00 hrs 9th September 1940

Luftwaffe Casualties	Combat A	16.40 - 18.00 hrs

III/JG2 Me109E-1 Wn.2947 Landed at Beaumont-le-Roger 30% damaged. Ff: safe.

4/JG3 Me109E-1 Wn.6138 Started from near Calais at 16.00 hrs escorting bombers to the London Docks. The formation consisted of about forty bombers and an escort of sixty mixed Me109s and Me110s. As the bombers were heading for London, there was a slight engagement with fighters near Dover at 16.50 hrs and shortly afterwards the engine of this aircraft began to fail. Escorted by his wingman in the Rotte (Feldwebel Kortlopel), the pilot turned for home. At 22,000 feet his escort dived steeply, under control and for no apparent reason, leaving this pilot to his fate. He tried to reach the French coast but was forced to ditch six miles off Newhaven, East Sussex. Ff: Fw August-Wilhelm Müller PoW.

7/JG3 Me109E-1 Wn.6316 White 6+ Started at 16.15 hrs on a free-lance patrol of one Staffel along the English coast. While flying at 25,000 feet over the coast, they were surprised by a fighter coming out of the sun and this aircraft was hit from behind through the engine. The aircraft landed at Cooper's Field, Rosemary Farm, Flimwell, East Sussex, with its undercarriage retracted and was in good condition. Ff: Uffz Matthias Massmann PoW.

Below: White 6 of 7/JG3 photographed at Farnborough whilst under evaluation.

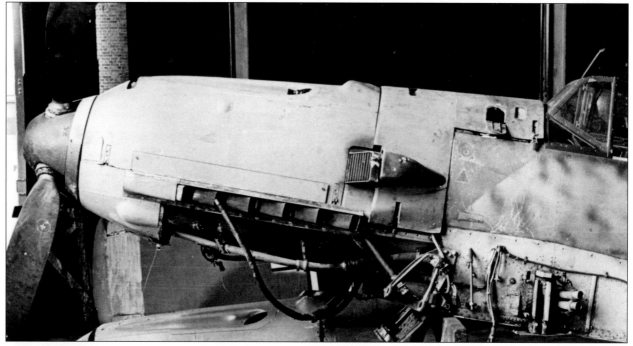

7/JG3 Me109E-4 Wn.5351 Fell into the Channel. Ff: Fw Josef Bauer missing.

Stab I/JG27 Me109E-4 Wn.1394 < + While flying at about 16,000 feet two fighters suddenly appeared above and this aircraft was shot through the radiator with the first burst. Turning for home the engine began to overheat and the aircraft was landed in good condition on Knowle Farm, Mayfield, East Sussex. Ff: Oblt Günther Bode PoW.

Left: Oblt Günther Bode's Me109 photographed shortly before being shot down on 9 September.

Opposite page: The same aircraft after its forced landing at Knowle Farm. It remained in the field for a few weeks, so was covered in camouflage netting to stop it being attacked from the air.

Opposite page inset: Oblt Günther Bode.

Left: When Günther Bode's Me109 was finally moved, it went on display in Ashford, note how the yellow cowling colour was not painted over the uppersurface camouflage.

Luftwaffe Casualties

16.40 - 18.00 hrs 9th September 1940

5/JG27 Me109E-1 Wn.3488 Black 13+ Started from Calais, escorting bombers to London. Following an attack by a fighter at 20,000 feet from below and astern, the radiator and petrol tank were hit, and the pilot landed on Charity Farm, Cootham, West Sussex. Ff: Oblt Erwin Daig PoW.

6/JG27 Me109E-1 Wn.6280 Yellow 7+ Flying between 19,000 and 21,000 feet, the pilot got careless and dropped too far behind. He was shot down and dived to 10,000 feet before he baled out. Aircraft fell at Mounts Farm, Benenden, Kent. Ff : Uffz Georg Rauwolf PoW.
See report of P/O Whitbread, 222 Squadron.

Above: Erwin Daig's Black 13 on display to the public, possibly in the West Midlands.

7/JG27 Me109E-4 Wn.1617 Shot down in a dog-fight and fell at Roman Gate Cottage, Rudgwick, West Sussex. Pilot baled out but found dead. Ff: Uffz Karl Born killed.
See report of Sgt Frantisek, 303 Squadron, and F/O Peterson, 1 (RCAF) Squadron.

1/JG51 Me109E-1 Wn.3614 Crash-landed at Abbeville 80% damaged. Ran out of fuel. Ff: Fw Erwin Fleig safe.

1/JG53 Me109E-4 Wn.1508 White 5+ Escorting bombers attacking an aerodrome east of London. This aircraft was the left support of a Kette flying in Vic, which was itself the left Vic of a Staffel, at 22,000 feet. On the return flight the formation was attacked by five fighters from the rear, port side. The first burst set fire to this aircraft, and the pilot baled out, suffering severe burns. The aircraft fell at Cherry Tree Farm, Old Jail Inn, Biggin Hill, Kent. Ff: Fw Heinrich Höhnisch badly burned PoW.
See reports of the 'Duxford Wing'.

4/JG53 Me109E-4 Wn.963 Fell into the Channel. Ff: Oblt Günther Schulze-Blank killed.

8/JG53 Me109E Wn.6139 Black 1+ Shot down at Sundown Farm, Ditcham, Hampshire. Ff: Gefr Peter Becker killed.

I/JG54 Me109E-1 Wn.6103 Fell into the Channel. Ff: Fw Karl Biber missing.

3/JG54 Me109E-1 Wn.3906 Fell into the Channel. Ff: Fw Adolf Strohauer rescued by the Seenotdienst.

9/JG54 Me109E-4 Wn.0972 Landed at Guines 20% damaged. Ff: Uffz Karl Kempf safe.

1/JG77 Me109E-4 Wn.4055 Landed at Fécamp 30% damaged ran out of fuel. Ff: Lt Heinz Escherhaus safe.

1/JG77 Me109E-4 Wn.3753 Landed at Fécamp 30% damaged ran out of fuel. Ff: Fw Heinz Ettler safe.

3/KG1 He111 H-3 Wn.5713 V4+BL This crew picked up their escort over Guines en-route to attack an aerodrome near London, the whole of I/KG1 taking part. They bombed the target successfully and during the return flight were attacked by fighters from the rear that damaged the cooling system and wounded two of the crew. One engine stopped and the intercom was shot away. The flight engineer baled out, but the rest of the crew remained in the aircraft, which crashed at Sundridge, Kent, with its undercarriage retracted. The crew tried to set fire to the aircraft with an incendiary bomb but this failed to operate. Both airscrews showed .303 strikes, also on starboard nose, port upper surface of fuselage, twenty in the starboard wing, fifty on the port lower side of the fuselage and six on the port wing and engine. Ff: Oblt Erich Kiunka, Bo: Uffz Anton Stumbaum, Bf: Uffz Erich Marks (wounded), Bm: Ofw Alfred Heidrich (baled out) and Bs: Gefr Heinrich Reinecke (wounded) all PoWs.
See reports of Sgt Burnell-Phillips, 607 Squadron and P/O Zimprich, 310 Squadron.

Right: Heinkel 111 V4+BL of 3/KG1 which crashed at Sundridge in Kent and was subsequently put on display in Sevenoaks.

Luftwaffe Casualties

16.40 - 18.00 hrs 9th September 1940

6/KG1   He111H-2   Wn.5124   V4+AW   Landed due to engine failure. Crew safe.

6/KG1   He111H-2   Wn.2729   V4+KW   Landed at Glisy 35% damaged by AA fire over London. Crew safe.

Stab KG30 Ju88A-1   Wn.0274   4D+AA   Target London Docks. Took off with four 250 kg bombs, the same mission having been carried out successfully the previous day. Fifteen aircraft set out all flying in a Ketten Vic astern led by Oberleutnant Metzatin. Although the Geschwaderkommandeur, Oberst Rieckhoff, should have been flying in this aircraft, he was actually with Oberleutnant Gollnesch in 4D+FA. Before reaching the target, the formation was attacked by twelve fighters. The canopy, together with the machine guns, was jettisoned and the oil radiators hit. The pilot made a landing at Church Field, Newells Farm, Nuthurst, West Sussex. Ff: Oblt Rolf Heim, Bo: Uffz Josef Beck, Bf: Fw Albert Fuchs and Bs: Uffz Walter Baustian all PoWs. See report of 66 Squadron.

Below: Two views of Junkers Ju88 4D+AA which force landed at Newells Farm, Nuthurst. In the bottom photo, the aircraft has been significantly dismantled ready for transportation.

Stab II/KG30 Ju88A-1 Wn.8032 4D+FB Fell into the Channel. Uffz Stahl, Uffz Fecht, Uffz Hallert and Gefr Goerth all missing.

Stab II/KG30 Ju88A-2 Wn.5074 4D+KK Target London Docks carrying four 250 kg bombs. Before reaching the target, this aircraft was intercepted by several fighters at 16,000 feet. With both engines hit, the pilot made a forced landing at Bannisters Farm, Barcombe, East Sussex. Ff: Lt Hans-Gert Gollnisch, Bo: Uffz Willi Rolf, Bf: Uffz Willi Hamerla all PoWs. Bs: Uffz Ernst Deibler killed. *See report of 66 Squadron.*

Stab III/KG30 Ju88A Wn.333 4D+AD Target Woolwich. The starboard engine and both radiators were hit and the pilot landed in shallow water in Pagham Harbour, West Sussex. Ff: Major Johann Hackbarth and Bo: Ofw Hans Manger both badly wounded. Bf: Uffz Willi Sawallisch and Bs: Gefr Friederich Petermann both killed. *See reports of 602 Squadron.*

Below and right: Three photos of another KG30 Ju88, this time 4D+AD which force landed in shallow water at Pagham Harbour. The photo immediately below shows the body of one of the crew, Friederich Petermann, who was killed during the fighter attack.

Luftwaffe Casualties

16.40 - 18.00 hrs 9th September 1940

8/KG30 Ju88A-5 **Wn.3195** **4D+LS** Fell into the Channel, probably off Bognor Regis. Bo: Uffz Otto Hettinger and Bf: Ogefr Fritz Baumgarten killed. Ff: Fw Ludwig Jung and Bs: Uffz Wilhelm Vette both rescued.

Stab III/KG53 He111 H-2 **Wn.2630** **A1+ZD** At 18,000 feet the aircraft was suddenly attacked by fighters. Collided with the Hurricane of P/O Forrester, 605 Squadron. One wing came off and the aircraft crashed in a spin on Southfield Farm, Chawton, Hampshire. Ff: Oscar Broderix baled out PoW. Bo: Oblt Kurt Meineke baled out wounded PoW. Bf: Fw Ernst Wendorff, Bm: Fw Wilhelm Wenninger and Bs: Fw Willi Döring all killed. *See also report of F/Lt McKellar, 605 Squadron.*

8/KG53 He111H-2 **Wn.3306** **A1+AS** Returned with 10% damage from AA fire over London. Bo: Uffz Reinhold Cott and Bm: Fw Michael Köpferl both wounded. Rest of crew safe.

8/KG53 He111H-2 **Wn.5548** **A1+DS** Returned with 20% damage from fighters over London. Bf: Oberfw Ernst Pflüger badly wounded - on 16th September. Ff: Oberfw Ludwig Eck and Bo: Fw Eduard Kemper both wounded. Rest of crew safe.

15(Z)/LG1 Me110C-4 **Wn.3298** **L1+DL** Attacked by two Hurricanes and dived steeply into the ground at the Maori Sports Club, Old Malden Lane, Worcester Park, Surrey. Ff: Uffz Alois Pfaffelhuber and Bf: Uffz Otto Kramp both killed. *See report of P/O Currant, 605 Squadron, and P/O Tamblyn, 242 Squadron.*

7/ZG76 Me110C-2 **Wn.2137** **2N+FM** Escorting KG1 to London. Hit by AA fire from the 1/58 AA Battery at Twydall. The crew baled out, but one was killed by shrapnel and the other left it too late to bale out. Aircraft fell at Munsgore Lane, Borden, Kent. Ff: Uffz Georg-Alfred Bierling and Bf: Uffz Friedrich Kurella both killed.

9/ZG76 Me110C-2 **Wn.3108** **2N+BP** Escorting KG1 to London between 13,000 and 21,000 feet. When near London, the formation was attacked by fighters, the wireless operator being wounded. The pilot tried to get back to France, but was attacked a second time by Hurricanes off Newhaven and eventually came down in the sea five miles off the coast. Ff: Fw Hermann Koops PoW. Bf: Uffz Christian Weiher killed.

9/ZG76 Me110C **Wn.3207** **2N+EP** Escorting KG1 to London. Collided with the Hurricane of F/O Boulton, 310 Squadron, and fell in a garden at Woodcote Park Avenue, Woodmansterne, Surrey. Ff: Lt Eduard Ostermünchner and Bf: Gefr Werner Zimmermann both killed.
See reports of 310 Squadron and P/O Currant, 605 Squadron.

9/ZG76 Me110C-4 **Wn.2081** **2N+CP** Landed 60% damaged at Quoeux-Haut-Mainil after being damaged by fighters over Croydon. Crew safe.

Above: Alois Pfaffelhuber who was killed in action aboard Me110 L1+DL during this combat.

Below: Although officially recorded as 2N+EP, this photo of Me110 Wk Nr 3108 conclusively shows that it was 2N+BP which was shot down on 9 September.

10 SEPTEMBER

224 RAF fighters fly 73 patrols.   Luftwaffe - 48 bomber and 32 fighter sorties

Weather: Cloudy with some showers.

COMBAT A: 72 Squadron Spitfires scramble to intercept individual raids

Night operations 9/10 September

65 bombers Luftflotte 2 and 130 bombers Luftflotte 3. 232 tonnes of bombs dropped. Target docks and industry along the Thames. Large fires seen. 10 bombers of Luftflotte 3 were sent to Liverpool.

Luftwaffe Casualties

4/KG4   He111P-4   Wn.2869   Crashed on the railway line between Eindhoven and Best on return. Ff: Lt Heinz Arnold, Bo: Gefr Albert Nowack, and Bs: Gefr Willi Hain all killed, Bf: believed baled out safely.

5/KG54   Ju88A-1   Wn.3093   Crashed at St-André-de-l'Eure on return from London. Ff: Lt Wilhelm Fischer and Bs: Gefr Friedrich Kuhn both killed. Bo and Bf believed to baled out safely.

4/LG1   Ju88A-1   Wn.5106   L1+BM   Landed at Orléans-Bricy on return - 40%. Crew safe.

Wellingtons sent to Berlin turned back due to bad weather and bombed secondary targets. At least one aircraft found II/KG4's airfield near Eindhoven at 03.51 hrs: Six He111P-4 destroyed 100%: Wn.2972, 2933, 2935, 2939, 3079 and 3080. Two damaged 85% Wn.2635 and 2637. Three damaged: Wn.2140, 2919 and 2792.

Below: A victim of the 9 September bombing raids was this London bus, illustrating the strength of the bomb blast that must have hit it.

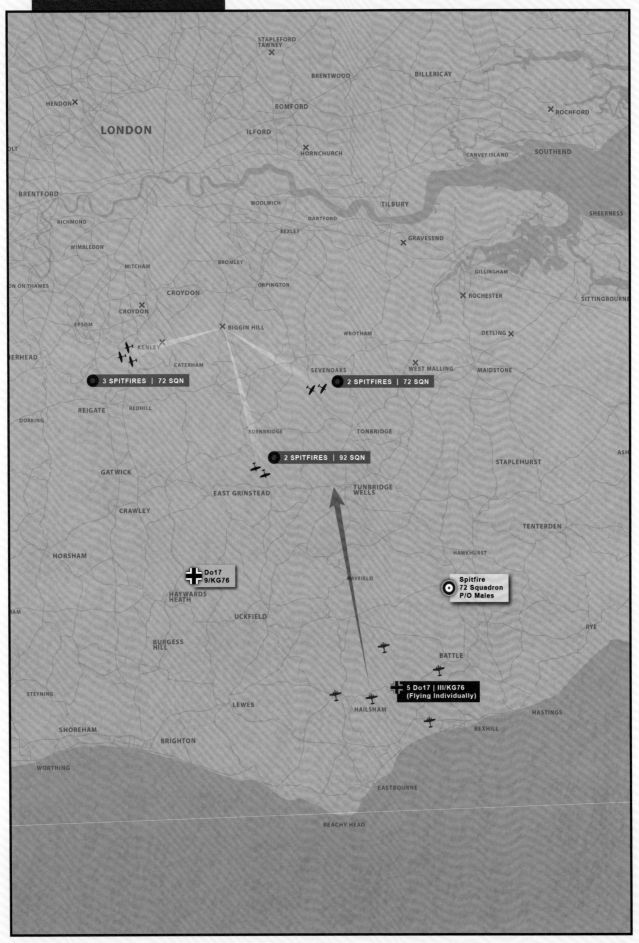

3 SPITFIRES | 72 SQN

2 SPITFIRES | 72 SQN

2 SPITFIRES | 92 SQN

Do17
9/KG76

Spitfire
72 Squadron
P/O Males

5 Do17 | III/KG76
(Flying Individually)

A Quiet Day
17.45 - 18.05 hrs 10th September 1940

The Luftwaffe sent a small number of bombers flying individually over south-east England, using the cloud cover to evade Fighter Command. Bombs were scattered widely over the countryside but only one incident was reported near London when bombs fell at Woolwich. One aircraft machine gunned Tangmere airfield as it passed over. Only one aircraft was successfully intercepted.

Luftwaffe Summary
London: Between 13.00 and 17.45 hours single aircraft attacked Millwall, Croydon and oil tanks north east of London. 5 bombers dropped 5 x SC250, 1 Flambo, 16 x SC50 and 14 BSK. Due to the poor weather in the south east 43 bombers and 32 fighters were sent to Great Yarmouth, Cambridge, and other areas.

RAF Victory Claims		Combat A	17.45 – 18.05 hrs
72 Sqn	F/O J W Villa	Do215 destroyed*	East Grinstead
72 Sqn	P/O E E Males	- shared -	
72 Sqn	P/O N C H Robson	Do215 destroyed*	south of Weybridge
72 Sqn	Sgt J S Gilders	- shared –	
92 Sqn	Sgt R H Fokes	Do17 destroyed	Biggin Hill - East Grinstead
92 Sqn	P/O T S Wade	Do17 destroyed	Biggin Hill

As only one aircraft was brought down, as described by 92 Squadron, it can be seen that these claims should have been for aircraft 'damaged'.

Luftwaffe Victory Claims

None

72 SQUADRON INTELLIGENCE REPORT

Five aircraft from No.72 Squadron were ordered to patrol Redhill. Five aircraft took off from Croydon at 17.40 hours. While on patrol control gave information that bandits were approaching Rastus at Angels 10. Red Section, after orbiting, saw enemy east of Biggin Hill flying in south-west direction at 10,000 feet. The leader ordered a No.1 attack, which results in one Do215 being shot down, and, as confirmed by Army Officer it crashed in a field near East Grinstead.

In the meantime Yellow Section pursued a Do215 and made contact over Weybridge. A quarter attack was delivered at from 500 to 150 yards range. The enemy aircraft was seen in a steep dive through the clouds and was later reported as having crashed near Weybridge. Only two enemy aircraft were seen, and it is thought that Flying Officer J W Villa and Pilot Officer E E Males were jointly responsible for bringing down the one at East Grinstead, and Pilot Officer N C H Robson and Sergeant J S Gilders that at Weybridge*. One aircraft crash landed at Etchingham, but the pilot is uninjured.

Author's note: No aircraft fell at or near Weybridge.

COMBAT REPORT:
F/O J W Villa – Red 1, A Flight, 72 Squadron

I was Red One when I was ordered to patrol Redhill – Angels 3. While on patrol control informed me that bandits were approaching Rastus at Angels 10. I climbed to 10,000 ft and was vectored 135° for 1 minute. I was then ordered to orbit and again vectored 260°. Soon after altering course I sighted a Do215 below me just above the clouds. I ordered a Number 1 attack and dived down. E/A was flying a south westerly course. E/A dived into cloud. I followed E/A into cloud and saw him ahead of me in a clear patch. I fired two short bursts at 150 yds and broke away level and climbed up above cloud. Red Two (P/O Males) then attacked. I then did a quarter attack on E/A and followed through to astern position. E/A again went into cloud and I was able to continue firing in cloud as I had closed to about 30 yds. I fired one short and one long burst. E/A climbed steeply out of cloud and I closed into formation on him not experiencing any further return fire. I broke away and did further quarter attacks using the rest of my ammunition. E/A dived steeply into cloud and I could find no further trace of him. A Do215 has been reported crashed in the vicinity of the attack.

92 SQUADRON INTELLIGENCE REPORT

Two aircraft 92 Squadron ordered to patrol base below cloud. One aircraft at 17.50 and one aircraft at 17.55 hours.

At 17.55 hours Yellow 2 P/O Wade was told to intercept a bandit approaching from south-east. E/A was sighted by Yellow 2 at 7,000 feet, travelling north about 6 miles east of Biggin Hill.

Yellow 2 opened fire from astern at about 150 yards. Rear gunner of the Do17 opened fire first but was killed by the first burst from Yellow 2. E/A turned and dived for cloud, Yellow 2 followed underneath and about 10/15 yards behind. Coming out of cloud Yellow 2 fired medium bursts into starboard engine from about 50 yards, broke away and did beam attack and quarter attacks from the right and observed bits flying off the fuselage.

Yellow 2 by now expended all his ammunition and saw E/A lose height and speed and with starboard engine on fire. He therefore called up Red 2 Sgt Fokes and vectored him on to the bandit.

Red 2 found E/A at 1,500 feet about 10 miles south-west of base and observed that starboard engine was stopped, and when going on to make a head-on attack observed cannon fire from front of E/A. He therefore attacked three times from port quarter and put port engine on fire.

E/A crashed near Gatwick and broke up completely. Weather 5/10th cloud at 1,500 ft up to 5,000 ft.

Yellow 2 P/O T S Wade	Take off Biggin Hill 17.50 hours. Landed Biggin Hill 18.30 hours. Rounds fired 2800.
Red 2 Sgt R S Fokes	Take off Biggin Hill 17.55 hours. Landed Biggin Hill 18.30 hours. Round fired 2800.

COMBAT REPORT:
P/O T S Wade — Yellow 2, A Flight, 92 Squadron

As Yellow 2 at 17.50 hours ordered to patrol base below cloud. At 17.55 hours told one bandit approaching from south-east at 10,000 feet. Climbed up east of base and sighted bandit at 7,000 feet travelling north about 6 miles east of me. Went into stern attack and opened fire at about 150 yards. Return fire observed from top gunner before opening fire. Broke away to left after killed rear gunner. Bandit dived on a turn towards cloud so followed underneath and about 10/15 yards behind through cloud. After coming out of cloud fired medium burst into starboard engine from 50 yards. Broke away and did beam and quarter attacks from the right. Observed starboard engine stopped and bits flying off from amidships during attacks.

Bandit lost height and speed and Red 2 took up the attack at 1,500 feet. Bandit crashed in a wood clearing with starboard engine on fire and broke up. Observed no movement from enemy personnel after crash.

COMBAT REPORT:
Sgt R H Fokes — Red 2, A Flight, 92 Squadron

At 17.55 hrs I, Red 2, was ordered to patrol base at cloud base. Ground station then informed me that E/A was approaching base from south east at 10,000 ft. I climbed and proceeded in this direction meeting E/A at 5,000 ft being attacked by Yellow 2. The E/A was then diving in a westerly direction with Yellow 2 on his tail. I went after them but could not overtake before they entered cloud. I saw 4 or 5 black objects fall from the E/A in front of Yellow 2 just before reaching cloud. I called Yellow 2 on the R/T and again made contact with E/A who had starboard engine stopped. I made three port quarter attacks and on the third attack the port engine caught fire. The E/A dropped his port wing and nose-dived into a field, breaking up completely.

Cannon fire observed from the front gun.

RAF and Luftwaffe Casualties

17.45 - 18.05 hrs 10th September 1940

Luftwaffe Casualty	Combat A	17.45 – 18.05 hrs

9/KG76   Do17Z-3   Wn.2778   F1+ET Started from six miles north-west of Pontoise, on a lone armed reconnaissance of central London. Before reaching London it was engaged by fighters and driven towards Gatwick aerodrome at 1,500 feet where it was damaged by AA fire from the aerodrome. The bomb load was jettisoned during combat and it crashed at Lower Sheriff Cottages, Horsted Keynes, West Sussex. The wreckage showed about one-thousand .303 strikes all over the aircraft, which apparently had been hit in previous actions, the strikes being patched over with fabric. All four crew were in the aircraft when it crash-landed. Ff: Oblt Walter Domenig and Bf: Uffz Hans Strahlendorf both killed. Bm: Gefr Albert Greza PoW. Bo: Uffz Ernst Nürenberg was badly wounded with two broken legs, left shoulder blade and collar bone, due to his injuries he was repatriated to Germany in 1943 via the Red Cross.

RAF Casualty	Combat A	17.45 – 18.05 hrs

72 Sqn Spitfire K9841 RN-R   P/O E E Males – safe. Hit by return fire and landed at Little Hutchings Farm, Etchingham, East Sussex, where the undercarriage collapsed.

```
OTHER INCIDENT   HORNCHURCH   16.15 HRS
```

COMBAT REPORT:
F/Lt E N Ryder - Red 1, A Flight, 41 Squadron

I led Red and Blue Section in a diving attack on twin-engined formation with a view to cutting the formation into two. I fired on passing through at a Ju88 and had a glimpse of smoke coming from his port engine and at the same time his left wing dropped slightly. This happened very quickly and might have been his evasion. I then attacked another 88 by joining a circle and experienced very great return fire and by good evasion on E/A's part had to break off the engagement. I fired at a third and was fired on from astern, part of my hood at this moment flew off. Ordered by control to patrol Home Base and engage 50 plus E/A, I returned but did not engage before pancake order.

Other RAF Casualties		

25 Sqn Blenheim L1440   Sgt K B Hollowell – safe. Propeller fell off during a patrol and the aircraft was belly-landed at North Weald.

312 Sqn Hurricane L1644   Sgt J Keprt – safe. Pilot baled out south of Cambridge.

Night 10th - 11th

One concentrated attack was launched by 148 bombers that dropped 175 tonnes of bombs aimed at Silvertown, Commercial and London Docks, Woolwich Arsenal and Woolwich, Barking Power Station and Beckton Gas Works. Other attacks were made by eight bombers on Liverpool (160 x SC50), Cardiff, Bristol, Newport and Southampton by two bombers each.

RAF Casualties	Night 10th - 11th September	

602 Sqn Spitfire L1040   Sgt D W Elcome - safe. Crashed Felpham Golf Course during night-flying practice
20.45 hrs. Aircraft a write-off.

602 Sqn Spitfire L1002   P/O O V Hanbury - safe. Damaged forced-landing at Tangmere following night-flying training 21.15 hrs.

602 Sqn Spitfire X4270   P/O C J Mount - safe. Slightly damaged landing at Tangmere after night-flying 21.15 hrs.

Luftwaffe Casualty	Night 10th - 11th September	

II/KG54   Ju88A-1   Wn.6092 Crashed on landing at St André de l'Eure. Crew safe. 30% damaged.

6/KG54   Ju88A-1   Wn.4146   B3+DP Crashed near Climont during night sortie to London. Ff: Oblt Karl John, Bo: Uffz Siegfried Schauer, Bs: Uffz Gustav Flamm and Bf: Gefr Hans Weiler all killed.

Stab/KG55 He111P-2   Wn.2683   G1+BA Crashed and burned out near Versailles on approach to Villacoublay airfield following sortie over London. Ff: Uffz Walter Lange, Bo: Fw Kurt Eckert and Bf: Ogefr Artur Windmann all killed. Bm: Gefr Franz Koller injured.

11 SEPTEMBER

678 RAF fighters fly 114 patrols.   Luftwaffe - 96 bombers and 570 fighters / Zerstörer

Weather: Cloudy, particularly over the Channel.

COMBAT A: KG26 Heinkels head home under constant fighter attack.

421

London Again

11 September 1940

As had become expected in recent days, the morning passed without incident save for lone reconnaissance aircraft. Fighter Command's controllers had to wait until mid-afternoon before the now familiar build-up of aircraft over the French coast heralded another raid. A plot of 12+ and another of 25+ appeared south of Cap Gris Nez and crossed the Channel near Folkestone at 15.10 hours. The raid flew west, then north to Maidstone, but the speed of the raid meant that few squadrons had time to scramble and it left over North Foreland without interception. It was believed that it had been a feint to distract the Fighter Command Controller from a larger raid forming again over Cap Gris Nez. In response, seven squadrons began to be scrambled:

46 Squadron - 12 Hurricanes up from Stapleford to intercept over Dover. TO 15.10 hrs.
504 Squadron - 10 Hurricanes up from Hendon to patrol Gravesend. TO 15.15 hrs.
253 Squadron - 10 Hurricanes up from Kenley to patrol Maidstone. TO 15.15 hrs.
41 Squadron - 11 Spitfires up from Hornchurch to patrol Maidstone. TO 15.15 hrs.
603 Squadron - 12 Spitfires up from Rochford to patrol Maidstone. TO 15.16 hrs.
92 Squadron - 13 Spitfires up from Biggin Hill to intercept over Dungeness. TO 15.20 hrs.
501 Squadron - 11 Hurricanes up from Kenley to patrol Maidstone. TO 15.20 hrs.

By 15.35 hours three raids had appeared on the plotting tables; 100+ and 50+ with He111s from I and II/KG1 approaching South Foreland, and 50+ He111s of I and II/KG26 approaching the Dover - Folkestone area.

Three more squadrons had by now been scrambled, six from 11 Group and four from 12 Group; the 'Big Wing':
72 Squadron - 11 Spitfires up from Croydon to patrol Gravesend. TO 15.25 hrs.
249 Squadron - 12 Hurricanes up from North Weald to patrol East London. TO 15.27 hrs.
222 Squadron - 13 Spitfires up from Hornchurch to patrol base. TO 15.28 hrs.
303 Squadron - 12 Hurricanes up from Northolt to patrol Biggin Hill. TO 15.30 hrs.
229 Squadron - 12 Hurricanes up from Northolt to patrol Biggin Hill. TO 15.25 hrs.
238 Squadron - 12 Hurricanes up from Middle Wallop to patrol Weybridge. TO 15.30 hrs.

Duxford Wing
19 Squadron - 10 Spitfires up from Fowlmere to patrol Hornchurch - North Weald. TO 15.30 hrs.
266 Squadron - 6 Spitfires up from Duxford to patrol Hornchurch - North Weald. TO 15.30 hrs.
611 Squadron - 12 Spitfires up from Duxford to patrol Hornchurch - North Weald. TO 15.30 hrs.
74 Squadron - 5 Spitfires up from Duxford to patrol Hornchurch - North Weald. TO 15.30 hrs.
As the raids crossed the English coast it became clear that two separate attacks on London were going to be made simultaneously; KG1 heading along the north Kent coast from South Foreland towards Gravesend, and KG26 from Dover towards Tunbridge Wells.

The 11 Group Controller then ordered his remaining six squadrons into the air.

66 Squadron - 10 Spitfires up from Gravesend to intercept raid over Kent. TO 15.35 hrs.
17 Squadron - 12 Hurricanes up from Debden to patrol Rochford. TO 15.45 hrs.
73 Squadron - 12 Hurricanes up from Castle Camps to patrol Rochford. TO 15.38 hrs.
1(RCAF) Squadron - 12 Hurricanes up from Northolt to patrol Gatwick. TO 15.40 hrs.
605 Squadron - 12 Hurricanes up from Croydon to patrol base. TO 15.43 hrs.
257 Squadron - 8 Hurricanes up from Martlesham Heath to patrol North Weald. TO 15.45 hrs.

Part of the raid that had crossed the coast near Dover bombed between there and Deal and then turned back as planned, leaving two streams of He111s heading towards London.
The bombers were all He111s from KG1 and KG26, escorted by around 120 Me110s from ZG26, II and III/ZG76 and V(Z)/LG1 with 450 Me109s from JG2, JG3, JG26, JG27, JG51, JG53, JG54 and I/LG2. *
The fighter escort, however, had been given incorrect information about the timing and routes to be taken by the bombers and most of the fighters turned back early.

Surviving Luftwaffe documents do not specify the number of fighters, but this can be estimated from the units known to have been involved.

Right: Today was the first day that RAF pilots encountered bombers with large white stripes painted on the fins and wings. They are believed to have been used for the assembly of the various waves of bombers sent out on this day.

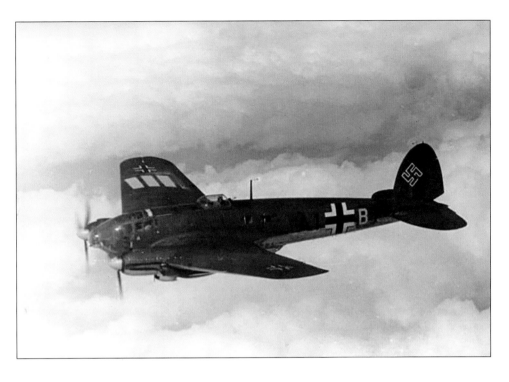

KG1's Attack - North Kent - Target London Docks

46, 504, 92 and 253 Squadrons were first to engage with the force over North Kent, yet none of the squadrons was aware of the others. 72 Squadron then found the raid near Maidstone and the anti-aircraft guns around the Thames Estuary went into action. 222 Squadron and 605 Squadron engaged and, as the raid flew over the Estuary, the Duxford Wing's four squadrons (19, 74, 266 and 611) attacked. Undeterred, the raid swung west along the Thames where 249 Squadron saw it bombing the London Docks, before heading back out across North Kent chased by 501, 17, 66 and 73 Squadrons, until it re-crossed the coast.

KG26 - West Kent - Target London Docks

The force of 50+ that crossed the coast between Dover and Folkestone, later than the North Kent raid, headed north towards Tunbridge Wells. Most of Fighter Command's squadrons had by now been ordered to the east of London, leaving just four squadrons based to the west of London, plus 41 and 603 Squadrons from east of London, to intercept this raid. The raid had divided into two formations flying a few minutes apart. The Northolt Wing consisting of 303 and 229 Squadrons met the raid near Reigate at 16.10 hours. 41 and 603 Squadrons then engaged near Sevenoaks and 238 Squadron over Croydon. The leading formation was broken-up short of London itself, but the second element of this raid was said to have slipped through to bomb London unhindered. 1(RCAF) Squadron then chased the raid south.

Note: Although in the early stages it is possible to identify the RAF squadrons that were directed to engage the 'North Kent' and 'Tunbridge Wells' raids, when combat was joined and the aircraft scattered the combat became a 'free-for-all'.

Luftwaffe Intelligence Summary

54 aircraft dropped bombs on targets between Dover and Deal at 15.45 hours.

Operations Against London

96 bombers dropped 83 tonnes of bombs including 8 x 1,000 kg between 16.00 hrs and 16.10 hours aimed at Silvertown, Commercial and London Docks, Woolwich Arsenal, Barking Power Station and Beckton Gas Works. A 1,000 kg bomb was seen to explode on the Woolwich Arsenal.

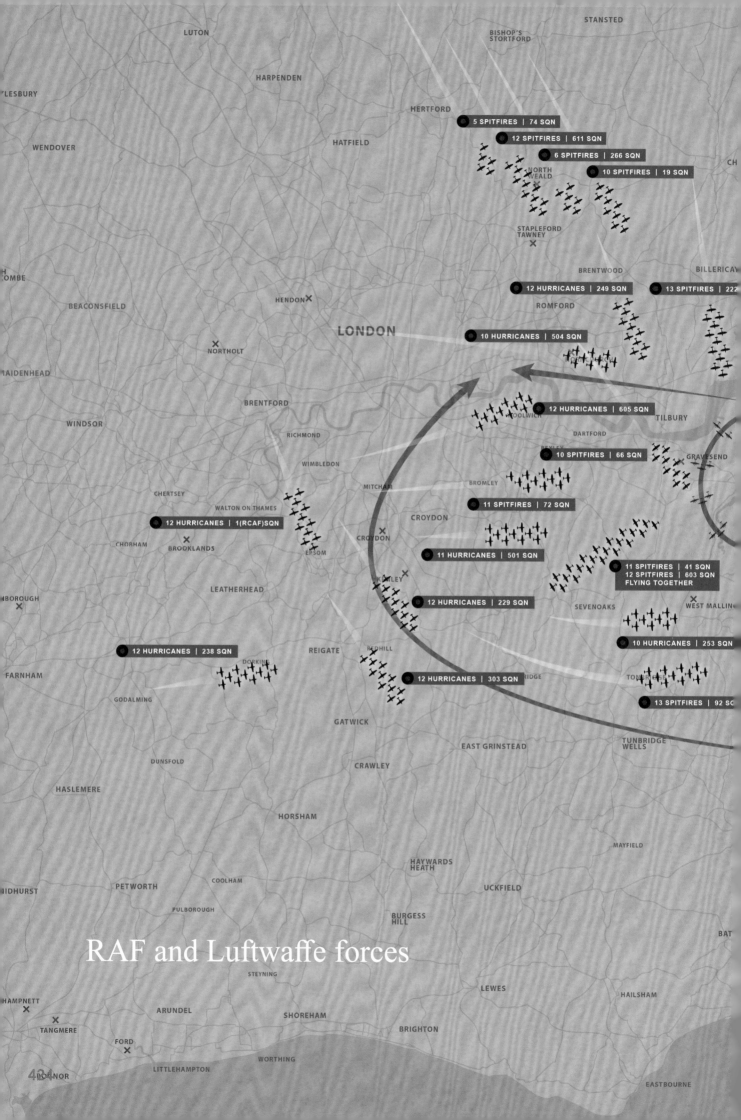

RAF and Luftwaffe forces

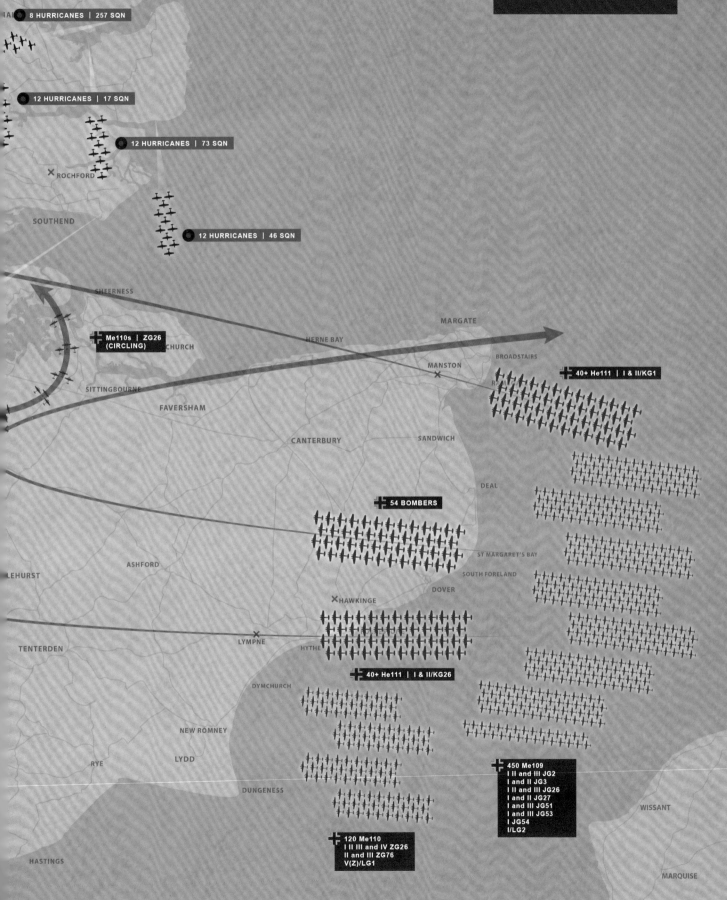

CLACTON

8 HURRICANES | 257 SQN

12 HURRICANES | 17 SQN

12 HURRICANES | 73 SQN

× ROCHFORD

SOUTHEND

12 HURRICANES | 46 SQN

SHEERNESS

MARGATE

Me110s | ZG26
(CIRCLING)

HERNE BAY

CHURCH

BROADSTAIRS

MANSTON ×

40+ He111 | I & II/KG1

SITTINGBOURNE

FAVERSHAM

CANTERBURY

SANDWICH

DEAL

54 BOMBERS

ST MARGARET'S BAY

ASHFORD

SOUTH FORELAND

LEHURST

DOVER

× HAWKINGE

TENTERDEN

× LYMPNE

HYTHE

40+ He111 | I & II/KG26

DYMCHURCH

NEW ROMNEY

450 Me109
I II and III JG2
I and II JG3
I II and III JG26
I and II JG27
I and III JG51
I and III JG53
I JG54
I/LG2

RYE

LYDD

DUNGENESS

WISSANT

120 Me110
I II III and IV ZG26
II and III ZG76
V(Z)/LG1

HASTINGS

MARQUISE

BOULOGNE-SUR-MER

RAF Victory Claims	North Kent and Thames Estuary Force (KG1)		
46 Sqn	P/O A E Johnson	Me110 damaged	10 miles north of Dungeness
46 Sqn	Sgt R L Earp	Do215 destroyed	10 miles north of Dungeness
504 Sqn	S/Ldr J Sample	Do215 probable	Lympne
504 Sqn	F/O W Royce	- shared -	
504 Sqn	F/Lt M E A Royce	Do215 probable	north west of Folkestone
92 Sqn	S/Ldr P J Sanders	He111 damaged	Dungeness
92 Sqn	S/Ldr P J Sanders	Me109 destroyed	Tonbridge
92 Sqn	F/Lt C B F Kingcombe	He111 destroyed	Dungeness
92 Sqn	F/Lt J A Paterson	Me110 destroyed	north of Dungeness
92 Sqn	F/O J F Drummond	Me109 probable	Dungeness - Rye - London
92 Sqn	P/O T S Wade	He111 destroyed	Maidstone
92 Sqn	P/O G H A Wellum	He111 destroyed	Dungeness
92 Sqn	P/O D G Williams	He111 destroyed	Dungeness – London
92 Sqn	P/O A R Wright	He111 destroyed	east London
92 Sqn	Sgt P R Eyles	He111 destroyed	Dungeness
253 Sqn	Acting S/Ldr G R Edge	Me109 destroyed	Maidstone
253 Sqn	Acting S/Ldr G R Edge	He111 probable	Maidstone
253 Sqn	Acting S/Ldr G R Edge	Do215 destroyed	Maidstone
253 Sqn	F/Lt J H Wedgewood	- shared -	
253 Sqn	F/Lt J H Wedgwood	Do215 damaged	Maidstone
253 Sqn	P/O G C T Carthew	Do215 destroyed	Maidstone
253 Sqn	P/O W M C Samolinski	- shared -	
253 Sqn	P/O L C Murch	- shared -	
253 Sqn	P/O A R H Barton	- shared -	
253 Sqn	P/O T Nowak	- shared -	
253 Sqn	Sgt E H C Kee	- shared -	
253 Sqn	Sgt W B Higgins	- shared -	
253 Sqn	Sgt R A Innes	- shared -	
253 Sqn	Sgt A S Dredge	- shared -	
253 Sqn	Sgt W B Higgins	Me109 destroyed	Maidstone
253 Sqn	Sgt R A Innes	He111 damaged	Maidstone
253 Sqn	Sgt R A Innes	He111 damaged	Maidstone
253 Sqn	Sgt W B Higgins	Me110 damaged	Maidstone
72 Sqn	F/Lt E B Graham	Me109 damaged	east of Maidstone
72 Sqn	P/O R D Elliott	He111 destroyed	east of Maidstone
72 Sqn	Sgt N R Norfolk	Do17 destroyed	east of Maidstone
72 Sqn	Sgt J White	Do17 destroyed	south of Sevenoaks
72 Sqn	Sgt J White	Do17 probable	
72 Sqn	Sgt W T E Rolls	Do17 destroyed	Cranbrook
72 Sqn	Sgt W T E Rolls	Do17 probable	
72 Sqn	Sgt J S Gilders	Me110 destroyed	east of Maidstone
222 Sqn	F/O B Van Mentz	Ju88 destroyed	Hornchurch
222 Sqn	F/O B Van Mentz	Me109 damaged	Hornchurch
222 Sqn	P/O J W Broadhurst	Ju88 probable	Hornchurch
222 Sqn	Sgt S Baxter	He111 probable	Maidstone
222 Sqn	Sgt E Scott	He111 destroyed	Hornchurch
222 Sqn	Sgt I Hutchinson	He111 probable	Gravesend
222 Sqn	Sgt S Baxter	Ju88 destroyed	Hornchurch
222 Sqn	Sgt R G Marland	Ju88 destroyed	Hornchurch
222 Sqn	Sgt A W P Spears	Me109 damaged	Hornchurch
605 Sqn	F/Lt A A McKellar	He111 destroyed	Sittingbourne
605 Sqn	P/O R E Jones	- shared -	
605 Sqn	F/Lt A A McKellar	He111 probable	south east of London
605 Sqn	F/O C F Currant	He111 destroyed	south east of London
605 Sqn	P/O T P M Cooper-Slipper	He111 damaged	south of Eltham
605 Sqn	Sgt J Budzinski	Me109 destroyed	south of Bexley
605 Sqn	Sgt W J Glowacki	Me110 destroyed	Rochester
605 Sqn	Unknown pilot	He111 damaged	south east of London
605 Sqn	Unknown pilot	He111 damaged	south east of London
605 Sqn	Unknown pilot	He111 damaged	south east of London
605 Sqn	Unknown pilot	He111 damaged	south east of London

F/Lt J A Paterson 92 Sqn

P/O W M C Samolinski 253 Sqn

F/O B Van Mentz 222 Sqn

19 Sqn	S/Ldr B J E Lane	Me110 destroyed	Gravesend
19 Sqn	S/Ldr B J E Lane	Me110 probable	Gravesend
19 Sqn	S/Ldr B J E Lane	He111 damaged	Gravesend
19 Sqn	F/O L A Haines	Me110 destroyed	Gravesend
19 Sqn	P/O W J Lawson	He111 destroyed	east-south east of London
19 Sqn	F/Sgt G C Unwin	He111 probable	east London
19 Sqn	F/Sgt G C Unwin	Do215 damaged	east London
19 Sqn	Sgt B J Jennings	Me110 destroyed	Gravesend
19 Sqn	Sgt H A C Roden	Me110 probable	south west of Gravesend
19 Sqn	Sgt B J Jennings	He111 probable	Gravesend
19 Sqn	Sgt D G S R Cox	Do215 probable	Biggin Hill - Dungeness
74 Sqn	F/Lt J C Freeborn	Do215 destroyed	south east of London
74 Sqn	F/O H Szczesny	Me110 destroyed	London
74 Sqn	F/O J C Mungo-Park	Ju88 damaged	London Docks
74 Sqn	F/O J C Mungo-Park	He111 destroyed	London Docks
74 Sqn	P/O H M Stephen	Ju88 destroyed	London
74 Sqn	P/O D Hastings	Ju88 probable	south east of London
74 Sqn	P/O P C B St John	He111 destroyed	south of London
74 Sqn	P/O E W G Churches	He111 probable	London
74 Sqn	P/O D Hastings	Me110 damaged	south east of London
74 Sqn	P/O H M Stephen	Me109 damaged	London
266 Sqn	F/Lt S H Bazley	Do17 probable	Gravesend
266 Sqn	P/O W S Williams	He111 probable	east of London
266 Sqn	P/O R B J Roach	He111 probable	south east of Hornchurch
266 Sqn	P/O W S Williams	He111 damaged	Dungeness
266 Sqn	P/O H M T Heron	Do215 damaged	Dartford
266 Sqn	Sgt R G V Barraclough	He111 damaged	south east of London
611 Sqn	F/Sgt H S Sadler	Me110 destroyed	Gravesend
611 Sqn	P/O J W Lund	Me110 probable	south of London
611 Sqn	Sgt A D Burt	He111 probable	London - Dungeness
611 Sqn	Sgt S A Levenson	Ju88 destroyed	London
611 Sqn	Sgt S A Levenson	Me109 probable	London
249 Sqn	W/C F V Beamish	He111 probable	London
249 Sqn	F/Lt D G Parnall	He111 destroyed	south of London
249 Sqn	P/O W B Pattullo	- shared -	
249 Sqn	F/O T F Neil	He111 destroyed	London
249 Sqn	Sgt W L Davis	Ju88 destroyed	London
249 Sqn	Squadron	4 He111s damaged	2 miles south east of London
501 Sqn	F/O R C Dafforn	Do215 destroyed	Thames Estuary
501 Sqn	F/Sgt P F Morfill	- shared -	
501 Sqn	F/O S Witorzenc	- shared -	
501 Sqn	3 unknown pilots	- shared -	
501 Sqn	Unknown pilot	He111 damaged	Biggin Hill
501 Sqn	Unknown pilot	He111 damaged	Biggin Hill
501 Sqn	Unknown pilot	He111 damaged	Biggin Hill
501 Sqn	Unknown pilot	He111 damaged	Biggin Hill
17 Sqn	F/Lt A W A Bayne	Me110 destroyed	Girdler Light Vessel
17 Sqn	F/O M B Czernin	Me110 destroyed	Thames Estuary
66 Sqn	S/Ldr R H A Leigh	E/A destroyed	north of Rye
66 Sqn	F/O R W Oxspring	E/A destroyed	Walland Marshes
66 Sqn	P/O A B Watkinson	Do17 destroyed	Walland Marsh
66 Sqn	P/O C A W Bodie	He111 destroyed	Romney Marshes
66 Sqn	Sgt D A C Hunt	E/A destroyed	3 miles east of Rye
73 Sqn	S/Ldr M W S Robinson	Me110 destroyed	Herne Bay
73 Sqn	F/Lt M L ff Beytagh	Me110 damaged	Herne Bay
73 Sqn	P/O J D Smith	Me110 destroyed	5 miles north of Herne Bay
73 Sqn	P/O R A Marchand	Me110 probable	2 miles east of Margate
73 Sqn	P/O J D Smith	Me110 damaged	Herne Bay
73 Sqn	Sgt A E Scott	Me110 damaged	Herne Bay

F/Lt J C Freeborn 74 Sqn

F/O T F Neil 249 Sqn

P/O J W Lund 611 Sqn

Contemporary Accounts 504 Sqn

11 September 1940 - 15.30 - 16.00 hrs Combat A.

504 SQUADRON INTELLIGENCE REPORT

At 15.15 hours, 10 Hurricanes of No.504 Squadron left Hendon to meet No.46 Squadron over North Weald and patrol Gravesend at 15,000 feet. After several vectors they met a formation of enemy bombers and fighters near Lympne at about 15.45 hours. The bomber formation was flying north at 15,000 feet and consisted of about 40 He111s and Do215s in 4 vics of about 9 aircraft each, the aircraft in each vic being about 2 spans apart and the vics being about 100 yards apart.

The whole formation formed roughly a flat vic. The enemy aircraft adopted no evasive tactics. The enemy fighters escort consisted of:

(i)   Three stepped up vics each of about 12 Me109s and 110s flying above and behind the bombers, the first vic about 300 feet above and behind the bombers, the second about 1,000 feet above and behind the first, and the third similarly positioned to the second.

(ii)   About 12 Me109s and 110s circling level with and to the port of the bombers.

Red Section, 504 Squadron in echelon starboard attacked the starboard vic of the bombers. Red 1 (S/Ldr Sample) observed hits on one Do215, large pieces of the fuselage and cowling breaking off. Red 2 (F/O M E A Royce) hit the starboard engine of another Do215 and the engine slowed down and emitted smoke and flame. Yellow and Blue Sections attacked the front vic of the bombers. The vics attacked broke up. Almost immediately after Blue Section's attack, Blue 1 (F/Lt W B Royce) saw two bombers (one from starboard vic and one from leading vic) dive straight down apparently out of control, and a third (from starboard vic) with petrol streaming from starboard wing turned homewards. This machine was immediately joined by 6 Me109s which broke from the leading escort formation and escorted the lone machine. Green Section took no part in the combat having separated from the remainder of the squadron while weaving.

9 Hurricanes landed at Hendon between 16.12 and 16.20. Shortly before the combat it was noticed that Dover was being bombed by other e/a.

Our casualties: Personnel -   P/O A W Clarke missing.
                                        Aircraft - 1 Hurricane missing.

COMBAT REPORT:
F/Lt M E A Royce - Blue Section, B Flight, 504 Squadron

At 15.45 hours 10 miles north-west of Folkestone sighted large enemy formation escorted by fighters. Delivered an attack on leading bomber formation with no visible immediate result. After breaking away I continued to follow enemy for a short distance on their starboard quarter. During this time I saw two enemy machines, one from the leading formation and one from the starboard formation, dive straight down apparently out of control. I also saw another machine from the starboard formation which had petrol streaming from the starboard wing break formation and turn back southeast. This machine was immediately joined by 6 Me109s which broke from the leading escort formation and continued to escort the lame machine.

COMBAT REPORT:
S/Ldr J Sample - Red 1, A Flight, 504 Squadron

While patrolling in company with No.46 Squadron, sighted formation of enemy bombers escorted by fighters in 4 vics of about 9 each flying north at a point about 10 miles west of Folkestone. My Section (Red) carried out beam attack on the starboard vic of bombers close on the heels of No.46 Squadron. Fired short burst at one bomber, then changed to another one which was closer. Opened fire when on his starboard bow and continued firing until on his starboard rear quarter. Saw my cone of fire start on his starboard engine and slowly move back along the fuselage to a point halfway along. Large pieces of fuselage, cowling etc, fell off and his starboard engine gave off a little black smoke. I broke away at that point and did not see what happened to him. The enemy aircraft vic broke up.

92 SQUADRON INTELLIGENCE REPORT

13 aircraft of 92 Squadron were ordered off from Biggin Hill at 15.20 hours to intercept raid coming in over the coast by Dungeness. Squadron encountered a large formation of bombers with fighters above. Squadron was split up over Maidstone and all our aircraft carried out individual attacks on a large formation of Heinkel 111s and fighters, Me109 and 110. The individual aircraft carried out a series of beam, quarter and head-on attacks.

Six He111s were shot down round about Rye and Dungeness and have been confirmed by the Irish Fusiliers. Further, one Me109 was seen crashing and the pilots also claim one Me109 and two Me110s as probable.

Eleven aircraft landed at Biggin Hill about 17.30 hours; one aircraft landed at Brooklands aerodrome. One aircraft - Pilot Officer Hargreaves - is missing.

P/O Edwards reported that he fired at an Me110 from head-on over Dungeness and saw something explode underneath him. P/O Edwards took off again at 17.45 hours and has been missing since.

COMBAT REPORT:
F/Lt C B F Kingcombe - Red 1, A Flight, 92 Squadron

I was patrolling with Yellow 2 when I sighted a very large formation of enemy bombers with a large fighter escort of Me109s and Me110s above and behind. They were crossing the coast over Dungeness when I first sighted them. With Yellow 2 I made a head-on attack on the lower layer of the bomber formation. One aircraft, an He111, started to smoke but I had no time to notice whether it crashed or not. I broke away downwards, climbed up behind, and started an astern attack on the lower layer of the bomber formation when my engine cut, so I broke off the attack.

COMBAT REPORT:
P/O T S Wade - Red 3, A Flight, 92 Squadron

I sighted He111 at 16.00 hours near Maidstone after the squadron had broken up. Attacked from astern after seeing Hurricane break away with smoke coming from it. Broke away after firing short burst and attacked from starboard quarter, stopping starboard engine. Did two more quarter attacks and watched enemy aircraft crash land in a field with smoke and flames coming from starboard engine. Three of crew got out dragging one body to side of field. Observed white letter A on the left side of fuselage. E/A crashed west-north-west of Lympne. Landed at Lympne to rearm and re-fuel but neither was available. Took off and landed at Hawkinge with Green 2. After re-arming and re-fuelling returned to base at 15,000 feet looking for stragglers.

COMBAT REPORT:
P/O D G Williams - Green 2, B Flight, 92 Squadron

I was Green 2 on patrol with 92 Squadron over Maidstone. After the squadron had broken up individually at Angels 15, I saw an He111 being attacked by another Spitfire (P/O Wade) at about Angels 12. I joined in the attack with the other Spitfire. We succeeded in first making his starboard engine useless and forcing him down until it crashed through a hedge in a field and came to a standstill. I did beam, quarter and head-on attacks on the Heinkel. I observed fire at first from the rear gunner but later it stopped. After crashing, three of the crew got out and dragged the fourth to a hedge. Civilians then came on the scene. The aircraft was painted black, had a large white square on the top of the starboard wing and the letter A in white on the side of the fuselage. Position of crash was somewhere west of Lympne. I fired all my rounds and sustained no damage.

Contemporary Accounts 92 Sqn

11 September 1940 - 15.30 - 16.00 hrs Combat A.

COMBAT REPORT:
P/O A R Wright - Green 1, B Flight, 92 Squadron

I took off 15.20 hours and lost squadron at 15.40 hours. I climbed from 15,000 to 25,000 feet and positioned myself over Croydon. After about 30 minutes saw very large formation approaching London from direction of Ramsgate. I did a head-on and quarter attack at leading formation and last formation of bombers before Me109s came into vicinity. I dived away and saw one twin engine aircraft of the leading formation break away with smoke coming from engines. I climbed again to 20,000 feet towards the sun, turned, and saw the bombers returning towards Dungeness. I could not catch them up but did an astern and head-on on an He111 with three other Spitfires of LZ (66 Squadron). This crashed intact beside another in flames on Dungeness peninsula*. Returned home and landed.

Editor's note: See opposite page

COMBAT REPORT:
Sgt P R Eyles - 92 Squadron

I took off after the squadron with our remaining serviceable machine and climbed to 20,000 feet over the aerodrome where I joined a Spitfire formation thinking it was my own. We proceeded to the south coast and from there west of Dungeness. I observed the enemy formation crossing the coast. I broke away from the formation I was with having recognised it as a squadron other than my own. I dived down on the bombers from approximately 1,000 feet above. I gave a full deflection shot on to the first machine and passed through the enemy bomber formation behind the second section of three. These front machines were He111s. I climbed and turned in front of the formation and again approached out of the sun, turning sharply into a head-on attack, breaking away sharply underneath. I used the same tactics again on another head-on attack and saw that one of the Heinkels had broken formation and was losing height with smoke coming from one engine. This was approximately over Tonbridge. On my third attack my ammunition ran out a split second before I broke away downwards, so I continued diving being almost directly above my home aerodrome.

COMBAT REPORT:
F/O J F Drummond - Green 3, B Flight, 92 Squadron

As No.3 of Green Section I was patrolling over Maidstone with squadron. I heard 'Snappers' on the R/T. I became separated from the squadron and climbed to 28,000 feet. I patrolled at this height for about 20 minutes over base, then flew southeast towards Dungeness. I encountered 3 Me109s at 20,000 feet. I dived on No.3 and did a quarter attack breaking away to the right. I did not see the effect of my fire. I saw an Me109 attacking a Hurricane. I attacked the 109 as he broke away from the Hurricane. I followed the 109 doing a quarter attack and finished off my ammunition. I looked round and saw two more Me109s diving on me. I did a half roll and dived down. As I broke away I saw smoke coming from the tail of the Me109.

Place of attack 10 miles northwest of Dungeness.

COMBAT REPORT:
P/O G H A Wellum - 92 Squadron

Having lost the squadron, I was flying near the coast at 9,000 feet when I saw and engaged an He111. The port engine was out of action. I did one quarter attack and was met with fire from top and bottom guns on the e/a. I did a second quarter attack and this time met with fire from the top gun only. Black smoke began to come from the starboard engine. I did one more quarter attack and then went in astern. White smoke came from the starboard engine and the enemy aircraft lost height slowly. Having finished my ammunition I broke off the engagement.

66 SQUADRON INTELLIGENCE REPORT

10 a/c (Spitfires) of 66 Squadron left Gravesend at 15.35 hours to intercept a raid approaching from the south-east.

P/O A B Watkinson was slightly late in taking off owing to a leak in the oil pipe of his own plane which necessitated changing planes, and on becoming airborne he was unable to contact the squadron. He, therefore, patrolled alone and soon sighted an e/a (Do17) flying singly. See pilot's combat report.

Meanwhile the remainder of the squadron sighted a large formation of bombers with fighter escort: they were attacked and forced to break formation in pairs. Later two sections reformed. The others not making contact with the squadron or successful contact with the enemy. These two sections were proceeding south-east towards Dungeness at about 8,000 feet when enemy bomber of unknown type was seen proceeding due south, 3,000 feet below about 10 miles north of Rye, at about 180 mph.

The CO (Squadron Leader R H A Leigh, Blue 1) himself led the squadron into attack, whereupon e/a went into a steeper dive and turned slightly to port, Green 1 (F/O R W Oxspring) having overshot, did an S-turn over e/a and attacked with full deflection from above. He was followed by Green 3 (Sgt D A C Hunt) who fired a short burst when e/a was 50 yards from the ground. No return fire was experienced from e/a which force landed in a field, broke up and caught fire on Walland Marsh about 3 miles east of Rye. None of the crew were seen to escape.

At the time this plane was sighted, P/O C A Bodie (Green 2) saw another enemy straggler in obvious difficulties, see pilot's combat report.

Below: 66 Squadron pilots clearly helped shoot down two Heinkels within a few hundred yards of each other near Dungeness. The main photo shows V4+RW of 6/KG1, the inset shows the columns of smoke from both aircraft.

COMBAT REPORT:
P/O C A W Bodie, Green 2, B Flight, 66 Squadron

I was flying Green 2 in a squadron formation going south towards Dungeness at about 8,000 ft when we sighted a twin-engined E/A on our starboard, 3,000 ft below, travelling south, the CO dived to attack, and as we were going down I saw a Heinkel 111 almost beneath us, travelling south, obviously in difficulties with one or both engines. There seemed to be plenty of machines to deal with the first one sighted, so I broke to port, half-rolled and delivered a diving beam attack at the Heinkel, commencing my burst at 200 yds, allowing plenty of deflection, he went right through my sights and as I passed behind him I saw that his port engine was stopped and the starboard prop to be just ticking over. He successfully force landed in a field (on his belly), and three crew got out wearing light brown flying suits. They seemed uninjured, standing near the tail and chatting and the machine was in good order.

Another e/a was burning fiercely ¼ mile south of the Heinkel, I could not make out its type, and a mile east another was also burning.

Contemporary Accounts 66 Sqn

11 September 1940 - 15.30 - 16.00 hrs Combat A.

COMBAT REPORT:
F/O R W Oxspring, Green 1, B Flight, 66 Squadron

E/A was sighted at 16.30 proceeding in a shallow dive on a southerly course and camouflaged in the normal dark green with swastika and black crosses on wings. E/A went into a steeper dive and turned slightly to port as the section attacked. Overshooting, I did an 'S' turn above E/A and then attacked with full deflection from above. Both engines now appeared to be ticking over and it was obvious that it was going to land. E/A then pancaked in a field and burst through a fence and ditch and six or seven seconds after halting the whole aircraft burst into flames. No personnel were seen to leave it before the fire.

Sun SW. 3/20 cloud about 5,000 ft thick but considerably larger to NE.

No return fire was experienced and combat took place over Walland Marsh.

> *E/A sighted at about 5,000 ft diving shallowly in southerly direction at a position 10 miles north of Rye. Speed 180 mph approx and camouflage blackish green with small swastikas at wing tips on upper surfaces. E/A on being engaged by other member of the squadron proceeded to dive and turned gently to port. When E/A was about 50 ft from ground a short burst was fired full deflection, after which E/A just continued to pancake in a field, breaking up and catching fire. No return fire experienced. No one saved from wreck.*
>
> Sgt D A C Hunt, Green 3, A Flight, 66 Squadron

Below: The other Heinkel was also a KG1 aircraft, this time V4+FA of the Geschwader Stab.

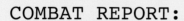

COMBAT REPORT:
P/O A B Watkinson - B Flight, 66 Squadron

I was patrolling by myself after losing my squadron in the approximate vicinity of Tunbridge Wells at 8,000 feet when I saw e/a at 6,000 feet travelling on a straight course of approximately 160 Magnetic. I immediately carried out a series of quarter and beam attacks. After my first burst of two seconds, I saw black smoke pouring from e/a starboard engine. I then concentrated on the port engine, giving it one and two second bursts. After a short while I noticed that both engines were smoking and that the airscrew had stopped and the e/a was gliding towards the coast. My ammunition was finished so I flew round the e/a keeping it in sight when I noticed a few AA bursts behind the e/a. The e/a eventually crash-landed in a field in Walland Marsh and three of the crew climbed out and appeared to stand around and wait. I noticed a number of army troops arrive on the scene so I returned to base.

COMBAT REPORT:
S/Ldr R H A Leigh - Blue 1, B Flight, 66 Squadron

I was Blue 1 leading 66 Squadron which took off from Gravesend at 15.35 hours to intercept a raid. We climbed as ordered and when at 20,000 feet we sighted a bomber formation proceeding north-west with fighter escort. While manoeuvring into position we were attacked, and broke formation in pairs. I succeeded in reforming Blue and Green Sections and we were re-climbing, at the same time flying towards Dungeness when at 8,000 feet we saw an enemy bomber of unknown type (at first I took it to be a Ju52, but it was only twin-engined) flying singly about 3,000 feet below us. We were then about 10 miles north of Rye. I led the formation down to attack, and myself fired two bursts of 2 - 3 seconds, closing to 150 yards. E/A proceeded to dive and turn to port. I broke off and other members of the squadron continued the attack, after which e/a force-landed in a field on Walland Marsh, and almost immediately broke into flames.

11 SEPTEMBER

253 SQUADRON INTELLIGENCE REPORT

10 Hurricanes 253 Squadron left Kenley 15.15 hours to orbit base at 5,000 feet then ordered to vector 090 degrees at 20,000 feet to intercept Raid 44. After several further vectors squadron were told to orbit when formation of some 30 He111s and Do215s escorted by approximately 50 Me109s and Me110s above were sighted at 16,000 feet some 30 miles east over Dover heading north-west. Squadron headed north-north-east climbing to about 1,000 feet above the bombers, changing the formation to sections echelon starboard, and delivered a beam attack on to the bomber formation who were then at 15,500 feet, out of the sun. The result of this was that 3 bombers were seen to be in flames followed by a number of parachutes opening. Several pilots also report that a number of e/a were smoking badly. The bombers signalled to their fighter escort by firing a red rocket.

After the main attack several pilots had individual combats in which 2 e/a were destroyed and further ones damaged. Visibility was exceptionally good with no cloud but a slight ground haze. No evasive tactics employed by enemy who apparently did not see our fighters until attack was being delivered.

1 Hurricane landed Kenley 16.15 hours as he was not receiving any oxygen (believed regulator broken) and 9 Hurricanes landed Kenley between 16.20 - 16.50.

COMBAT REPORT:
Acting S/Ldr G R Edge - Red 1, A Flight, 253 Squadron

I was Red Leader when a large enemy formation was sighted about 30 miles east over Dover heading north-west. I vectored north-north-east to intercept and delivered a beam attack from about 1,000 feet above on to the bomber formation in sections echeloned starboard. Smoke was pouring from three of them and some parachutes were seen to be in the air. I endeavoured to reform the squadron but although in touch on the R/T with several could not make contact. I then climbed up to 18,000 feet ahead of the bombers and delivered a head-on diving attack on an He111 at the port side of bomber formation. Bullets were seen to enter the pilot's cockpit which smashed the Perspex and probably killed the pilot as almost immediately he spiralled away. It was not possible to follow it as I was engaged by Me109s. Diving away from them to about 8,000 feet I saw an Me109 heading south-east at about 6,000 feet. As I approached he dived down and endeavoured to take evasive action by flying very low and then pulling up doing a half roll and diving in another direction. This latter made it very easy to overtake and as he was diving out of his fifth roll he crossed in front of me at about 50 yards. I gave about ½ second to 1 second burst and as he pulled out smoke was seen to be coming out. A few moments later he crashed in flames by the side of a farm house near Wadhurst. Circling round, incendiary ammunition was seen to be exploding in the fire.

> " *I attacked a Do215 and before I broke away I observed black smoke pouring from its port engine. Later I observed three Do215s on fire and coming down rapidly also about five enemy airmen descending by parachute, one parachute being on fire.* "
>
> *F/Lt J H Wedgwood - Yellow 1, A Flight, 253 Squadron*

COMBAT REPORT:
Sgt R A Innes - Red 3, A Flight, 253 Squadron

I was Red 3 flying in squadron vic when we sighted a formation of bombers on our port side at 15,000 feet. Sections went into line astern and we attacked on the beam. I broke downwards and not being able to pick up any other aircraft I climbed again. As I climbed northwards I saw an He111 approaching from the north, flying south at 14,000 feet. As it passed on my starboard side I turned out of the sun but was rather late in doing so and I had to attack from astern. I gave it a burst of 4 - 5 seconds and observed the port engine on fire. I then broke away into the sun and on turning saw a formation of bombers going south just on the coast. I flew after them snd chose an He111, which was slightly separated from the rest, as my target. After my burst I saw black smoke pouring from the machine but did not observe which part it was coming from. It appeared to be coming from underneath the centre section of the wings but I could not confirm this.

COMBAT REPORT:

Sgt W B Higgins - Yellow 2, A Flight, 253 Squadron

I was Yellow 2, the squadron attacked a large formation of enemy bombers in sections echelon. The break-away from each individual attack (carried out over Maidstone, the e/a proceeding towards London) was so swift, no-one was able to ascertain the extent of his own particular burst. However 3 or 4 of the bombers did definitely go up in flames. After this first attack I was separated from the remainder of the squadron, finding myself very busy in a duel with an Me109 which I finally set on fire inland near Newhaven, when e/a crashed in flames. I then returned towards the Thames Estuary making contact with 12 Me110s, manoeuvring myself until it was possible to get in a 2 seconds burst, the result being clouds of white smoke issued from the rear. It was impossible to ascertain the real extent of the damage as I was attacked by several Me109s from which I broke away to return to my base.

Right: William Higgins' 'duel' was with the experienced C/O of 2/ JG51 Ernst Wiggers. Apparently the chase was at extremely low level, even under electric wires, only ending when Wiggers was killed when he hit rising ground near Lewes, (below).

Higgins was killed in action just three days later.

11 September 1940 - 15.30 - 16.00 hrs Combat A.

72 SQUADRON INTELLIGENCE REPORT

No.72 Squadron were ordered to patrol base at Angels 15. Eleven aircraft took off from Croydon at 15.25 hours. The formation consisted of three sections (Blue leading) with two sections of three aircraft each (Red and Green) and a rear guard of two aircraft (Yellow).

A large formation of enemy aircraft consisting of 60 Do17s and He111s, 60 Me109s and 30 Me110s were encountered at 21,000 feet flying north-west, in the Maidstone - Gravesend area. The bombers were in vic line astern formation with the fighter escort on their port side. The Squadron Leader ordered line astern and then echelon starboard, and a quarter attack was delivered out of the sun. Fire was opened at 300 yards closing almost to point blank range, in bursts of two to six seconds. Bursts of AA fire assisted in intercepting the enemy, whose return fire was not very effective.

COMBAT REPORT:
F/Lt E B Graham, Tennis Leader, Blue Section, 72 Squadron

On order to patrol base at angels 15 the squadron took off with a leading section of 3 (Blue), two more sections of 3 (Red and Green) and a rear guard of 2 a/c (Yellow). We patrolled Black Line at 25,000 ft and then sighted the large formation of E/A to the east, bunched together and flying in vics, line astern. I ordered the squadron line astern and then echelon starboard and delivered a quarter attack out of the sun. Just as I drew a bead on the leading Do17 an Me109 shot right across my nose, so I gave him a burst and am certain it went home. 4 Me110s and about the same number of Me109s had singled me out and I had to dogfight, finally going into a spin, from which I did not recover until about 7,000 ft. I then returned home.

COMBAT REPORT:
Sgt J S Gilders, Red 3, A Flight, 72 Squadron

Enemy a/c were flying NW when intercepted. I was Red 3 and as we approached the enemy bombers went into echelon, the Me109s came down after our attack. As they came down I saw one do a steep turn to port of me, as he turned I followed him round in the turn. I gave him a long burst and saw the fire going into his fuselage. He spun round and went on spinning until he hit the ground. He smashed into small pieces in a field near some high-tension wires, the approximate position of the crash being roughly near Cranbrook.

Round fired 800 approx.

COMBAT REPORT:
Sgt W T E Rolls, B Flight, 72 Squadron

3.30 pm. I took off from Croydon and we met the enemy in the Ashford region where they were flying on a north west course. We attacked them from the beam and by the time our section had got into position we were attacking dead astern of the Do17. We dived down from 25,000 to 20,000 ft and made our attack. I saw return fire from the Do17 and immediately I opened fire it stopped and I saw pieces flying away from the machine and smoke start coming from the engine. I closed range at about 25 to 30 yds as it heeled to starboard and went on its back as I did a steep turn to watch it go down. It continued to spin with smoke and flame coming from it and I saw it crash near a wood and lake at an estimated position of Cranbrook. I started to climb up again and I saw the other enemy machines above me. I continued to climb up below then from astern and saw the Me109s above me but they did not attack then. I was about 300 yds below them and I aimed full deflection on the leading machine and directly I fired I saw pieces flying off the underneath of it. I pulled the stick back gradually and finally saw the machine slip in but no smoke or fire came from it. By then I had stalled and found myself in a spin. When I had pulled out I saw 3 Me109s coming down towards me and I had to get them off my tail. They opened fire and I got hit in the tail plane and I kept doing steep turns and finally got rid of them at 3 to 5,000 feet and I then dived down to about 800 feet and came back home to Croydon. I had 13 rounds left in each gun approx. Before I fired my guns I saw Yellow 1* hit a Do17, which went down below the hills near my own Do17.

Note: It has not been possible to establish who 'Yellow 1' was, presumably either Sgt White, or Sgt Norfolk, but Sgt Norfolk's combat has not been found.

COMBAT REPORT:
P/O R D Elliott, Yellow 2, 72 Squadron

I was flying as Yellow 2 and acting as rear guard to the squadron. As the squadron attacked the E/A formation I followed in and attacked an He111 who immediately turned and flew on a due easterly course. On my first astern attack the starboard engine caught fire and the wheels dropped out. I continued to attack until his port engine caught fire and the E/A, still flying east, commenced to lose height and when about 12 miles east of Ramsgate, both engines completely stopped and E/A glided down onto water. I then returned to base. Only very little return fire was experienced.

P.S. Quarter attacks - astern attacks from below and above were carried out.

COMBAT REPORT:
Sgt J White, B Flight, 72 Squadron

At 15.30 I took off from Croydon. We intercepted the enemy near Ashford flying on a north westerly course at 22,000 ft. We came in from their port side and I opened fire from astern. I saw white smoke coming from the starboard engine and bits began to fly from the fuselage and wings. I then broke away downwards. I then climbed up to 18,000 feet and saw a single Do17 flying south with 2 Me109s flying close behind it and above. I flew underneath the Me109s and fired a long burst from astern. I broke away and I then saw white smoke coming from the port engine and the wheels came down and the machine fell into a vertical dive and crashed south of Sevenoaks.

501 SQUADRON OPERATIONS RECORD BOOK

At 12.00 hours on 10th September instructions were received for the squadron to move from Gravesend to Kenley. The movement was carried out without a hitch until the squadron arrived at Kenley, few preparations had been made for the reception of the squadron and accommodation had to be found for some of the personnel at a late hour in an adjacent hotel. The move of aircraft, personnel and equipment was completed by midnight.

501 SQUADRON INTELLIGENCE REPORT

11 Hurricanes of No.501 Squadron took off from Kenley at 15.20 hours in company with No.253 Squadron (Hurricanes) to patrol Maidstone at 1,500 feet ... from Maidstone they were vectored to Chatham and they turned south-west towards a point between Biggin Hill and Maidstone. When they were about 10 miles south of Biggin Hill the squadron was attacked by 3 or 4 of a large number of Me109s, causing the squadron to break up ... Seven of the squadron reformed and three of them, together with three Spitfires, attacked and destroyed a Do215 .... This was a straggler from a force of twenty Dorniers, which came in towards Kenley and turned towards the Thames Estuary ... The remaining five Hurricanes attempted to re-join them, but could not find them. Yellow 3 sighted a formation of about 30 plus He111s with fighter escort, coming in from the east, and attacked the second vic of the bomber formation, damaging two of them. He then climbed to a height of 18,000 feet and sighted a force of He111s coming in from the east approximately over Maidstone and travelling south at 16,000 feet. He did a beam attack on the leading vic of the formation, out of the sun, and damaged one of the bombers. His machine was hit in the oil tank.

Blue 2 engaged a single Heinkel at 10,000 feet near Biggin Hill and damaged it ... One pilot was forced to bale out after the attack by Me109s.

10 Hurricanes returned to Kenley at 16.50 hours.

Enemy casualties.   1 Dornier 215 destroyed, four Heinkels 111 damaged.

Our casualties.   1 Hurricane lost ... Pilot Sgt Pickering baled out and has since returned to unit.

Contemporary Accounts 222 Sqn

11 September 1940 - 15.30 - 16.00 hrs Combat A.

222 SQUADRON INTELLIGENCE REPORT

13 Spitfires took off from Hornchurch at 15.28 hours to patrol base at 15,000 feet. A large number of He111s, Ju88s and Me110s, escorted by Me109s were seen and the squadron climbed above the bombers to 28,000 feet, the enemy being about 4,000 feet lower. The squadron attacked the bombers in line astern formation and inflicted considerable damage on the enemy, until compelled to break away owing to the attention of the 109s.

P/O Assheton had to force land, owing to engine trouble. The remaining 12 machines landed at Hornchurch by 17.00 hours.

COMBAT REPORT:
Sgt I Hutchinson - A Flight, 222 Squadron

After the squadron had delivered an attack upon an enemy bomber formation, I noticed an He111 behind the formation on its own. As I went into attack it, another Spitfire delivered a short attack, whereupon the e/a lowered its undercarriage and black smoke emitted from its engines. The Spitfire broke away and I watched the e/a, who commenced to raise his undercarriage, and the smoke ceased. I therefore delivered an attack myself. On the second burst his undercarriage dropped again and glycol and oily smoke poured from his starboard engine. I transferred my attack to the port engine with the same result. As the lower rear gunner was firing I finished my ammunition at him; then as I was attacked by an Me109, I broke away. As I went down I could still see the He111 with both motors smoking and dropping behind and below the formation, and its undercarriage was still dropped. On landing I noticed my a/c was covered in dirty oil from his coolers for which I aimed.

COMBAT REPORT:
Sgt R G Marland - A Flight, 222 Squadron

At approximately 17.00 hours, I was patrolling with 222 Squadron at 30,000 feet. Enemy bombers were sighted below and, as we attacked in line astern formation, I saw one enemy bomber about 8,000 feet below me, which I took to be a Ju88 travelling in a south-easterly direction. I dived vertically and opened fire at approximately 400 yards range, closing to 150 yards, when I broke away. As I broke away, my goggles blew off my eyes and I was momentarily blinded with tears. When I regained proper control, I could not see the enemy bomber at all, but a few minutes later saw a column of smoke and went to investigate. I then saw a bomber in flames on the ground, which I took to be the same machine which I had attacked. The approximate position of this machine was about 10 to 15 miles north-west of Dungeness.

COMBAT REPORT:
Sgt E Scott - A Flight, 222 Squadron

I was flying in line astern when I saw what appeared to be a broken formation of 12 - 15 He111s going south. I dived on one and commenced a beam to astern attack, opening fire at 300 yards and closing into about 10 yards. The e/a began to dive steeply, but I was unable to follow it down because my hood was hit by either a piece of metal from the bomber or by fire from another e/a, which I assume was an Me109. The hood was completely smashed and I was rather blinded for a few seconds by what appeared to be a flash.

I commenced a steep dive with evasive action to rid myself of any following e/a. On reaching 500 feet I began to check my a/c to see if the damage was any greater than the hood. My a/c seemed to be in perfect condition, so I began to climb when I noticed a burning enemy wreck. I circled it to try and confirm it as the He111 that I had attacked, but the wreckage was spread over such a wide area I could not be certain as to what type it was.

I had circled the wreckage for a minute or so when I saw two parachutists descending. They were immediately pounced upon by farmers or the L.D.V.

605 SQUADRON INTELLIGENCE REPORT

12 Hurricanes of No.605 Squadron left Croydon 15.43 hours on 11th September 1940 with orders to patrol base angels 15, Yellow 3 returning 15.55 with suspected glycol leak which proved to be unfounded. The squadron were flying with sections echelon port, 'B' Flight, leading at about 18,000 feet when they saw 40 He111s at about 16,000 feet escorted by about 40 Me109s on both sides and above and by 20 Me110s behind and above. The enemy bomber formation was flying in vics of five, line astern approaching from east-south-east.

Blue 1, coming out of the sun and apparently unseen by the bombers attacked the leader of the port outside vic from quarter ahead to beam and saw it spiral out of the formation and spiral down a few miles south of Gravesend. This was confirmed by Green 1, but neither saw it actually hit the ground or break up.

Blue 3 attacked the leader of the main formation and Blue 2, attacked another enemy aircraft in the same formation with beam attacks, but with no visible effect.

Yellow 1, following in, attacked an He111 in the same vic with a diving beam attack, opening fire at 300 yards closing to 50 yards with one ring deflection and a four second burst. The enemy aircraft streamed white smoke and vapour from the port engine and turned left out of the formation.

No.605 Squadron broke away under the formation and climbed again into the sun. Yellow 1, attacked the leading vic head-on, opening fire at 600 yards with a 4 second burst, aiming at all the leading He111s. As he broke away he noticed the right-hand enemy aircraft of the vic was streaming white smoke and losing height and jettisoned two large bombs and numerous incendiaries near Eltham.

Red 3, who had broken away to the right, attacked one of a formation of four He111s from 250 yards to 30 yards with a four to five seconds burst, seeing his fire enter the enemy aircraft along the starboard wing, engine and side of the fuselage, causing much white vapour to be emitted.

Meanwhile Yellow 2, and Blue 2, who had broken right away after the second attack by the squadron, were attacked by an Me110, and Me109 respectively. Yellow 2, made a dive attack from astern on the Me110 which Yellow 2 had evaded after the Me110's attack on him with a 5 second burst from 350 yards closing to 150 yards. The enemy aircraft dived into the ground between Rochester and Gravesend. Blue 2 also made a diving attack from astern on the Me109 with a 5 second burst at 250 yards. The enemy aircraft broke up and dived into the ground also between Rochester and Gravesend. The effect of these attacks was to turn the enemy formation off their westerly course towards the south.

Yellow 1 climbed again into the sun and opened fire head-on from 700 yards with a 4 second burst at the two leading He111s of a vic, both of which were last seen streaming white vapour in large quantities, losing height and flying south-east. Yellow 1 then opened fire at another He111 to the left of the two leaders with a head-on attack closing to 150 yards. This enemy aircraft spiralled down in the vicinity of Addington and Hayes and was confirmed by 605 Intelligence Officer from Croydon aerodrome. After the formation had turned south, Red 2 encountered a few miles east of Croydon heading south, a Ju52 with about 10 Me110s above and behind him, circling and weaving. The Ju52 must have been with the main bomber formation all the way, but no one else appeared to have seen it. Red 2 did a 5 second beam attack on the Ju52 from 500 yards, but with no visible effect. As the enemy formation were turning their course towards the south, Blue 1 and Blue 3 twice climbed up into the sun each doing beam attacks upon an He111, Blue 1 putting its starboard engine out of action. The top rear gunner baled out as well as another member of the crew. By now both Blue 1 and Blue 3 were out of ammunition, but continued doing feint attacks in the hope of forcing the enemy aircraft to come down on land. The machine, however, crashed in the water south of Beachy Head.

10 aircraft 605 Squadron returned Croydon 16.15 - 16.50 hours, Green 2 landing Redhill and one aircraft being Cat.2.

Red 1 was slightly wounded.

Cine gun was used by Blue 1.

Red 1	S/Ldr Churchill	Red 2	P/O Ingle	Red 3	P/O Cooper-Slipper
Yellow 1	P/O Currant	Yellow 2	P/O Glowacki	Yellow 3	P/O Milne
Blue 1	F/Lt McKellar	Blue 2	Sgt Budzinski	Blue 3	P/O Jones
Green 1	F/O Passy	Green 2	F/O Hope	Green 3	P/O Watson

Contemporary Accounts 605 Sqn

11 September 1940 - 15.30 - 16.00 hrs Combat A.

COMBAT REPORT:

F/Lt A A McKellar - Blue 1, B Flight, 605 Squadron

I was leading the squadron from Blue Section and was told to rendezvous with another squadron 16,000 feet above base, I to lead both squadrons. This other squadron never, as far as I could see, joined me. At 14,000 feet I saw large bomber formation, plus escort fighters to the east still some distance away and at about 18,000 feet flying west-north-west. I informed the squadron and Runic of this and carried on climbing. When I had gained about 1,000 feet above the bombers, I instructed the squadron to prepare for a beam attack out of the sun, which was just behind us and of great value, as I consider that the bomber formation never saw our approach due to the sun in their eyes. The bomber formation was composed of vics of five aircraft in squadron formation a little south of Gravesend, I therefore attacked the leader of the port outside vic from quarter ahead to beam and saw it break out of the formation and spiral down, confirmed by Green 1. As I was fairly close I had to break through the formation (this bomber formation was flying in much wider formation than that previously noticed and I consider that this may be due to the fear of head-on attacks doing damage to several aircraft if they are flying too close together). On climbing up again I noticed near Chislehurst one enemy aircraft at 15,000 feet much behind and carried out a beam attack from the west and stopped his starboard engine (this aircraft had four vertical white strips on his fin and also about quarter way up the port wing tip and what appeared to be a Blue Bear on a white shield just behind the Perspex nose - no other squadron markings were noticed. I did one more attack from a slight dive and behind as the enemy aircraft was heading south, in an attempt to put out the port motor, thereby expending all my ammunition, and then saw the top rear gunner bale out and another member of the crew as well. What appeared to be maps etc were also being thrown overboard some miles south of Tunbridge Wells. I also noticed another Hurricane flying near me during these two attacks (Blue 3). As by now I had no ammunition left, I called up this other aircraft who I knew to be one of my flight, to finish the enemy aircraft off, but was informed that he also had no ammunition. We both then kept diving very low over him in an endeavour to force him lower and down on land. He was losing height very rapidly even on one engine (I think perhaps due to my and Blue 3's low flying tactics). This machine however crashed on the water south of Beachy Head, having crossed Beachy Head at 1,000 feet. I landed Croydon 16.50 hours.

COMBAT REPORT:

Sgt J Budzinski - Blue 2, B Flight, 605 Squadron

I left Croydon 15.43 hours with 605 Squadron, 'B' Flight leading, 'A' Flight in echelon left, we met the He111s at 18,000 feet near Addington going north. They were in vic formation, a vic of 3 leading followed by vics of 5, with many Me109s each side of them, and 1,500 feet above with 20/30 Me110s over and behind the bombers. I attacked an He111 in the second formation with a beam attack from 400 yards, with a 3 seconds burst with no visible effect. I broke underneath it and saw an Me109 coming towards me. I made a head-on attack but with no effect. The Me109 then dived and turned right-handed, I turned into him and dived after it to 10,000 feet I was then in a position to make an astern attack from above. I fired a 5 seconds burst from 250 yards, the enemy aircraft broke up and dived down to the ground south-east of Gravesend. I then met another Hurricane and returned to Croydon aerodrome.

Left: McKellar and Jones's victim was almost certainly this Heinkel, 1H+KH of 1/KG26 which actually made it back across the Channel after the pilot baled out! According to the RAF pilots, the aircraft had four white stripes on the fin along with white stripes on the port wing. See the full story on page 480.

COMBAT REPORT:
P/O R E Jones - Blue 3, B Flight, 605 Squadron

Attacks commenced 4 miles north of Farningham, Kent. I followed Flight Commander and attacked leader of leading formation of 5 He111s at 18,000 feet from the port beam allowing 1 ½ to 1 ring deflection, saw burst entering leader's aircraft - broke and did not observe result of attack. Broke to the left and pulled up below one He111 and did a number 5 attack and followed with a beam. By this time I had expended all my ammunition. Flight Commander also attacked this enemy aircraft which lost height rapidly and came down in the sea off Beachy Head. After I had expended ammunition I continued feint attacks hoping to draw fire so the Flight Commander could bring the machine down. After it was obvious that neither of us had any ammunition left and two of the enemy aircraft's crew had left the machine, we continued diving attacks hoping to force enemy aircraft to crash on land. The enemy aircraft had 4 white lines on fin and white slashes down the port wing. Underneath duck egg blue. 1 He111 claimed as shared with F/Lt McKellar.

COMBAT REPORT:
P/O T P M Cooper-Slipper - Red 3, A Flight, 605 Squadron

I was Red 3 of 605 Squadron, ordered to scramble at 16.55 hours at 17,000 feet in the vicinity of Rochester, a large formation of enemy aircraft was sighted heading west. 'A' Flight followed 'B' into a beam attack, but I was rather cramped for space and only a short burst could be fired at one of the He111s. I broke downwards and then climbed up again on the right-hand side of the bombers. I did a beam attack on one of a formation of 4 He111s and after the attack observed white vapour coming from the starboard engine of the enemy aircraft. My attack began at 250 range closing to about 30 yards in a 4/5 seconds burst. I saw my fire entering the aircraft along the starboard wing, engine and side of fuselage. A large amount of cannon fire was coming from astern so I carried out evasive tactics and in doing so lost the bomber formation. I cruised around for a time in search of other aircraft but did not see any, so I proceeded to Croydon and landed at 17.55 hours.

COMBAT REPORT:
Sgt W J Glowacki - Yellow 2, A Flight, 605 Squadron

I left Croydon 16.53 hours with No.605 Squadron, 'B' Flight leading 'A' Flight. We were in echelon port just before beginning our attack on the He111s. We met the enemy formation coming from the east near Rochester. I attacked the port aircraft of the leading vic of 3 He111s from the port side with a diving quarter attack from 300 yards closing to 100 yards with 3 very short bursts with no visible effect - I then broke under it and circled left and climbed parallel to and above the leading bomber.

I again attacked the same He111 with a diving head-on attack without effect. At that moment I noticed an Me110 behind me and diving on to me so I broke away down and to the right. The Me110 was following me. I then did a climbing turn to the right and saw the Me110 break away below me to the left, so I continued my turn and dived upon it from astern firing a 5 seconds burst from 350 yards - 150 yards when its port engine began to smoke and it turned sharp left and dived into the ground from about 8,000 feet between Rochester and Gravesend. Then I was by myself so climbed and searched for other enemy aircraft. I saw an He111 going south-east, being attacked by a Spitfire with a diving attack from astern, so I joined in also with a diving attack from astern. The Spitfire breaking left and I broke right climbing again to attack. When I made my second attack there were about 7 Hurricanes and Spitfires also attacking. The He111 dived about 8 or 10 miles south-east of Maidstone, 3 of the crew baling out - 2 appeared to land safely but the parachute of the third did not open. I then returned to Croydon.

Contemporary Accounts Duxford Wing

11 September 1940 - 15.30 - 16.00 hrs Combat A.

DUXFORD WING INTELLIGENCE REPORT

The Wing, consisting of three squadrons with 36 aircraft, left Duxford just before 16.00 hours on the 11th September and patrolled North Weald at 23,000 feet. AA fire in the direction of Gravesend drew their attention to at least 150 E/A flying north at 20,000 feet. The enemy were coming north in waves of tight formations of Do215s, He111s and Ju88s with protecting fighters, the Me110s immediately behind the bombers and a large number of Me109s behind them at 24,000 feet. It had been arranged that the two Spitfire squadrons in the lead (a composite squadron composed of 19 and 266, and 611 Squadrons) were to attack the fighter escort whilst the other squadron (74) attacked the bombers. As 74 Squadron went into the formation of Ju88s they were attacked by enemy fighters (He113s) diving on them, but continued their attack on the main formation. AA fire which had drawn our fighters' attention to the enemy was troublesome during the engagement and hampered the plan of attack. In spite of this 74 Squadron stuck to their task and inflicted considerable losses on the enemy bombers, while the other two squadrons joined in the general melee and engaged both fighters and bombers.

19 SQUADRON OPERATIONS RECORD BOOK

Squadron along with wing on usual evening tea party. Led by S/Ldr Lane and P/O Lawson. S/Ldr Lane shot down an Me110 also damaged an He111, P/O Lawson an He111, Sgt Jennings an Me110 and probable He111, Sgt Roden an Me110, P/O Haines got an Me110, Sgt Cox a probable Do215, P/O Dolezal an Me109 probable, F/Sgt Unwin was himself shot down but made a wizard forced landing with undercarriage down!!! 611 Squadron who came in place of 310 shot down one.

Quite a successful party.

" *I sighted the enemy formation to port, right over Central London. I attacked an Me109 which turned after a Spitfire. I got between the Me109 and the Spitfire, flying towards the former, and gave it a burst of 3 seconds. Black smoke poured from the e/a and it turned away to port. I turned after it but in doing so got a full burst from the rear. My cockpit became full of oil and I had to break away and land at the aerodrome, being slightly wounded in the right knee by a splinter. My aircraft suffered the following damage: undercarriage pump shot through, and trim cable shot through.*

P/O F Dolezal - B Flight, 19 Squadron "

Below: Brian Lane not only spotted that the Heinkels had white stripes on the rudder but also that the Me110s had white noses up to the windscreen. This tactical marking was introduced around this time and can be seen here on U8+HL of 2/ZG26 which was shot down in this combat.

COMBAT REPORT:
S/Ldr B J E Lane, Red 1, A Flight, 19 Squadron

I took off from G.1. with 19 Sqdn at 15.40 hrs and formed up a wing of 19, 611 and 74 Squadrons. I climbed to 23,000 ft over North Weald. I then sighted AA fire south of Gravesend and observed a large formation of E/A flying north at 20,000 ft. I turned south and dived in a head-on attack on the leading formation of approx 12 He111s. I turned to port and observed E/A turning south east over Sittingbourne. There were now only 7 He111s in formation with 2 more ½ mile ahead and 2 Me110s, 1 astern and 1 to port. I attacked rear Me110 from astern and saw large pieces flying off his starboard engine which stopped. I broke away and attacked again from astern. The starboard engine caught fire and E/A was last seen in a dive. The 2nd Me110 then opened up and left the He111s. I carried out head-on and beam attacks on E/A without visible effect and then an astern attack on rear He111. The starboard engine was seen to catch fire. I had no more ammunition left and returned to base. Vis was good, 1/10 cloud 15,000 ft. Camouflage appeared dark green, only He111s had two white stripes on rudder. Me110s had white noses up to windscreen. Little rear fire experienced from He's. None from Me110. AA fire was accurate but 500 ft high at first and a trifle dangerous for fighters. Range opened approx 300 yds, closed to 50 yds. Speed of E/A approx 250 mph.

COMBAT REPORT:
Sgt H A C Roden, A Flight, 19 Squadron

Made an astern attack on the rearmost machine of about 30 Me110s which were milling round in a large circle. I was about 1,000 feet higher and dived with the sun behind me - I came up from below into the astern position. I gave him a burst of about 5 seconds and as other aircraft were coming up behind I broke away down. Pieces of the target aircraft flew off from the port mainplane and he continued straight and level for about another 50 yds and then smoke came from the port engine and he started a shallow dive. My position was not very healthy and I had to remove my attention from him. I tried to follow his flight a minute or two later but could see no sign of him.

Contemporary Accounts 19 Sqn

11 September 1940 - 15.30 - 16.00 hrs Combat A.

" *I closed to 200 yards and opened fire. The e/a's starboard engine burst into flames and it broke formation. I followed it and gave it a long burst when the port engine caught fire and lots of pieces came away from the fuselage and port mainplane. I had observed no rear fire but was continually having to evade attacks by Me109s - which were painted yellow from spinner to cockpit - which dived on me from above.*

After the combat I noticed several bullet holes in both mainplanes, but as the aircraft appeared quite normal in flight, I climbed and endeavoured to engage some more Me110s. E/A went into a defensive circle on sighting me and when I tried to get above them they climbed also. I kept in their vicinity and they gradually climbed from 15,000 feet to 20,000 feet, and made their way towards the coast. I had to leave them over Beachy Head, not having been able to engage one unfortunately.

My aircraft crashed on landing as both tyres had been punctured by bullets. I had taken off from G.1 and crash landed at G.1.

F/O L A Haines - Green 1, B Flight, 19 Squadron "

Below: A 19 Squadron Spitfire is guided to dispersal by groundcrew in mid September 1940.

COMBAT REPORT:

Sgt D G S R Cox, Blue 2, Flight, 19 Squadron

I was Blue 2 in the Flight. I was line astern of Blue 1 when we attacked E/A. I was attacked from astern by an Me109 and had to break away. I then attacked an Me110 which was the end machine of a section of about 20. I fired one burst but without success and had to break away on being attacked by another Me110. I then climbed up and spotted a Do215 a little way behind the rest of an enemy formation. I climbed above the E/A and attacked out of the sun from about 2,000 feet above. I made three attacks and at the third time observed that his starboard engine had stopped. I had then finished my ammunition. The last I saw of E/A was that he was losing height as he crossed the coast at about 7,000 feet near Dungeness.

Took off G.1. 15.30 landed Tangmere 17.00 hours

COMBAT REPORT:
Sgt B J Jennings, Red 2, A Flight, 19 Squadron

I was Red 2 and took off from G.1. at 15.30 hrs, at 16.15 hrs we intercepted 12 He111K, we did a head-on attack, I turned after firing, and saw my He111K with his starboard engine burning. I fired again and he went down apparently out of control, so much tracer was flashing past that I didn't stay to watch him crash. I lost the rest of the formation, so I attacked a rear end Me110 out of a formation of about 15, this one fell back from the rest of the formation with smoke pouring out of his starboard engine, I did another attack from above and behind and he crashed down in a wood, south west of the railway line, between Sittingbourne and Maidstone, approx. I didn't see anybody jump by parachute.

I chased 11 Me110s out to sea, finished my rounds and returned home, without any visible result.

COMBAT REPORT:
F/Sgt G C Unwin, Red 4, A Flight, 19 Squadron

I was Red 4 with S/Ldr Lane. I sighted a large enemy formation on our starboard and below. We attacked in line astern, forming echelon port. I attacked an He111 and fired a 7 or 8 second burst at 50 yds range. Bits came off both engines and the A/C went into a steep spiral. I did not see him crash as I immediately attacked a Do215. I opened fire from below at 100 yds closing to 50 yds. I fired all my rounds into him, but did not see any result, owing to the fact that my windscreen and engine were shot up by the fire from his bottom gunner. My engine was running badly as I dived away and was pouring out smoke which was in my opinion glycol. I switched off and force landed with my wheels down. No damage was done to the A/C on landing. Place of landing 1 mile north of Brentwood near searchlight site E.C 11.

Contemporary Accounts 266 Sqn

11 September 1940 - 15.30 - 16.00 hrs Combat A.

266 SQUADRON OPERATIONS RECORD BOOK

6 aircraft sent to Duxford from Wittering.

Ordered to patrol London at 25,000 ft from Duxford as part of wing formation. Shortly after leaving ground a formation of 30 Do215s were sighted over Dartford and Gravesend flying north west at about 240 mph at 22,000 ft. Further behind was a wave of 30 He111s with approx 10 Me109s 2,000 to 3,000 ft above. The 215s were being hotly engaged by AA fire. Our aircraft in twos line astern attacked the starboard wing of the 215s, out of the sun from above, ahead and to port. Enemy casualties:- 3 probably destroyed. 5 damaged. Spitfire P.7313 piloted by P/O R J B Roach hit by cannon fire and crashed near Billericay, Essex. Pilot baled out over Billericay and spent the night at North Weald returning to squadron next day.

COMBAT REPORT:
F/Lt S H Bazley - B Flight, 266 Squadron

Flying directly astern of a flight of Spitfires from 19 Squadron I saw a large formation of e/a flying west at approximately 10,000 feet in the locality of Gravesend. The Wing Leader put fighter a/c into line astern and attacked out of the sun from above and ahead the centre vic of approximately 30 Dornier Do215s which immediately before had been hotly engaged by AA fire which was of the greatest assistance in locating e/a.

I dived on the starboard wing of the enemy's vic formation from above, ahead and to port using deflection. I opened fire at approximately 400 yards and firing straight down the arm of the 'V' closed to approximately 50 yards or less.

I observed one e/a, about half way down the arm of the 'V', emit clouds of white smoke as my bullets hit. P/O Williams and Sgt Barraclough, of Green and Blue Sections, 266 Squadron respectively both observed a Do215 dropping out of formation and emitting white smoke at this time.

No enemy fire was encountered although Me110s were in formation to starboard of the e/a attacked - there was no cloud, but slight ground haze. The entire enemy formation appeared to turn towards the south at the first attack but took no other evasive action. No cine camera gun was fitted.

COMBAT REPORT:
Sgt R G V Barraclough - B Flight, 266 Squadron

Attacked 12 Me110s. Opened fire on one machine from astern and the formation took evasive action by forming into a circle. Machine attacked did not appear to be hit and no return of fire experienced. Later attacked a lone He111 flying south-east in direction of Dover. Attacked from astern twice and after the second burst of approximately 5 seconds the He111 was losing height and there appeared to be a trace of black smoke from both engines. Enemy aircraft was at a height of approximately 12,000 feet. Noticed return fire from rear gunner.

Before this engagement I sighted a formation of about 20 Do215s which squadron attacked from dead ahead. The enemy aircraft were in extended vic formation and immediately after the attack I saw one enemy aircraft break away from formation and dive steeply with a Spitfire on its tail. There was a great deal of anti-aircraft fire in the vicinity which hindered fighter (our) aircraft attacking. Cine gun not fitted. Weather clear - practically no cloud, slight haze near ground.

Opposite: 266 Squadron airborne towards the end of the Battle of Britain.

COMBAT REPORT:
P/O H M T Heron - Green 3, B Flight, 266 Squadron

I was Green 3 flying with Blue and Green Section as part of a wing formation over Dartford, flying at 22,000 feet. A vic formation of about 30 Dornier 215s was flying northwest at about 21,000 feet approximately 240 mph. They appeared to be wholly black in colour except for a black cross outlined in white on the side of the fuselage. As I dived to make a front attack with about 3 other Spitfires the e/a turned west. The damage apparent after first attack, e/a then formed protective circle. I then carried out 3 quarter-to-stern attacks (commencing with 1 length of Dornier 215 as deflection). On second attack and other two quarter-to-stern attacks small pieces fell off the e/a (aileron on one, tail unit on other two). One machine went on its back then lost height in a spiral. The other two Dornier 215s continued to circle with their formation. As my ammunition was then finished I broke off combat into the sun and returned to base.

I did not observe any return fire from the Dornier 215s.The AA bursts helped me to locate the e/a which were slightly above the smoke puffs. The weather was very clear and sunny with no cloud. Cine camera gun was not fitted. Sun was almost in west.

COMBAT REPORT:
P/O R B J Roach - Blue 2, B Flight, 266 Squadron

I was Blue 2 and my squadron was ordered to patrol London at 25,000 ft. As enemy aircraft were sighted I paired off with Blue 1 in line astern. I saw eight He111s and proceeded to carry out an attack from astern. I attacked the E/A on the starboard side of the formation of eight which were in a large vic flying at a speed of 250 mph heading NW. I opened my first burst of six seconds at 300 yards closing in fairly rapidly. I gave my second burst of five secs from 200 closing to 150 yards with the starboard engine issuing black smoke and E/A losing height from his formation. Just before I broke off my attack I received two heavy thuds, gun fire from one of the other E/A, as I could see flashes coming from him while carrying out my attack on the starboard aircraft. Camouflage on top of E/A appeared to be black. I received no fire from the attacked aircraft. AA fire was excellent, but did not stop immediately when our fighters attacked E/A. E/A appeared to be firing a cannon from above. I was hit on the port side which put my engine out of order, and proceeded to glide clear of London, with my cockpit getting very hot, so decided to bale out. Air Raid Wardens witnessed my baling out then saw my aircraft come down in flames and crash in a field.

The weather was excellent. No cine-gun fitted.

I saw no enemy fighters escorting bombers, but noticed one E/A fighter painted bright yellow, going in opposite direction 1,000 feet below bombers.

Contemporary Accounts 611 Sqn

11 September 1940 - 15.30 - 16.00 hrs Combat A.

611 SQUADRON OPERATIONS RECORD BOOK

Clear day, but a cold wind again. The squadron (12 aircraft) off at 06.45 to G.1. From there they took off at 15.30, along with two other squadrons, on patrol over the London area, and ran into a very large enemy formation. The fighting soon became confused. The intelligence Officer's summary reads as follows:

At 15.30 hours 611 Squadron left G.1 Duxford and went into position as second squadron of the wing formation which was ordered to patrol in a southerly direction towards the Thames Estuary. At about 15.50 when in the vicinity of southeast London, 611 Squadron formed up in three sections of four aircraft in line astern. 100 plus enemy aircraft were seen coming north in the direction of our fighters. Our aircraft were then at 20,000 feet. The enemy formation consisted of 15 to 30 Dornier 215s and a number of Heinkel 111s at 18,000 feet and a mass of Me110s stepped up behind at 20,000 feet, with a large number of Me109s behind them at 24,000 feet. Our aircraft altered course, making a left-handed turn, coming in to attack on the beam of the enemy formation. 611 Squadron attacked the Me110s. Pilots report that from the moment of contact with the enemy it was impossible to keep formation, and a general melee ensued.

F/Sgt Sadler, who was No.4 of Yellow Section, got separated from his section and attacked an Me110 giving two long bursts closing from 500 yards to 100 yards, and using nearly all his ammunition. The fuselage was seen to catch fire, and the e/a was last seen losing height.

P/O Lund, No.4 of Blue Section – See Combat Report.

Sgt Burt – See Combat Report.

Squadron landed at Duxford at approximately 16.20 hours to refuel and rearm, and left for Digby where squadron arrived at dusk.

Sgt F E R Shepherd and his Spitfire P7298 are missing.

Sgt S A Levenson force landed near Kenley and returned to Digby by train on 12.9.40. See Combat Report.

Pilots report that R/T was working well during combat. Reflector type sight used. Me110s were very dark in colour, Me109s were painted yellow from nose to cockpit. Combat took place above 1/10 cloud in good visibility.

An additional summary forwarded by the Intelligence Officer reads as follows:

F/O D H Watkins followed 19 Squadron into an attack on a large formation of Me109s and 110s. He fired a short burst at full deflection into an Me110 from less than 100 yards range but owing to his rapid approaching speed he saw no result. He broke away climbing towards the sun and lost the formation. At 16.15 hours he sighted a formation of about 40 Do215s, being directed onto them by AA fire. As he was about to attack these aircraft two bursts upset his aircraft in its dive and the engine stopped. He force landed at Hornchurch and later returned to Duxford and thence to Digby.

S/Ldr McComb followed by P/O Williams were preparing to attack an Me110 when they were themselves attacked by an Me109 and climbed away from the formation to evade. They did not find other targets.

F/Lt Stoddart attacked an Me109 at long range firing 1784 rounds without observed result. He then returned to base.

F/O Hay who was covering his rear followed him back to Duxford he did not open fire on the Me109 as he never got within range.

P/O D H O'Neil fired 174 rounds into a Do215 without result. The general confusion and AA fire prevented him from making a further attack and P/O Adams made no attack for similar reasons.

P/O Lund's stoppage was due to a faulty feed chute.

F/Sgt Sadler's stoppage was due to a jammed transporter guide.

Sgt Burt had two stoppages, one after 180 rounds and one after 4 rounds, both due to cross feed.

The total bag claimed therefore is 1 Me110 and 1 Ju88 destroyed, and 1 He111, 1 Me110 and 1 Me109 probable, to set off against 1 Spitfire considerably damaged (P7321, Sgt Levenson) and 1 missing (P7298, Sgt Shepherd).

COMBAT REPORT:
Sgt A D Burt, Red Section, A Flight, 611 Squadron

Wing (Squadron) were ordered to intercept 100 Huns coming into London area from Dover. E/A were sighted at approx 15.45 by formation leader over SE London. I lost formation in sun and then saw them above me, at approx 21,000 ft (my height 20,000 ft), an Me109 with yellow spinner and dark camouflage pursued by Hurricane. E/A left Hurricane behind and then manoeuvred to get on my tail. I took violent avoiding action, lost sight of E/A then saw below formation of bombers approx 18,000 ft consisting of about 12-15 Do215 or 17 with single He111K Mk V in rear about 200 yds behind, protected by approx same number of Me110 1,000 ft above. I manoeuvred into position for attack on the He111 with sun at my back about 5,000 ft above him, then dived, opening fire at about 400 yds and maintaining fire to about 200 yds or less when it became necessary to take violent avoiding action again (a) to avoid hitting the target (b) because I glimpsed fighter aircraft, type unknown, on my tail. Burst was about 5 to 6 secs in duration and apparently put rear gunner out of action since tracer fire ceased almost immediately. Having made a steep climbing turn I presently observed the same formation heading towards Dungeness, and on closing range again observed that the He111K was no longer with the formation. From moment of breaking off attack I did not see the above mentioned E/A again.

Following this attack I shadowed formation almost to Dungeness, when it turned east. I attacked one of the escorting Me110s from above and out of the sun, when it got out of formation momentarily. I opened fire at about 500-450 yds, when E/A did left-hand turn, and I followed round, giving 5 to 6 seconds deflection burst, but with no positive results observed. Other escorts then attacked me and I was forced to get away quickly, so could not observe any result of my attack.

Observed at long range an aircraft which appeared to be of Focke-Wulf 198* type, but was not sure of this as aircraft made off too quickly. I observed one fighter, type unknown, going down in flames and one bomber going down with one engine ablaze, again, type unknown. Very effective AA barrage at 20,000 ft east of London appeared to be too high to catch bombers.

Note: This is as written in Sgt Burt's original report.

COMBAT REPORT:
Sgt S A Levenson, Blue Section, B Flight, 611 Squadron

Enemy sighted 15.45 hours approaching London area from the SE. About 50-60 Ju88 were in one large formation - i.e. very close Vic - about 5-8 aircraft in each Vic. There appeared to be no escorting fighters and the enemy remained in close formation on a set course through intense AA fire. After flying around formation once I observed Me109s in line astern (with distinctive yellow noses) circling the formation in the opposite direction to myself and about 500 feet below me. I being about 2,000 ft above bombers. As we converged I made ready for a quarter attack. I opened fire on the leading a/c at 200 yds giving about 60 degrees deflection and allowed both a/c to fly through the sights. After breaking away the leader dived steeply but appeared to be under control. I saw no apparent effect of my fire. The second a/c followed its leader down for about 500 ft and then flicked over onto its back, dived and slowly began to spin. I then lost sight of the a/c.

I returned to above the enemy bomber formation and decided to carry out a quarter attack from head-on. I flew to about 1,500 ft above the enemy formation and dived down and engaged the foremost a/c on the starboard side. I kept the button pressed and allowed the whole formation to fly through the sights. No fire was returned and no attacks were made by enemy fighters. I broke away and observed two a/c break away and down to starboard. I followed one which appeared to be losing height the more quickly of the two. I carried out a short burst on a quarter attack. No enemy return of fire. Smoke appeared from the starboard engine and a/c continued to glide down, losing about 10,000 ft in 10-15 miles. I was flying alongside e/a in formation about 100 yds away, no fire from E/A. When AA opened fire I broke away at once but black smoke appeared from under the instrument panel and from the bottom of the cockpit. I intended to jump and undid the straps, but although smoke increased there were no flames. I therefore remained with the a/c and I intended to land at Kenley aerodrome. When engine finally stopped and by the time I re-fastened my straps, I was too low to make the aerodrome and had to land in a field with wheels up. It was reported to me by the OC Searchlights at a nearby camp that the a/c I was following crashed in flames about 6-10 miles south of Kenley.

Contemporary Accounts 249 Sqn

11 September 1940 - 15.30 - 16.00 hrs Combat A.

249 SQUADRON INTELLIGENCE REPORT

At 15.27 hours on 11.9.40, 11 aircraft of 249 Squadron and Wing Commander Beamish, Station Commander, left North Weald first to patrol base at 15,000 feet, then to intercept raid 54 with 257 Squadron and then to patrol Maidstone to Mayfield at 10,000 feet.

About 2 miles south-east of London 249 Squadron engaged a large compact vic of 50 plus He111s at 19,000 feet. They were heading west when seen, but they turned north just as we engaged them, dropping bombs on the London docks and then turning south. The large vic was composed of vics of three.

An unusual occurrence was that there appeared to be only a very small fighter escort (Me109s or He 113s) which was flying 10,000 feet above enemy bombers. In consequence our fighters were more or less unmolested in their first attack. They attacked from ahead and at least 4 enemy bombers were seen to drop behind, streaming glycol. These are claimed as 'damaged' by the squadron as a whole.

Blue 2 (P/O Neil) destroyed an He111, which crash landed in a field about 20 miles south-east of London.

Green 3 (P/O Pattullo) and Red 1 (F/Lt Parnall) each claim a Heinkel 111 which crashed in a field by a railway station near Tonbridge. It was clearly the same e/a and it has been awarded as shared between them.

Wing Commander Beamish accounted for an He111 'probable', witnessed by P/O Beazley. He was the only pilot to be engaged by enemy fighters.

10 aircraft and Wing Commander Beamish returned to North Weald by 16.40 hours, Sgt Davis having (it is believed) baled out. He is safe and only slightly injured.

Below: The Heinkel claimed by 249 Squadron's pilots which came down in a field was this one V4+KL of 3/KG1, seen here on display to the public shortly after.

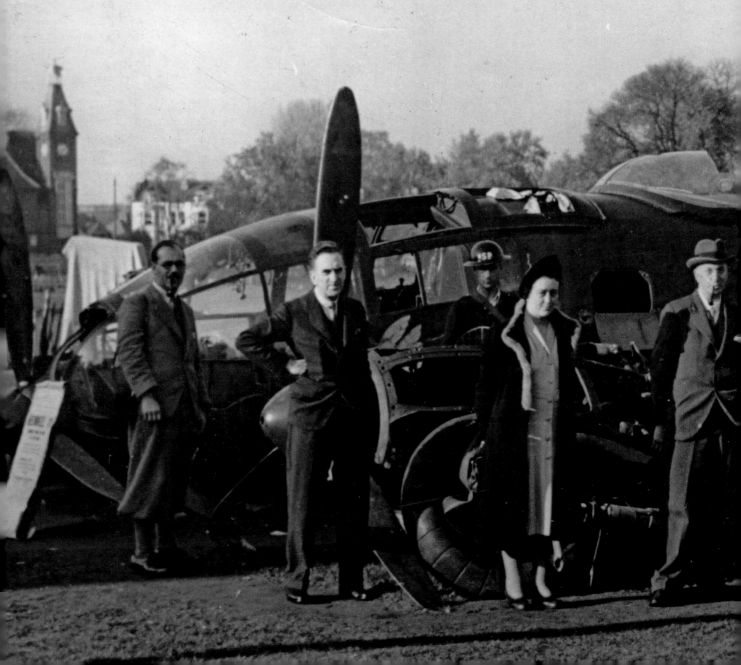

COMBAT REPORT:
P/O W B Pattullo, Green 3, B Flight, 249 Squadron

Having made a head-on attack in formation with the squadron, my position being Green 3, I broke away and attacked one Heinkel 111 which was slightly behind the main formation. The return fire ceased after I had attacked once, and on my second attack one engine gave off white smoke, presumably glycol. During my attacks I noticed another Hurricane attacking this machine, which eventually pancaked in a field by a railway station about 5-10 miles SE of London. This machine was definitely destroyed but three of the crew climbed out after the forced landing. A parachute also broke out when the machine hit the ground. This machine may have been destroyed by either myself or the second Hurricane.

COMBAT REPORT:
F/Lt D G Parnall, Red 1, A Flight, 249 Squadron

I (F/Lt Parnall) was Red 1 on patrol with 249 Squadron over London when Squadron attacked about 30 He111s and then broke away. I then attacked 1 He111 that had dropped slightly behind the main bomber formation now heading due south and so climbed up and attacked from the sun, beam to full astern slightly above. I fired a steady 5 sec burst before breaking away to the sun once again, noticed no return fire after beginning of bursts; e/a continued a steady course. I then did an exactly similar attack beam to full astern slightly above when firing a steady burst; both engines gave out oily smoke one quite slowly and the e/a went into a steady glide at about 160-170 yds. I felt quite certain the e/a was bound to crash and so flew a steady course 500 yds on the sun side of it ready to fire again if necessary as I did not wish to use all my ammunition. At about 5,000 ft or so another aircraft did astern attack on the He111 without any apparent effect in its flying ability. At 1,000 ft glycol streamed from the motor and in the same steady glide the He111 turned east and crashed in a field just north of the Redhill -Tonbridge railway line a few miles west of Tonbridge, when 4 of the crew climbed out. A parachute streamed from the Heinkel immediately prior to it crashing. At no time did the e/a catch fire.

I claim this He111 destroyed.

Contemporary Accounts 74 Sqn

11 September 1940 - 15.30 - 16.00 hrs Combat A.

74 SQUADRON OPERATIONS RECORD BOOK

Aircraft operating from Duxford. Interception patrol took place over London. All aircraft returned to base - Coltishall - safely.

Left: A rare photo of a ZP coded 74 Squadron Spitfire in flight during the Battle of Britain.

COMBAT REPORT:
P/O E W G Churches, Red 4, A Flight, 74 Squadron

I was Red 4 of 74 Sqn when I saw E/A at 17,000 feet over south London. Two other a/c attacked an He111 and I followed up the attack with a 6 sec burst from 150-50 yds range. I saw the E/A was being hit badly by my gunfire, pieces falling off the wing root and side of the fuselage. I further shot pieces off his tail-planes and when I broke away his port motor had practically stopped, whilst there was heavy black smoke coming out of it.

COMBAT REPORT:
P/O H M Stephen, Blue 3, B Flight, 74 Squadron

I was Blue 3 of 74 Sqn. Sqn intercepted E/A at 18,000 feet. I attacked Ju88 and put 8 second burst into him causing the undercarriage to fall down and port engine to stop. I broke away and was about to attack again when a Hurricane nipped in and finished him off. He was then left diving towards the ground. I was attacked by an Me109 and he swept past me in a dive so I turned onto his tail and gave him a burst of 2 secs when I saw my de Wilde entering his fuselage. I think he was armour plated or he should have gone down and rather than lose too much height myself I broke off the engagement.

COMBAT REPORT:
F/O J C Mungo-Park, Blue 1, B Flight, 74 Squadron

I was Blue 1 of 74 Sqn sent off to intercept enemy raid. I sighted formation of 30 Ju88s, carried out attack and saw pieces fall off the bomber of second section leader. I broke away and climbed to 20,000 ft and attacked flank machine of several He111s from slightly above, setting starboard engine on fire and saw it diving away steeply to ground.

Right: John Mungo-Park and Harbourne Stephen posing for a series of Press photos.

17 SQUADRON INTELLIGENCE REPORT

12 aircraft of No.17 Squadron took off from Debden at 15.43 hours, and joined 73 Squadron over the mouth of the Thames, the intention being that No.73 Squadron should attack the bombers, No.17 Squadron acting as escort.

The squadrons circled in sections of vic in line astern, and at 16.09 hours saw about 12 Me110s in line astern in the vicinity of Girdler Lightship flying east at 14,000 feet, with about 8 He113s above them. After No.73 Squadron had gone into attack, Yellow 1 (F/O Count Czernin, DFC) saw three Me110s apparently escaping, and led Yellow Section consisting of Sgt Bartlett (Yellow 2) and Sgt Chew (Yellow 3) to attack.

An He113 dived on Yellow 2 as he was about to attack, and a cannon shell went into the fuselage of his aircraft, tearing away most of the fabric behind the pilot's seat, and denting, but not piercing, the armour plating. Machine gun bullets also entered port mainplane, and fuselage. Yellow 1 fired a 2 seconds burst in a beam attack on one of the Me110s which dived into cloud with black smoke pouring from it. Yellow 1 followed e/a below cloud, and as he did so saw an Me110 which had been attacked by Blue 1 dive into the sea between Girdler Lightship and Margate Sands. Yellow 1 continued to chase the Me110 he had previously attacked in and out of cloud, and in a clear gap got within 400 yards, and gave it a 7 to 8 seconds burst from astern.

The e/a dived into the sea about 10 miles east of Margate. A large yellow stain was seen to spread over the sea where the e/a went in. Yellow 3 attacked another of the Me110s but did not observe the result.

Blue 1 (F/Lt Bayne) also led his section consisting of Polish pilots (F/O Niemiec Blue 2 and P/O Kumiega Blue 3) to attack Me110s. Blue 1 gave a 4 seconds burst at one Me110 from astern at 250 yards range, and saw e/a dive for cloud with white smoke coming from starboard engine, but was unable to observe results owing to low cloud. In breaking away he became separated from his section, and coming out below cloud saw another Me110 approaching him head-on. He gave the e/a a 5 seconds burst at a slight angle from the head-on position, and saw it going down in a spiral dive. The e/a was seen to crash into the sea by Yellow 1.

The remainder of the squadron stayed above as escort, and were not engaged in combat.

Weather was fine, visibility excellent, but slight haze up to 8,000 feet. Cloud 3/10ths at 3,000 feet.

COMBAT REPORT:
F/Lt A W A Bayne, Blue 1, B Flight, 17 Squadron

I saw about 8 Me110s circling in the vicinity of the Girdler Lightship in line astern. Attacked one from astern, and gave it a 4 second burst, and saw white stuff come from starboard engine. I dived down through clouds and sighted another Me110 coming practically straight at me, gave a 5 second burst from slightly off the head-on, the machine went down in a spiral, but did not follow it as I half rolled, came out below cloud, and saw one go in - and observed another patch of oil about a mile away to the east, which I presume was another crashed machine. Yellow 1 confirmed the second Me110.

COMBAT REPORT:
F/O M B Czernin - Yellow 1, A Flight, 17 Squadron

I was Yellow 1 and the squadron was escorting 73 Squadron. We first sighted e/a flying east down the Thames Estuary at about 14,000 feet. We were at 17,000 feet. I saw 73 Squadron going into them. I saw 3 Me110s trying to get away. I led the section into a beam attack on these three, but Yellow 2 left me owing to a cannon shell removing most of his A/C from under him. This was fired from an He113 which had dived down onto us. I pursued the one I had gone for and as he dived below the clouds I saw another Me110 dive into the sea. I continued chasing mine as he made for the sea. I must have got his port engine with my first burst as the whole time thick black smoke was pouring from it. With my plug pulled I finally got within range of him, but he was dodging in and out of the clouds at 3,000 feet. There was a clear gap and I opened up on him from astern and gave him a 7 - 8 seconds burst, after which he dived straight into the sea about 10 miles east of Margate near some sands on which there were 2 wrecks. When the e/a went into the sea a large yellow stain appeared on the surface of the water. I then returned to base and landed at 16.55 hours.

Contemporary Accounts 73 and 257 Sqns

11 September 1940 - 15.30 - 16.00 hrs Combat A.

73 SQUADRON INTELLIGENCE REPORT

'A' and 'B' Flights (12 Hurricanes) led by S/Ldr Robinson took off from Castle Camps at 15.38 hours with orders to join up with 17 Squadron over Debden and operate together in patrolling Rochford area, Angels 15. At about 16.15 hours approximately 12 to 15 Me110s or Jaguars were sighted flying in an easterly direction near Herne Bay in a straggling line astern formation at 10,000 feet approximately. Prior to being attacked, enemy aircraft went down lower and started milling round in circles.

Red Section (S/Ldr Robinson, Sgt Marshall and Sgt Scott) led attack out of the sun on to enemy aircraft at 8,000 feet. Yellow Section (F/O Smith, P/O McFadden and Sgt Brimble) and Blue Section (F/Lt Beytagh, P/O Marchand and Sgt Plenderleith) following in sections line astern.

At about 16.26 hours S/Ldr Robinson made an astern attack on one Me110 from above, firing one short burst and one very long burst at 350 yards, whereupon he saw the tail unit of the enemy aircraft break clean away and enemy aircraft falling into cloud below over the sea. Last seen by S/Ldr Robinson at 4,000 feet, but F/O Smith Yellow 1 and Sgt Scott, Red 3 each saw e/a later with tail end floating down towards sea and main part of enemy a/c falling some 200 yards away. One Me110 destroyed.

Red 2 Sgt Marshall claims no enemy casualties except that he silenced rear gunner and believes killed him. Red 2 states e/a was manoeuvred very well and escaped by turning inside him.

Sgt Scott Red 3 singled out an Me110 and got in one short burst at 300 yards with no effect. E/A camouflage light battleship grey with green zig zag lines across its back. Sgt Scott broke away and climbed with intention of carrying out a head-on attack on another Me110 but states that it was shot down by S/Ldr Robinson. Sgt Scott then spotted another Me110 on his starboard beam and made a steep turn, catching e/a with two bursts of 3 seconds at 300 yards and 200 yards respectively. Port engine caught fire but e/a disappeared into cloud below before Sgt Scott could complete his turn. One Me110 damaged.

P/O Smith Yellow 1, was fired on at 200 yards by an Me110. By turning inside enemy a/c and closing to 300 yards, P/O Smith fired one short burst causing rear gunner to cease fire. Two short bursts of less than 2 seconds each at 200 yards caused port engine of e/a to burst into flames and e/a to dive for cloud below. One further burst of 2 seconds from above and astern at 150 yards and e/a pulled up in a stall, whereupon P/O Smith put another short burst into e/a which caused starboard engine to stop and airscrew to freewheel. By this time smoke as well as flame was coming from port engine. E/A fell in vertical dive through cloud towards sea. One Me110 destroyed. While diving after e/a, P/O Smith noticed another Me110 about 1,000 feet below approaching him from in front about 800 yards away. Head-on attack giving 2 bursts of 2 seconds each caused numerous pieces to break away from fuselage. E/A went into a shallow dive and P/O Smith pulled out, narrowly avoiding a collision. P/O Smith had a 'blackout' and on regaining his sight could see nothing of e/a or any other e/a in vicinity. One Me110 damaged. Both e/a had light coloured camouflage resembling dull olive and battleship grey. Enemy fire stated to be accurate - tail of Hurricane being hit. 850 rounds of ammunition expended.

F/Lt Beytagh Blue 1 (See Pilot's Combat Report).
P/O Marchand Blue 2 (See Pilot's Combat Report).

Green Section (P/O Langham Hobart, Sgt Ellis and Sgt Webster) at about 16.25 hours sighted eight or nine He111s heading east at 14,000 feet in a position a few miles south of Detling, Kent. This section was to the rearmost of the squadron and apparently lost the other three sections. Green Section climbed to 18,000 feet and carried out an astern attack on e/a which were almost in line abreast in two sections of three and one of two.

Sgt Webster Green 3 was unable to keep up with leader and made an individual attack from astern on the left most e/a at 300 yards. Sgt Webster experienced no fire until he had closed to 150 yards when the enemy formation as a whole fired two bursts. Sgt Webster (Sgt Ellis Green 2 confirms) is of the strong opinion that enemy fire was controlled by one individual either by R/T or some other means, as the cross fire was too intense and was so well harmonised. Sgt Webster broke off attack and re-joined his section leader and experienced nothing noticeable until about 10 minutes later when his a/c caught fire and he baled out near Detling uninjured.

Green 2 Sgt Ellis had his machine hit but returned safely to base.

Weather cloudy in vicinity of Thames Estuary. 7/10ths cloud around Herne Bay at 6,000 feet.

Opposite: 73 and 17 Squadrons tangled with Me110s of ZG26 like this one, seen here taxiing out for another sortie over England.

257 SQUADRON OPERATIONS RECORD BOOK

Shortly before 16.00 hrs the whole squadron took off for North Weald which they patrolled at 15,000 ft. They landed shortly after 17.00 hrs. Sgt Fraser crashed in the precincts of the aerodrome.

COMBAT REPORT:
P/O R A Marchand – Blue 2, B Flight, 73 Squadron

Enemy sighted about 16.15 hours. Saw 2 Me110s proceeding towards Margate from Sheerness. Me110s were light grey on top, and greenish blue underneath, black crosses on white background. Enemy was flying straight and level, and an astern attack was delivered. E/A's port engine was hit, and gave out white smoke in which were intermittent puffs of black smoke until ultimately the whole port engine was giving a stream of black smoke. No enemy aircraft fire was experienced. The e/a dived into cloud for evasive action, and executed steep turns. Result of combat was e/a's port engine giving out black smoke while the e/a was diving, and flying level and diving again. Attack was stopped about 8 miles off Margate with the e/a still going down. Last observed e/a's height at 4,000 feet. Weather was one large patch of 8/10th cloud over Herne Bay. Sun was in the west. Took off 15.40 hours. Landed 16.55 hours. Shell bursts assisted in intercepting enemy aircraft but burst far too close to our aircraft for comfort. Fire was opened at 300 yards closing to 100 yards. Bursts of 3 seconds.

COMBAT REPORT:
F/Lt M L ff Beytagh – Blue 1, B Flight, 73 Squadron

E/A sighted milling at 12,000 feet and above near Herne Bay. I put my section in line astern and made a head-on attack on one Me110. After my first burst of approximately 2 seconds at 350 yards he turned away and dived for the clouds. I was unable to catch him but kept firing short bursts of about 2 - 3 seconds at a range which finally increased to about 600 yards. His port engine started smoking and just before he got to the cloud I could see that it had stopped. I followed him into the cloud but was unable to contact again. Markings of e/a were light under parts and dark upper parts. Some fire from rear gunner which stopped after my third burst. Enemy speed must have been about 350 - 360 in dive and was heading for France when last seen. AA did not help in interception. I attacked out of the sun and do not think I was spotted till I opened fire.

Time of take-off 15.40 hours.   Time of landing 17.00 hours.

RAF Victory Claims

11 September 1940 - 15.30 - 17.30 hrs Combat A. The South East

RAF Victory Claims	West Kent and London Docks Force (KG26)		
303 Sqn	F/Lt A S Forbes	Do17 destroyed	Horsham-sea
303 Sqn	F/Lt A S Forbes	Do17 destroyed	Horsham-sea
303 Sqn	F/Lt L W Paszkiewicz	Me110 destroyed	Horsham-sea
303 Sqn	F/O Z Henneberg	He111 destroyed	Horsham-sea
303 Sqn	F/O Z Henneberg	Me109 destroyed	Horsham
303 Sqn	P/O J Zumbach	Me109 destroyed	Horsham-sea
303 Sqn	P/O W Lokuciewski	Me109 destroyed	Horsham-sea
303 Sqn	P/O W Lokuciewski	Do17 destroyed	Horsham-sea
303 Sqn	Sgt M Brzozowski	He111 destroyed	Horsham
303 Sqn	Sgt M Brzozowski	He111 destroyed	Horsham
303 Sqn	Sgt J Frantisek	He111 destroyed	Horsham
303 Sqn	Sgt E Szaposznikow	Me110 destroyed	Horsham-sea
303 Sqn	Sgt E Szaposznikow	Me110 destroyed	Horsham-sea
303 Sqn	Sgt S Wojtowicz	Me109 destroyed	Horsham
303 Sqn	Sgt S Wojtowicz	Me109 destroyed	Horsham
303 Sqn	Sgt J Frantisek	Me109 destroyed	Horsham
303 Sqn	Sgt J Frantisek	Me109 destroyed	Horsham-sea
229 Sqn	F/Lt W A Smith	He111 destroyed	Reigate
3 Spitfires		- shared -	
229 Sqn	P/O G L J Doutrepont	Me110 damaged	Reigate
229 Sqn	P/O V B S Verity	- shared -	
229 Sqn	P/O V B S Verity	Me110 damaged	Reigate
229 Sqn	P/O J M F Dewar	Ju86 damaged	Reigate
229 Sqn	P/O V M Bright	He111 destroyed	south-south east of Redhill
229 Sqn	P/O G L J Doutrepont	- shared -	
229 Sqn	P/O R F Rimmer	He111 probable	Reigate
229 Sqn	P/O J M F Dewar	He111 probable	Reigate
229 Sqn	P/O E Smith	He111 probable	Ramsgate
229 Sqn	P/O K M Carver	He111 damaged	Maidstone
229 Sqn	P/O K M Carver	He111 damaged	Maidstone
229 Sqn	P/O J W Hyde	Do215 destroyed	Reigate
229 Sqn	P/O G L J Doutrepont	- shared -	
1 Spitfire		- shared -	
1(RCAF) Sqn	P/O H de M Molson	He111 destroyed	south east of Gatwick
1(RCAF) Sqn	F/Lt G R McGregor	He111 destroyed	south east of Gatwick
1(RCAF) Sqn	F/O B E Christmas	He111 damaged	south east of Gatwick
1(RCAF) Sqn	S/Ldr E A McNab	He111 damaged	south east of Gatwick
1(RCAF) Sqn	F/O A Yuile	Ju88 destroyed	Tunbridge Wells
238 Sqn	F/Lt M V Blake	Ju88 destroyed	Brooklands - Croydon
238 Sqn	P/O W Rozycki	He111 destroyed	Brooklands - Croydon
Unknown pilot		He111 destroyed	Brooklands - Croydon
603 Sqn	F/O C J Boulter	He111 damaged	north west of Dungeness
603 Sqn	P/O W A A Read	Me110 damaged	south west of London
603 Sqn	P/O B G Stapleton	Me109 probable	south of London
603 Sqn	P/O B G Stapleton	Me109 damaged	south of London
603 Sqn	P/O R Berry	Me109 damaged	south of London
603 Sqn	P/O F J MacPhail	He111 destroyed	south of London
603 Sqn	P/O B R MacNamara	He111 damaged	south of London
41 Sqn	P/O G A Langley	Ju88 damaged	15 miles south east of London
41 Sqn	P/O J N MacKenzie	He111 destroyed	south of West Malling
41 Sqn	P/O E S Lock	Ju88 destroyed	Kent
41 Sqn	P/O E S Lock	Me110 destroyed	Kent

F/Lt L W Paszkiewicz 303 Sqn

P/O R F Rimmer 229 Sqn

F/O B E Christmas
1 (RCAF) Sqn

Contemporary Accounts 303 Sqn

11 September 1940 - 15.30 - 17.30 hrs Combat A.

303 SQUADRON INTELLIGENCE REPORT

12 Hurricanes left Northolt 15.30 hours - 8 Hurricanes landed Northolt 17.10 - 17.40 hours. 2 Hurricanes were flown back at 20.00 hours on 11.9.40 and at 11.00 hours on 12.9.40.

Our casualties: F/O Cebrzynski killed - Sgt Wojtowicz killed.
                         1 Hurricane - Cat.3 - 1 Hurricane missing.

The squadron went on patrol to intercept enemy raiders coming from the south-east towards London, leading No.229 Squadron. When they met enemy No.229 Squadron, which was below and to their right, went straight on to attack the enemy bombers head-on.

No.303 Squadron wheeled round and attacked the centre and rear of the enemy formation, which appears to have been about 50 He111s and 30/40 Do215s strong, while Yellow Section of No.303 Squadron attacked the fighter escort above No.229 Squadron. It also appears that at least one other squadron was engaged with enemy fighters at a higher altitude. It seems clear from the reports that these attacks broke up the enemy bomber formation, and from conversation with pilots, large quantities of the bombs seem to have been jettisoned in wooded country - some 25 miles south of London.

F/O Cebrzynski jumped and fell near Pembury - his parachute did not open. It is believed that he was wounded if not killed, as he was getting out.

The following are the pilots' reports:

F/Lt Forbes (Blue Section)

The squadron took off with orders to lead Squadron No.229. We climbed up to 19,000 feet and were eventually vectored on 50°. We were due north of the enemy when sighted, and turned south, attacking from the east, up-sun. We were actually being vectored across the enemy's bow, and it was the wonderful eyesight of the Polish that spotted them some 6/7 miles on our right.

P/O Paszkiewicz spoke to me by R/T and wheeled round. Perceiving that No.229 were below and going in to attack the bombers, he led his section to engage the escort fighters above them. I brought up rear of the squadron as we wheeled. I therefore fired into the middle of the bomber formation which was now below me. There were 60/80 of them flying in vics of 3 and 5 line astern, with the Me110s above and Me109s around and above them, stepped up to over 25,000 feet.

As I dived into the attack I saw the crew of one bomber in the middle of the formation bale out, and as far as I could see, they were not being attacked (this is not the first time that members of my squadron have noticed a similar phenomenon, and we have also remarked that the German crews

Below: A photo taken on this day, 11 September at Northolt showing Group Captain Stefan Pawlikowski, the most senior Polish Air Force officer in the UK at the time, being shown a Hurricane cockpit by 303 Squadron personnel.

open their parachutes immediately, although they may be a great height up). I took on the left-hand bomber of a section and dived right in on the port wing and engine, which came adrift. I had difficulty in avoiding the wing top and drew out in order to attack the right-hand bomber of the next section. In fact, the slipstream of the bomber which I had just destroyed, threw me so far out that when I turned in again I found myself in the ideal position to attack the third machine up in the line. This left the bomber immediately in front of the destroyed one on my tail. I nevertheless pressed home the attack, and got in a very good burst from about 100 yards on the port engine, wing root, and cockpit. Large chunks fell away from all three, and the e/a immediately swung sharply to the left with its nose dropping. At this moment, I received a severe blow in the back of my right arm, and right thigh. My arm was thrown forward, and I went into a steep dive. When I neared ground level I started to return to base, flying with my left hand. On nearing Heston I began to feel faint and effected a landing. After treatment, I was driven back to Northolt. My machine, after small repairs, is being brought back.

Contemporary Accounts 229 Sqn

11 September 1940 - 15.30 - 17.30 hrs Combat A.

229 SQUADRON INTELLIGENCE REPORT

No.229 Squadron - 12 Hurricanes - left Northolt at 15.25 hours, and landed at Northolt at 16.30 hours on 11.9.40.

229 Squadron in conjunction with 303 Squadron were ordered to patrol Biggin Hill at 15,000 feet. At 16.10 hours four large formations of enemy aircraft flying at 20,000 feet were observed in the region of Reigate, flying towards London. The first wave of e/a turned back out to sea, and the squadron proceeded to attack the third wave head-on. No.303 Squadron, who were on their left, wheeled round and attacked the middle and rear of the enemy formation on the starboard side of 229, and travelling in the opposite direction. The head of the enemy formation consisted of some 30 He111s in large vics composed of smaller vics of 5 aircraft. Behind there were 25 Me110s, slightly higher than the bombers, and above all were 50 Me109s considerably higher.

S/Ldr Banham lead his squadron to attack in sections line astern straight at the leading bomber formation. He fired at two He111s but did not see the result, and was then attacked by fighters. As each section attacked, the enemy formation broke up and a series of fights developed between the Hurricanes and He111s, and Me110s with one or two Me109s.

In the initial attack **F/Lt Rimmer** probably destroyed an He111, which went down with starboard engine on fire. He returned to base with slight face injuries, resulting from an Me110 on his tail, which shattered his cockpit hood.

P/O Smith leading the last section also attacked an He111, and saw the port engine in flames before breaking away on account of a fighter on his tail.

P/O Barry flew straight through the formation, firing all his ammunition into several e/a but could not see the effect of his fire.

F/Lt Smith, after attacking the leading bomber section, broke away and followed one He111 which had detached itself from the formation. Two or three Spitfires were diving on this machine when he delivered a long attack from astern, and saw the He111 crash through a hedge in the Maidstone district. Two men got out.

P/O Bright first opened fire on the bomber formation and then on the Me110s attacking S/Ldr Banham. He then followed down one of our men descending by parachute until he was safe. Sighting an He111 at 6,000 feet with a Hurricane diving on it, he joined in with a diving attack and later with a No.1 attack from astern. Two minutes later he noticed e/a in flames on the ground just south-east of Redhill, between two railway lines. This Heinkel made no attempt at evasive action.

P/O Dewar attacked with Yellow Section and in breaking away blacked out, coming to about a mile away. He saw three He111s break away from the formation and attacked one which was 2,000 feet below him with no visible result. He then attacked another He111, and saw the port engine stop and later the starboard engine also stopped. The Heinkel was last seen in a steady glide towards Beachy Head at 17,000 feet. After this engagement Dewar sighted a Ju86 heading east, losing height, with port engine smoking; he attacked from starboard and after a two second burst had to break away owing to AA fire. This was between Maidstone and Chatham. This pilot, before attacking the He111, had observed large enemy formations at 20,000 feet in which several very large aircraft were escorted by strong contingents of fighters.

P/O Doutrepont (Belgian) after the initial attack by Blue Section saw an Me110 attacking F/Lt Rimmer. He put in a short burst at this machine and broke away; he thinks the rear gunner was killed by fire from **P/O Verity** who also attacked. After losing contact he went east at 10,000 feet and saw a Do215 at 6,000 feet pursued by several Hurricanes - its port engine was already smoking when he attacked. Three men baled out and just afterwards the Do215 went into a dive and crashed. Sgt Hyde also attacked this machine, his attention being drawn to its position by AA bursts. He made a long attack from astern at short range, and saw the crew bale out and later the machine crash and burst into flames somewhere between Lingfield and Edenbridge.

Sgt Hyde as Green 3 had been previously guarding the rear of the squadron with P/O Carver when they dived on the bomber formation. P/O Carver is missing.

P/O Doutrepont and Sgt Hyde then climbed together going north-west until they saw an He111 in a 30° glide. P/O Doutrepont turned and after catching up delivered a strong attack from astern. White smoke came from the port engine, and the e/a tried to weave about. A Spitfire and a Hurricane were also attacking this machine. P/O Doutrepont attacked again closing to less than 50 yards, and the e/a crash landed in a field about 10 miles east of the previous crash. Four men got out, one wounded.

Above: Belgian pilot Georges Doutrepont was in the thick of the action during this first engagement with the enemy for the newly arrived 229 Squadron. He was killed in action just four days later.

P/O Verity, after firing at 3 He111s in the formation, next fired at an Me110, which was about to attack F/Lt Rimmer. He saw pieces break off the rear cockpit, and the rear gunner did not return his fire. This gunner had been dropping red Verey lights in an attempt to damage our fighters. This machine had a distinctive blue nose and was leading a formation of four.

P/O Ravenhill has been reported in hospital, suffering from shock after baling out.

Nine aircraft returned to Northolt at 16.30 hours, and one at 17.50 hours.

During these operations the weather was fine with no cloud, but slight haze at 5,000 feet. This combined attack on the enemy mass formation caused the bombers to disperse and turn back so that very few of them arrived over their objectives in London. Large numbers of bombs were jettisoned at the scene of combat.

This is the first time No.229 Squadron has been in action, apart from isolated interception raids, since Dunkerque.

SUPPLEMENTARY INTELLIGENCE PATROL REPORT - No.229 Squadron.

Combat near Reigate at 16.10 hours on 11.9.40.

Below: The rarely photographed 229 Squadron pilots pose for the camera. L-R; P/O RAL Duvivier, F/O WA Smith, F/O VM Bright, Sgt RR Mitchell, F/O M Ravenhill, P/O RE Bary, F/O AS Linney, F/O RC Brown, Sgt SW Merryweather

P/O Carver who was protecting the rear of No.229 Squadron attacked a section of three He111s and damaged two of them. Whilst firing at the third one his machine was hit and burst into flames, forcing him to bale out. P/O Carver thinks his gravity tank was hit by a cannon shell coming from the rear of one of the two He111s he had just attacked. He went to hospital with burns on face and wrist.

P/O Ravenhill after taking part in the first attack on the He111s dived to deliver an attack from astern on a lone Do17. Whilst he was firing he was attacked from astern and to starboard by an unknown assailant. A piece of his port main plane broke off and glycol spurted all over the cockpit temporarily blinding him. He baled out and was taken to hospital with slight injuries.

Contemporary Accounts 1 (RCAF) and 238 Sqns

11 September 1940 - 15.30 - 17.30 hrs Combat A.

1 (RCAF) SQUADRON INTELLIGENCE REPORT

12 Hurricanes No.1 Canadian Squadron left Northolt 15.42 hours 11.9.40. 10 landed Northolt 16.35 - 17.00 hours.

The squadron led by S/Ldr McNab in sections line astern sighted a formation of about 20 He111s with fighter escort above, south-east of Gatwick at 16.15 hours and attacked, the order of battle being Blue, Green and Red Sections with Yellow acting as rear guard.

The enemy were about three thousand feet below, proceeding south, and the attack was opened from the beam and swinging to astern, breaking up the formation of the original attack after which the combat developed into individual dog-fights.

S/Ldr McNab damaged one of the bombers which had its starboard engine smoking and on his second attack fired a burst at an Me110 or Jaguar, which had evidently come down to join in the fight. No result was observed.

Blue 3 **F/O Christmas**, echeloned left on his leader, attacked an He111 the rear gunner of which stopped firing and the port engine started to smoke. No further observation was possible after his breakaway.

Yellow Section had no conclusive results.

Red 1 **F/Lt McGregor**, on his second attack by himself, firing from about 100 yards destroyed one of the e/a, one of the crew baling out. This bomber went into a spiral dive and he followed it down to 4,000 feet from where he saw it crash on land in flames.

Red 3 **F/O Molson** did not observe any result from his first attack, but in the ensuing dog-fight singled out an He111, which had smoke coming from its starboard engine, and after a short burst it lost height quickly in a right-hand turn which increased until it was out of control, hitting the ground and bursting into flames.

Green Section was the rear guard and did not join in the main attack, but subsequently all had actions with no apparent results to be reported, except F/O Yuile who, in company with two or three other of our fighters, one a Hurricane with markings VK*, came on a lone enemy bomber with vertical light blue and white strips on square rudder and fin, which he identified as a Ju52. This pilot has since studied silhouettes and pictures and is reasonably certain of the identification. He made three attacks with long bursts and finally observed black smoke emitting from between the fuselage, and starboard engine and the starboard undercarriage fell off. Several parachutes were noted floating down and the e/a dove straight for the ground where it exploded near Tunbridge Wells.

No report of their part taken in the action has been received from F/O Little, who baled out, is wounded and in hospital, nor from F/O Lochnan who crash landed and has not yet returned to the station.

The pilots report white vertical stripes on the fins of bombers.

Above: Gordon McGregor of 1 (RCAF) Squadron who claimed a He111 in this combat.

Our casualties:	1 pilot wounded (F/O Little), 2 Hurricanes Cat.3.
Enemy casualties:	2 He111s destroyed (F/Lt McGregor and F/Lt Molson)
	1 Ju 52 destroyed (F/O Yuile)
	2 He111s damaged (S/Ldr McNab and F/O Christmas)

* VK = 238 Squadron

238 SQUADRON OPERATIONS RECORD BOOK

15.25 - 17.08 12 sorties comprising the squadron patrolled Brooklands - Weybridge where Ju88s were found. Battle was joined in haze, and the squadron broke up. F/Lt Blake destroyed a Ju88 and P/O W Rozycki (Pole) also destroyed one. P/O Towers-Perkins baled out. Wounded in one leg, and suffering from burns, he was taken to Tunbridge Wells Hospital. F/Lt D P Hughes and Sgt S Duszynski 780764 (Pole) have not been seen since the engagement began and are missing. Owing to the haze the squadron became separated early in the engagement and a general melee ensued P/O W Rozycki landed in a field at Old Alresford owing to lack of petrol.

41 SQUADRON OPERATIONS RECORD BOOK

41 Squadron took off 15.15 - 16.45 hours 11.9.40 to patrol Maidstone. The enemy formation was sighted to port and below and consisted of about 70 - 80 twin-engined aircraft in close formation at 20,000 feet. F/Lt Ryder continued to lead the squadron across the leading bombers to look for the fighter escort, but no 109s were seen. Actually, two were seen with yellow noses prior to actual attack. F/Lt Ryder decided to lead Red and Blue Sections into the formation and endeavour to either break the rear half up or at least break the main formation in two.

The attack consisted of a steep diving astern approach. Most of the squadron got in a burst. Just prior to the breakthrough, and during which time they were under heavy return fire, they actually broke-up the rear half of the main formation and the squadron, now dispersed, continued to attack individual targets. About 25 Ju88s formed a defensive circle and F/Lt Ryder saw several Spitfire a/c diving through and firing short bursts at any e/a that presented a target.

The squadron was ordered to preserve its ammunition and about 10 minutes after the initial attack was told to patrol home base to engage about 50 e/a approaching from the south-east. Squadron a/c were reforming over home base angels 15 but were then given the order to 'pancake'.

COMBAT REPORT:
P/O E S Lock - Yellow 2, A Flight, 41 Squadron

I was patrolling with 41 Squadron as Yellow 2 when we sighted e/a. We went into echelon starboard - peeled off to port and dived on the enemy bombers which broke up. I attacked a Ju88 from astern giving several bursts. This had little effect so I then did a ¼ attack on same. Having carried out this attack it dived. I did not see any effect from this ¼ attack so I then attacked from below. This attack must have killed the pilot because it crashed in a field about 17 miles south of Maidstone. I circled it for a few minutes and noticed it was on fire. After about 5 minutes I saw it explode. I climbed back to about 6,000 feet when I was attacked by an Me110. After a dog-fight which lasted for twenty minutes he crashed with his starboard engine on fire, about ten miles south east of the Ju88. I received heavy fire from the rear gunner. I noticed that the Ju88 had white and black stripes painted on the tail fin. I force landed at West Malling as I had run out of ammunition and petrol. Port wing damaged - Cat 1.   I saw P/O Mackenzie's He111 on land.

COMBAT REPORT:
P/O G H Bennions - Blue 1, 'A' Flight, 41 Squadron

Leading Blue Section, 41 Squadron Red and Blue Sections dived onto the main formation of bombers and Me110 escort fighters in an attempt to break the formation. I attacked a section of 6 Me110s. The first one that I fired at turned over on its left side and dived away. My closing speed was so great that I could not see what damage if any had been inflicted. I continued to fire at the a/c in front, firing short bursts and then climbing slightly and diving on to the next one. After the third attack I received a good burst in the starboard side of my a/c and felt a short sharp pain in my left heel. I broke away and found that my guns would not fire owing to the air bottle having been pierced by bullets. My brakes, flaps and guns would not function and my top petrol tank was pierced, so I returned to base and landed.

COMBAT REPORT:
P/O G A Langley - Red 2, 'B' Flight, 41 Squadron

I was Red 2 in the leading section of 41 Squadron when we sighted the enemy 5,000 feet below us. We dived out of the sun and I fired a 5 seconds burst on a Ju88, hitting it on the port side - may have damaged port engine.

As I turned away I saw tracer bullets coming over my port wing, my machine went out of control and although I juggled with the controls for some time nothing happened. I baled out at approximately 6,000 feet to the north of Sevenoaks.

I finally landed in the middle of a large garden in Sevenoaks none the worse for wear.

Contemporary Accounts 41 Sqn

11 September 1940 - 15.30 - 17.30 hrs Combat A.

Above: This Spitfire is believed to be N3059 EB-B which Ted Howitt was flying on 11 September, the nose art shows a Pluto style dog.

COMBAT REPORT:
Sgt I E Howitt - B Flight, 41 Squadron

Single aircraft on recco at 32,000 feet at 16.00 hrs

At approximately 15.45 hours on 11.9.40, Mitor Squadron was ordered to patrol Southend. When in the air, I as Mitor 31, was detailed to vector 125 (Deal and Dover area) to patrol and observe and report any enemy raids approaching our coast. I climbed on vector 125, and at approximately 17,000 feet in the vicinity of west Maidstone, I observed a number of yellow-nosed Me109s proceeding in a northerly direction at approximately 15,000 feet. As far as I could see there were no bomber aircraft. The Me's numbered 12 to 15 aircraft. I reported this over the R/T. I then turned almost due south and climbed into the sun and finally took up a position over Dungeness at 32,000 feet. After a few minutes, I observed a large formation of bomber aircraft, presumably Ju88, escorted by Me109 and 110 fighters, crossing the coast south of Folkestone on a course of approximately 320 degrees. I reported this and while turning to starboard, observed another formation similar to the first approaching the coast off Dungeness, course 330 degrees approximately. Immediately after reporting this formation, I was attacked from behind, a cannon shell burst near the port main plane, a few holes appeared, but no serious damage was apparent. I used violent evasion but did not see attacking aircraft. Height at this time was 30 - 31,000 feet. Almost immediately, I observed another formation of enemy aircraft approaching Deal and Dover and another formation which appeared to be proceeding up the Thames Estuary from the east. I immediately reported this to base and was ordered to re-join my squadron over Southend at 25,000 feet. In all cases, enemy aircraft appeared to be at approximately 25,000 feet.

Owing to the number of enemy aircraft about, I decided to make a detour to the left and when in the vicinity of Tunbridge Wells, saw a single aircraft and turned to investigate. Almost immediately there was a violent thump from the engine and excessive vibration set in, accompanied by dense clouds of steam and it obscured the windscreen. I prepared to jump, but as the aircraft did not catch fire, I decided to force land it. My height was then about 20,000 feet. When down to 5,000 feet, I saw an aerodrome and managed to land aircraft without any further damage.

Examination of the aircraft showed that the oil cooler had been punctured. The engine sustained two broken connecting rods and seized solid.

COMBAT REPORT:
P/O J N MacKenzie 'A' Flight, 41 Squadron

I attacked formation of Ju88s south of London, dived on them but had too much speed and in too steep a dive to get accurate aim. I climbed to 30,000 feet after a steep right-hand turn climbing breakaway. I watched for an opportunity to attack from the sun and spotted an He111K behind the main formation going towards the coast. I came down in shallow dive and attacked from dead astern. The enemy aircraft dived and rear gun fired from top of enemy aircraft. Gave very long burst as I was short of petrol and would have no further chance of attacking enemy aircraft. As I broke away, I noticed smoke from port engine. Dived to ground level as I thought Me109 was on my tail (it was P/O Lock in Spitfire). P/O Lock watched enemy aircraft continue to glide down and force land. Also workman at West Malling aerodrome saw enemy aircraft gliding down with smoke from port engine, below trees. I landed at West Malling aerodrome with 7 gallons of petrol.

COMBAT REPORT:
F/Lt E N Ryder - Red 1, 'A' Flight, 41 Squadron

I led Red and Blue Section in a diving attack on twin-engined formation with a view to cutting the formation into two. I fired on passing through at a Ju88 and had a glimpse of smoke coming from his port engine and at the same time his left wing dropped slightly. This happened very quickly and might have been his evasion. I then attacked another 88 by joining a circle and experienced very great return fire and by good evasion on E/A's part had to break off the engagement. I fired at a third and was fired on from astern, part of my hood at this moment flew off. Ordered by control to patrol Home Base and engage 50 plus E/A, I returned but did not engage before pancake order.

603 SQUADRON OPERATIONS RECORD BOOK

12 a/c, 603 Squadron, left Rochford at 15.16 hours on 11.9.40. At 28,000 feet over Rochford they joined up with 41 Squadron. When just south of London they saw a large formation of Me110s and He111s in vics of 5, vics line astern at 20,000 feet going north. There were also some Me109s above.

41 Squadron dived to attack the bombers, followed by 603 Squadron in line astern. A dog-fight ensued and the enemy formation turned south, dropping their bombs in open country over Kent. It was noticed that the Me110s had very pale yellow noses. There seemed to be fewer Me109s than usual, and they made no attempt to assist the bombers when attacked. The Me109s had yellow noses.

COMBAT REPORT:
P/O F J MacPhail - A Flight, 603 Squadron

When on patrol with 603 Squadron and 41 Squadron I saw a large enemy bomber formation south of London moving in a north westerly direction.

The formation was protected by yellow nosed Me109s. I dived on an He111 from its port beam. The enemy immediately took evasive action, turning sharply to its port and I was forced to break away to its rear. I saw my burst enter the fuselage.

I climbed up and saw the enemy going southwards losing height. A Hurricane and Spitfire then dived and did stern attacks, one each, and the enemy turned to the right and I dived and did a head-on attack of 2 - 3 seconds, from a range of 150 yards to 50 yards, and saw tracer enter the centre of the fuselage. Two of the crew baled out, the wheels came down and the aircraft exploded on landing in the vicinity of Edenbridge.

The crew landed in two fields slightly to the southwest of the aircraft. I received an armour-piercing bullet in the gun channel heater of my inner starboard gun.

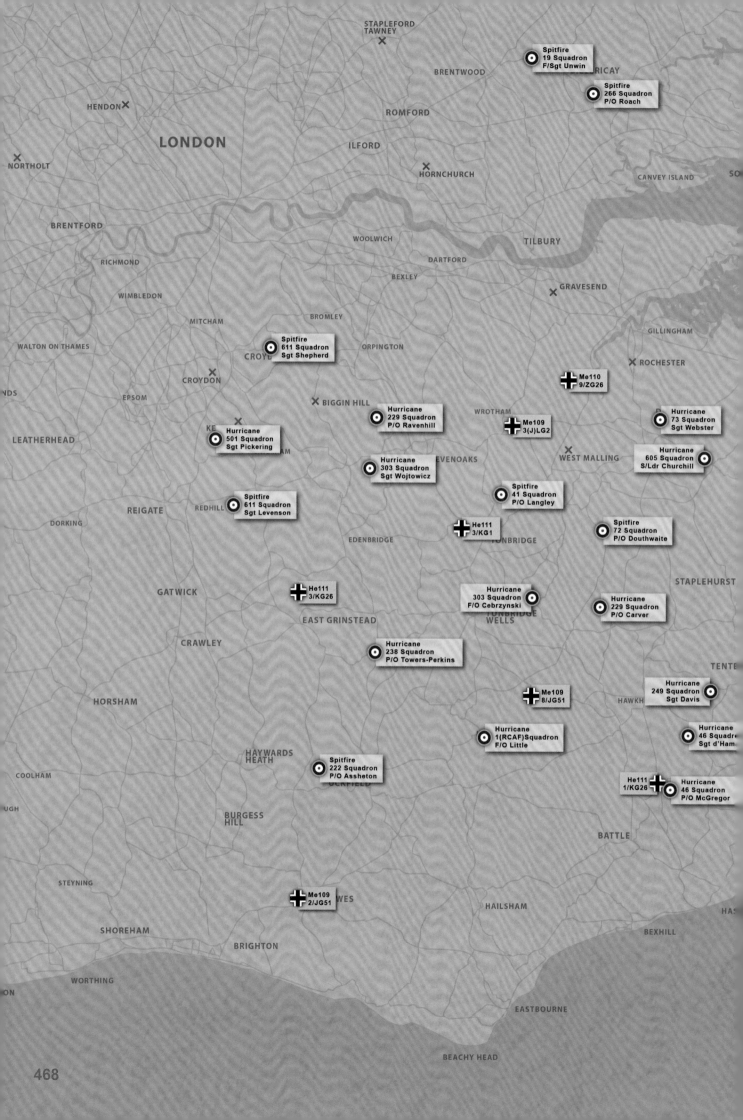

STAPLEFORD TAWNEY ✕

BRENTWOOD

RICAY

**Spitfire
19 Squadron
F/Sgt Unwin**

**Spitfire
266 Squadron
P/O Roach**

HENDON ✕

ROMFORD

LONDON

ILFORD

✕ NORTHOLT

HORNCHURCH ✕

CANVEY ISLAND

SO

WOOLWICH

TILBURY

BRENTFORD

DARTFORD

RICHMOND

BEXLEY

WIMBLEDON

✕ GRAVESEND

GILLINGHAM

MITCHAM

BROMLEY

ORPINGTON

WALTON ON THAMES

✕ ROCHESTER

CROYL

**Spitfire
611 Squadron
Sgt Shepherd**

NDS

CROYDON ✕

**Me110
9/ZG26**

EPSOM

✕ BIGGIN HILL

WROTHAM

**Hurricane
229 Squadron
P/O Ravenhill**

**Me109
3(J)LG2**

**Hurricane
73 Squadron
Sgt Webster**

LEATHERHEAD

KE

**Hurricane
501 Squadron
Sgt Pickering**

AM

**Hurricane
303 Squadron
Sgt Wojtowicz**

EVENOAKS

✕ WEST MALLING

**Hurricane
605 Squadron
S/Ldr Churchill**

**Spitfire
41 Squadron
P/O Langley**

REIGATE

REDHILL

**Spitfire
611 Squadron
Sgt Levenson**

**He111
3/KG1**

**Spitfire
72 Squadron
P/O Douthwaite**

DORKING

EDENBRIDGE

UNBRIDGE

STAPLEHURST

GATWICK

**He111
3/KG26**

**Hurricane
303 Squadron
F/O Cebrzynski**

**Hurricane
229 Squadron
P/O Carver**

EAST GRINSTEAD

UNBRIDGE
WELLS

CRAWLEY

**Hurricane
238 Squadron
P/O Towers-Perkins**

TENTE

**Hurricane
249 Squadron
Sgt Davis**

HORSHAM

**Me109
8/JG51**

HAWKH

**Hurricane
46 Squadre
Sgt d'Ham**

HAYWARDS
HEATH

**Hurricane
1(RCAF)Squadron
F/O Little**

**Spitfire
222 Squadron
P/O Assheton**

CKFIELD

**He111
1/KG26**

**Hurricane
46 Squadron
P/O McGregor**

COOLHAM

BURGESS
HILL

BATTLE

UGH

STEYNING

**Me109
2/JG51**

WES

HAILSHAM

HAS

SHOREHAM

BEXHILL

BRIGHTON

WORTHING

ON

EASTBOURNE

BEACHY HEAD

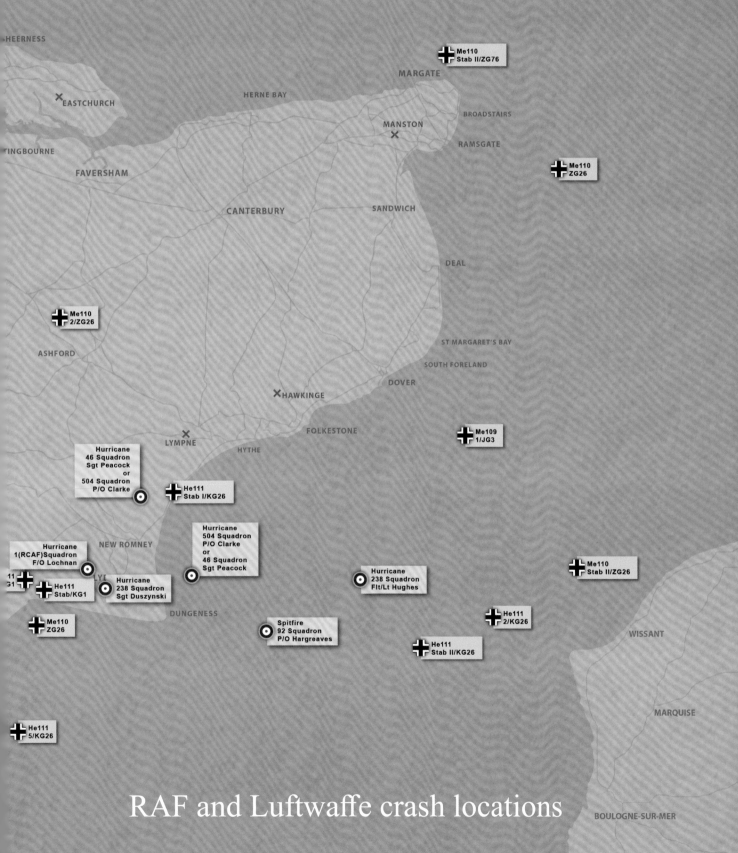

Me110
Stab II/ZG76

MARGATE

HERNE BAY

BROADSTAIRS

EASTCHURCH

MANSTON

RAMSGATE

Me110
ZG26

TINGBOURNE

FAVERSHAM

CANTERBURY

SANDWICH

DEAL

Me110
2/ZG26

ST MARGARET'S BAY

ASHFORD

SOUTH FORELAND

DOVER

HAWKINGE

Me109
1/JG3

LYMPNE

FOLKESTONE

HYTHE

Hurricane
46 Squadron
Sgt Peacock
or
504 Squadron
P/O Clarke

He111
Stab I/KG26

Hurricane
504 Squadron
P/O Clarke
or
46 Squadron
Sgt Peacock

NEW ROMNEY

Hurricane
1(RCAF)Squadron
F/O Lochnan

Me110
Stab II/ZG26

11
31

Hurricane
238 Squadron
Sgt Duszynski

Hurricane
238 Squadron
Flt/Lt Hughes

He111
Stab/KG1

DUNGENESS

He111
2/KG26

Me110
ZG26

Spitfire
92 Squadron
P/O Hargreaves

WISSANT

He111
Stab II/KG26

MARQUISE

He111
5/KG26

RAF and Luftwaffe crash locations

BOULOGNE-SUR-MER

RAF Casualties

11 September 1940 - 15.30 - 17.30 hrs Combat A.

RAF Casualties	Combat A	15.30 – 17.30 hrs

1 (RCAF) Sqn Hurricane P3534 YO-S F/O T B Little - wounded. Shot down whilst attacking He111s and crashed at Lakestreet Manor, Mayfield, East Sussex. Pilot baled out wounded in leg and landed at Rotherfield. Admitted to Kent and Sussex Hospital, Tunbridge Wells with burns to face and side. 23-year-old Canadian Thomas Little re-joined his squadron on 30th November.

1 (RCAF) Sqn Hurricane V6670 YO-Z F/O P W Lochnan - safe. Crash landed and burnt out on Romney Marsh, Kent, after attacking He111s.

17 Sqn Hurricane P3892 YB-I Sgt L H Bartlett - safe. Damaged over the Thames Estuary.

19 Sqn Spitfire N3046 F/O F Dolezal - wounded. Damaged over London. Pilot slightly wounded in leg, but he was flying again by the 18th.

19 Sqn Spitfire P9546 QV-H F/Sgt G C Unwin - safe. Landed at Canterbury Tye Spring, Shenfield, Essex, after being damaged by Me109s over London. After on-site repairs, Unwin flew the aircraft back to Duxford. Damaged included a bullet in the armoured windscreen.

19 Sqn Spitfire X4059 F/O L A Haines - safe. Crashed on landing with punctured tyres after being damaged over London.

41 Sqn Spitfire N3059 Sgt I E Howitt - safe. Landed at West Malling. The engine sustained two broken connecting rods and seized after the oil cooler was damaged by Me109s.

41 Sqn Spitfire X4325 P/O G A Langley - safe. Shot down whilst attacking bombers over Sevenoaks. Aircraft fell at Bewley Fm, Plaxtol, Kent. 24-year-old Gerald Langley baled out safely.

41 Sqn Spitfire X4343 P/O G H Bennions - wounded. Damaged by Me110s over Maidstone. Pilot slightly wounded in left heel.

46 Sqn Hurricane V6549 Sgt R E de Cannart d'Hamale - wounded. Shot down and crashed at School Fields, Sandhurst, Kent. Pilot baled out landing at Court Lodge, Bodiam, injured in forehead.

46 Sqn Hurricane V7232 Sgt W A Peacock - missing. Possibly the aircraft that fell at Rookelands, near Newchurch, Kent. A Browning machine gun found days after the crash was identified as being from V7232, but neither the aircraft nor pilot of the aircraft that fell at Rookelands have been identified to the satisfaction of the MoD and its pilot is still recorded as 'missing'. See also P/O Clarke of 504 Squadron.

William Albert Peacock (20)
Born: West Hartlepool.
Joined the RAF in January 1938.
Joined 46 Squadron on 18th July 1940 from 7 OTU.
Victory claims - 2:
3/9/40 Do17 damaged.
8/9/40 Me109 destroyed.

46 Sqn Hurricane P3094 PO-V P/O P R McGregor - wounded. Crash-landed and burned out in West Lordine Wood, Staplecross, East Sussex. 23-year-old Peter McGregor re-joined his squadron in December 1940.

72 Sqn Spitfire R6710 P/O B Douthwaite - wounded. Landed at Benover, near Yalding, Kent, and wrecked. Pilot suffered an eye injury.

73 Sqn Hurricane P2796 TP-U Sgt H G Webster - safe. Shot down by Me110s and crashed at Warren Farm, Boxley, Kent. Pilot baled out and landed two miles away.

73 Sqn Hurricane P3868 Sgt R V Ellis - safe. Damaged by Me110s over the Isle of Sheppey.

92 Sqn Spitfire K9793 P/O F N Hargreaves - missing. Shot down by Me109s and Me110s. Fell into the Channel off Dungeness.

222 Sqn Spitfire R6638   P/O W R Assheton - safe. Force-landed on Parsonage Farm, Fletching, East Sussex.

222 Sqn Spitfire P9364   Sgt E Scott - safe. Cockpit hood shattered by Me109 whilst attacking He111s over Tunbridge Wells.

229 Sqn Hurricane P3038 P/O M Ravenhill - safe. Shot down over Biggin Hill whilst covering his leader's tail. Aircraft fell at Polhill, Knockholt Pound, Kent. Pilot baled out and admitted to Langley Hospital, Maidstone, suffering from shock.

229 Sqn Hurricane P3463 RE-L   F/Lt R F Rimmer - wounded. Landed at Northolt after being attacked from behind by an Me109 whilst engaging an He111 over Biggin Hill. 20-year-old Reginald Rimmer suffered slight facial cuts from pieces of Perspex. Windscreen shattered, longeron damaged and rudder unserviceable.

Frederick Norman Hargreaves (21)
Born: Whitefield, Lancashire.
Joined the RAF in June 1939.
Joined 92 Squadron in March 1940.
Victory claims - none.

229 Sqn Hurricane N2466 RE-Z   P/O K M Carver - wounded. Set alight during engagement with He111s over Maidstone and crashed by the Goudhurst Road, Horsmonden. Kenneth Carver baled out with burns and re-joined his squadron in 1941.

238 Sqn Hurricane P3096 P/O W Towers-Perkins - wounded. Shot down south of Tunbridge Wells. Aircraft fell near Elkland Bridge, Hartfield, East Sussex. 22-year-old William Towers-Perkins baled out and landed 4 miles away near Withyham Post Office. He was admitted to Tunbridge Wells Hospital with burns to his face, hands and legs, and an injury to his left thigh. Later he was transferred to the Queen Victoria Cottage Hospital, East Grinstead, for treatment under Sir Archibald McIndoe and was discharged in April 1942 to the RAF Hospital, Torquay, but did not fly again. William Towers-Perkins had joined 238 Squadron straight from 6 OTU on 20th August 1940 and later became the first secretary of 'The Guinea Pig Club'.

238 Sqn Hurricane V7240 F/Lt D P Hughes - missing. Presumed to have fallen into the sea.

David Price Hughes (22)
Born: Reading, Berkshire.
Joined the RAF in February 1936.
Joined 238 Squadron on 4th August 1940 after converting to Hurricanes at 6 OTU.
Victory claims - 6:

8/8/40 Me110 destroyed.	13/8/40 Me110 destroyed.
11/8/40 Me109 destroyed.	13/8/40 Me110 destroyed.
13/8/40 Do17 destroyed.	13/8/40 Me109 probable.

238 Sqn Hurricane R2682   Sgt S Duszynski - missing. Shot down over the Romney Marsh. Aircraft crashed at Little Scotney, Lydd, Kent. The remains of Stanislaw's Hurricane and presumably human remains were dug up twice in 1973, once by a local group and subsequently by the RAF, but he remains officially 'missing'.

Stanislaw Duszynski (24)
Born: Torun, Poland.
After the fall of Poland he made his way to the UK.
Joined the RAF in February 1940.
Joined 238 Squadron on 2nd September 1940 from 6 OTU.
Victory claims - none.

RAF Casualties

11 September 1940 - 15.30 - 17.30 hrs Combat A.

238 Sqn Hurricane P3618   P/O W Rozycki - safe. Landed safely in a field at Old Alresford when out of fuel.

249 Sqn Hurricane V6682   Sgt W L Davis - wounded. Shot down whilst attacking He111s. Aircraft fell on the verge of New Pond Road, ¼ mile south of Benenden Cross Roads. 21-year-old William Davis baled out and was taken to No.7 Casualty Clearing Station Benenden. He re-joined his squadron in December 1940.

257 Sqn Hurricane V7338   Sgt R H B Fraser - slightly injured. Damaged on landing at Martlesham Heath after the pilot failed to turn on reserve petrol tank.

266 Sqn Spitfire II P7313   P/O R J B Roach - safe. Hit by return fire from He111s and abandoned. Aircraft fell at Well Farm, Great Burstead, Essex. 20-year-old James Roach landed safely at Pipps Hill, Basildon.

303 Sqn Hurricane V7465 RF-V   F/Lt A S Forbes - wounded. Force-landed at Heston after being damaged over south London. Shrapnel in right shoulder. Bullet hole in tailwheel.

Left: A recycled Hurricane! Athol Forbes's V7465 was taken away for repair and then reissued to 229 Squadron and coded RE-B. Note the overpainted 303 Squadron emblem just under the radio mast.

303 Sqn Hurricane V6667 RF-K   F/O A Cebrzynski - killed. Shot down and crashed at Hitchens Farm, Pembury, Kent. Pilot baled out, but suffered serious burns and later died in hospital. *Note: 303 Squadron's ORB incorrectly recorded the serial number as V6665 - which was lost on 27th September.*

Arsen Cebrzynski (28)
```
Born: Batumi (then Russia,now Georgia).
Fought with the Polish Air Force and with l'Armee de l'Air.
Joined the RAF in July 1940.
Joined 303 Squadron on 21st August 1940.
Victory claims - 7:
3 serving with the Polish Air Force.
3 serving with l'Armee de l'Air.
11/09/40 Do17 probable.
```

Casualty File   Accident to Hurricane V6667

The squadron took off at 15.30 hours to intercept enemy formations over the Horsham area. F/O Cebrzynski was killed in action and his body taken to the mortuary at Pembury Hospital. It has not been possible to obtain any information about his combat. He was shot in many places and one leg was blown completely off. It appears that his harness was severed and that he fell out of the aeroplane when it turned upside down. It is obvious that he could have been in no position to try to open his parachute.

303 Sqn Hurricane V7242 RF-B   Sgt S Wojtowicz - killed. Shot down by Me109s and crashed on Hogtrough Hill, Brasted, Kent.

Stefan Wojtowicz (24)
Born: Wypnicha, Poland.
Fought with the Polish Air Force and with l'Armee de l'Air.
Joined the RAF in June 1940.
Joined 303 Squadron on 2nd August 1940.
Victory claims - 4:
7/9/40 Do17 destroyed.
7/9/40 Do17 destroyed.
11/9/40 Me109 destroyed.
11/9/40 Me109 destroyed.

Casualty File

The squadron took off at 15.30 hours to intercept enemy formations over the Horsham area. Sgt Wojtowicz was believed to have been seen engaging a number of Me109s near Westerham. He was in fact shot in the forehead by a cannon shell and crashed in flames two miles east of Westerham Village, and his body taken to the mortuary there. Local Special Police state that during the few minutes of the combat two Me109s crashed in the neighbourhood of Westerham and there is reason to believe that they were accounted for by Sgt Wojtowicz

Eyewitness
Dennis Knight visited Hogtrough Hill in 1961 and interviewed people who vividly recalled the events 21 years earlier.

The Hurricane pilot had been in combat at low altitude and was chasing an enemy aircraft along the crest of a range of hills. The Hurricane came from the east, swept over Chevening Park up the low slopes of the hill, but failed to clear the trees bordering the wood that climbs over Hogtrough Hill.

Splintering treetops, the fighter dropped a few feet, dug its way into the ground, and cartwheeled into the 100 acre field above the chalk pits. The aircraft burst into flames and farm workers who raced up the hill were unable to reach the pilot because of the intense heat, and soon the aircraft was reduced to a tangle, with popping ammunition throwing sparks and fragments in all directions.

501 Sqn Hurricane P5200 SD-W   Sgt T G Pickering - safe. Shot down by Me109s over Kenley and crashed at Happy Valley, Old Coulsdon, Surrey. 20-year-old Tony Pickering landed safely on Caterham Guard's Barracks, where he was initially suspected of being a German.

Personal account of Tony Pickering in 1985

I remember the flight, and we as a squadron were scrambled from Kenley to intercept a large force of bombers. We carried out a head-on attack from about 10,000 feet. I felt the aircraft shudder violently, the engine poured out black smoke and after a short time I saw flames appearing. Not wishing to receive 'Hurricane Burns' I hastily went over the side. I was only 500 feet or so above the ground when I saw the aircraft hit the ground and I was probably only 800 -1,100 yards away, enjoying a grandstand view of the incident. I landed by parachute within the Guards Depot at Caterham. I vividly remember the Irish Guards officer with an eye patch who came over. As I was only dressed in a shirt, slacks, Mae West, no uniform and no boots, I had some difficulty in persuading him of my nationality! I was back at Kenley that evening having been posted temporarily as missing.

RAF Casualties

11 September 1940 - 15.30 - 17.30 hrs Combat A.

504 Sqn Hurricane P3429 TM-R   P/O M Rook - safe. Undercarriage collapsed on take-off.

504 Sqn Hurricane N2471   P/O J V Gurteen - safe. Oil pressure failure shortly after take-off.

504 Sqn Hurricane P3770   P/O A W Clarke - missing. Possibly the aircraft that fell at Rookelands, near Newchurch, Kent. Parts of a Hurricane were recovered from the crash site in the winter of 1972-1973. A pair of silk flying gloves were found bearing the name 'Clarke' but neither the aircraft nor pilot of the aircraft that fell at Rookelands have been identified to the satisfaction of the MoD and its pilot is still recorded as 'missing'. A memorial erected close to the crash site is dedicated to P/O A W Clarke.
Arthur Clarke had been a boarder at the same school as P/O Frederick Hargreaves of 92 Squadron, who was also shot down and killed this day.

Arthur William Clarke (20)
Born: Timperley, Cheshire.
Joined the RAF in March 1938.
Joined 504 Squadron on 7th April 1940.
Victory claims - none.

Casualty File   Accident to Hurricane P3770 piloted by P/O A W Clarke.

On 11th September, 1940 at approximately 15.45 hours, No.504 Squadron was patrolling over Kent in company with another squadron which it was following. A formation of enemy bombers escorted by fighters was seen crossing the coast south of Lympne at about 15,000 feet.

No. 504 Squadron followed the leading squadron into the attack and carried out a beam attack from the starboard side. On breaking away the squadron became split up and returned singly to base, but P/O Clarke did not return.

P/O Clarke was flying in the second section and none of the following sections or anybody else saw him shot down. The engagement took place about five miles inland. It can only be presumed that if P/O Clarke went down with his aircraft the aircraft was so broken up on hitting the ground that the pilot could not be identified, although no information has been received of any such crash. It is also possible that he might have landed by parachute in the sea as the wind was in such a direction that it would have blown him out to sea.

605 Sqn Hurricane P3828   F/O R Hope - safe. Landed at Redhill due to engine failure.

605 Sqn Hurricane P3588   S/Ldr W M Churchill - slightly wounded in one arm. Damaged and landed near Maidstone. Walter Churchill became operational again on 25th September.

611 Sqn Spitfire II P7321   Sgt S A Levenson - safe. Shot down by return fire from He111s and crashed attempting to land with a dead engine at Pendell Court, Bletchingley, Surrey.

611 Sqn Spitfire II P7298   Sgt F E R Shepherd - killed. Set alight during combat over Croydon. Abandoned aircraft crashed into No. 51 Hartland Way, Shirley. Pilot baled out with his parachute burning and was seen from the ground beating at his clothes in a desperate attempt to extinguish the flames. He fell from his harness and was found dead at Frylands Wood, off Featherbed Lane, Farleigh.

Frederick Ernest Richard Shepherd (22)
Born: Birkenhead.
Joined the RAF and 611 Squadron as an Aircrafthand pre-war.
Re-joined 611 Squadron after training on Spitfires on 1 September 1940.
Victory claims - none.

Casualty File

811129 Sgt Shepherd F E R

On 11/9/40 12 aircraft of this squadron, including Spitfire P7298 flown by 811129 Sgt F E R Shepherd, took off at 15.30 hours from the Duxford Satellite landing ground together with 2 other squadrons, for a patrol over the London area. I was leading the squadron, and Sgt Shepherd was No.4 in my section of 4 in line astern. Soon after 16.00 hours the squadron became heavily engaged at 20,000 feet with a number of Me110s which were escorting a large enemy bomber formation. From this engagement Sgt Shepherd failed to return, and no other pilot of the squadron had any reliable information about him.

On 14/9/40 it was learnt by a signal from Aston Down that RAF Croydon had informed them that Sgt Shepherd died on 11/9/40 - diagnosis multiple injuries.

An officer of this squadron attended the funeral on 24/9/40 at Whyteleaf Cemetery, Kenley. He was then informed verbally at Kenley that Sgt Shepherd was shot down in action on the 11th, that the aircraft crashed in flames at 16.15 hours in Kingswood Lane, Sanderstead, that the pilot had baled out but that his parachute had caught fire and that he had fallen close to the aircraft, and finally that from an engineer's examination of the wreckage, it appeared possible that the aircraft had been hit by anti-aircraft fire.

S/Ldr McComb
Officer Commanding
611 Squadron

Air Raid Precautions Committee

Air Raid on Croydon 11th September 1940, during this raid, one British fighter plane crashed. The engine fell in garden of No.32 Hartland Way, damaging the house. The main body of the plane crashed behind No.51, slightly damaging the house. Petrol flowed into air raid shelter, burning Mrs Weston, two children, and another woman, all of whom subsequently died in hospital. Further portion of plane fell in front of No.74 causing appreciable damage.

Civilian Dead
Mrs Winifred Neeves Weston - aged 28 years. Died in hospital on the 12th.
John Arthur Weston - aged 2 years. Died in hospital on the 11th.
Julia Mary Weston - aged 8 months. Died in hospital on the 12th.
Nancy Laura Davis - aged 17 years. Died in hospital on the 12th.
(From the Commonwealth War Graves, Record of Civilian War Dead)

Below: Fred Shepherd was flying a brand new, Castle Bromwich made, Spitfire MkII like this one. 611 Squadron was the first to receive the MkII and this and the loss of P7321 in the same combat are believed to be the first combat losses of MkIIs.

The Missing Pilots of Romney Marsh

11 September 1940

The Romney Marsh is an area of featureless, flat, land measuring about 10 miles by 10 miles square. It is low-lying, some actually below sea-level, and is criss-crossed by drainage ditches. It is quite unlike the rest of Kent and few people live there. In 1940 it was believed by the British Army to be at the centre of the expected German invasion, which indeed it was.

On 11th September, four aircraft fell on Romney Marsh: a Heinkel that force landed, a Hurricane from 1(RCAF) Squadron that crash landed and burnt out, and two other Hurricanes that dived into the ground with such force that they buried themselves deeply in the marsh. The identities of these two Hurricanes have proved to be among the most perplexing mysteries of the Battle of Britain.

The Hurricane at 'Rookelands'

Harry Flower, special correspondent for the The Daily Telegraph, watched the events unfold over the Romney Marshes on September 11th from a vantage point at Lympne. He recalled the events to veteran researcher Dennis Knight in 1960.

Left: Feldwebel Heinz Friedrich (left) walks away under guard from his Heinkel 111 1H+CB, which he has just force landed on Romney Marsh. Daily Telegraph correspondent Harry Flower was there with a Fox photographer to record what happened, as the burning Heinkel was circled by a Spitfire, (seen below).

The Missing Pilots of Romney Marsh

11 September 1940

The Daily Telegraph
12 September 1940

Soon a dozen Heinkels and Dorniers were heading back seawards in half a dozen different directions. On the tail of each was a Hurricane or Spitfire. And then they began to fall.

Three Dorniers with tell-tale whisps of smoke showing from their engines as they came lower dived for the sea in the hope of reaching the coast.

A Great Heinkel passed over my head flying low and in obvious distress following a rattle of machine-gun fire up in the sun. A Hurricane slipped over some tree tops on a hill. Poured a short burst into the Heinkel, which caused the bomber to lurch wildly and then 'hedge-hop' across field after field trying to find a safe landing.

Dennis Knight recorded how Harry Flower's story continued.

The Pressmen hurried off in their car towards the place where the bomber had disappeared behind trees. As a guide they had the lone Hurricane which was orbiting a dense cloud of oily brown smoke which climbed into the sky. With a policeman and a whole mobile column of troops they reached the field where the Heinkel had crashed and surged forward to apprehend the crew.

Four of the airmen climbed out and lifted out a fifth crew member who was wounded. One of the crew, a thick-set sergeant pilot, was inclined to be somewhat recusant, while the remainder seemed rather embarrassed by his swaggering. He and at least one other crew member wore the ribbon of the Iron Cross. Flower chatted with the pilot as he smoked a cigarette whilst the Fox photographer took a series of pictures, one being quite unique since it showed the German pilot with burning bomber in the background and the victorious Hurricane flying overhead.

Shortly after this a formation of Messerschmitts were engaged over the Kent Coast, and one aircraft fell like a stone out of the sky. When Flower reached the spot, all that remained was a pit made by the aircraft which had plunged bodily into the earth for many feet, leaving only a few pieces on the surface.

Of course, Harry Flower had no idea of the identity of either aircraft. The bomber proved easy to identify in post-war years; with the availability of information both German and British, it was Heinkel He111 1H+CB of Stab I/KG26 that had been landed by its pilot Fw Heinz Friedrich. But what of the second aircraft?

The Missing Pilots of Romney Marsh

11 September 1940

Harry Flower did not specify whether it had been German or British, but no Luftwaffe aircraft fell as he described in that area on that day. It must therefore have been an RAF fighter that had fallen reasonably close to the Heinkel at Burmarsh. Only one crash site fits his description, the site recorded by several independent sources as at Rookelands, south of Newchurch.

There are two possible identities:
504 Sqn Hurricane P3770   P/O A W Clarke – missing.
46 Sqn Hurricane V7232   Sgt W A Peacock – missing.

The 1976 Excavation

Mike Llewellyn of the nascent Kent Battle of Britain Museum was told of the crash at Rookelands in 1976 and arranged to excavate the wreck, which ultimately proved too difficult to recover fully with the equipment available. Several pieces of wreckage were found, among which was the map box from a Hurricane's cockpit and in the box was a pair of gloves bearing the name 'Clarke'.

With the knowledge available at that time it was clear that he had found the Hurricane of 20-year-old Arthur Clarke of 504 Squadron who had disappeared on 11th September 1940. Arthur's name appears on the Runnymede Memorial to missing RAF airmen and his family expressed their wish that he should be left to rest in peace in his aircraft. In accordance with the family's wishes, the wreck has never been further investigated and a memorial to Arthur was erected by the roadside within sight of the crash site.

New Clues

In 2014 The Ministry of Defence began to release the casualty files relating to airmen injured or killed during WW2. Among the many hundreds of files is that of Sergeant William Peacock, a Hurricane pilot with 46 Squadron, who had disappeared on 11th September 1940.

The documents contained within the file are routine, sad in their content and sadly routine. Sergeant Peacock had not returned from the combat, no one had witnessed his demise, the Air Council expressed their condolences to his parents. However, within the handwritten notes on the minutes sheet a remarkable, and seemingly hitherto unnoticed story, unfolds.

The day after the crash a salvage gang from RAF Hawkinge arrived to recover and identify the aircraft and its pilot. Equipped with a lorry to take away the wreckage, and a block and tackle to drag tubes and wires of the Hurricane's fuselage out of the ground, they went about their grim yet routine job. Shattered body parts were found, but nothing to identify the pilot, and several machineguns. Each Browning gun bore a serial number and these numbers were forwarded to the Air Ministry as a form of identification. At that time records were maintained of gun serial numbers so by 17th September Browning B.49375 had positively been identified as having being fitted to Hurricane V7232 flown by Sergeant Peacock. The last sentence reads, 'Therefore the body is identified as No. 808268 Sgt W A Peacock 46 Sqn'. However, what subsequently happened to the 'body' is not recorded and Sergeant Peacock remained listed as 'missing'.

80 years on, the identity of pilot who died at Rookelands cannot be confirmed.

The Hurricane at 'Little Scotney'

As Harry Flower was watching the air battle on the eastern edge of Romney Marsh, another Hurricane plummeted from the sky a few miles to the west on the other side of the marsh. The aircraft buried itself deeply in the ground at Little Scotney, Lydd. Whether the salvage gang from Hawkinge attended the site is not recorded, but if they did little if anything was recovered.

In 1973 Dave Buchannan was scouring the marshes for aircraft parts to display in his museum at Brenzett and was told of the crash at Little Scotney. His excavation proved that the Hurricane was almost completely buried and that the pilot was buried with it. Part of the Hurricane was found bearing the aerial number R2682, the aircraft in which the 24-year-old Polish pilot, Sergeant Duszynski of 238 Squadron had disappeared on 11th September 1940. Realising that Duszynski had no known grave and that this was an important discovery Buchannan informed the correct authorities and a few weeks later an RAF team arrived at the site to fully excavate it. Operating alone, the RAF team recovered the Hurricane and its pilot's remains. Anticipating news that Stanislaw Duszynski would be finally laid to rest, Dave Buchannan waited, but no news nor information was forthcoming, other than an overheard remark that the remains had been cremated in Ashford Hospital. Enquiries over many years met with silence - the body of Stanislaw Duszynski had seemingly 'disappeared'. He remains officially 'missing' to this day. The RAF's Casualty File on Sgt Duszynski AIR81/3201 is available, but contains no reference to the 1973 recovery or subsequent enquiries. Any post-war correspondence has been removed and placed in a separate file AIR81/3200 - and that file will not be made available until 1st January 2075.

Luftwaffe Casualties	Combat A	15.30 – 17.30 hrs

1/JG3 Me109E-4 Wn.5276 Collided with Ofw Hessel off Dover. Ff: Oblt Lothar Keller baled out and rescued.

1/JG3 Me109E-4 Wn.5341 Returned with 25% damage after collision with Oblt Keller Ff: Ofw Franz Hessel safe.

6/JG3 Me109E-4 Wn.5056 Landed at Wierre-au-Bois with 45% damage.

2/JG51 Me109E-4 Wn.1641 Black 6+ Crashed in flames at Houndean Bottom, Lewes. East Sussex. Ff: Hptm Ernst Wiggers killed. *See report of Sgt Higgins, 253 Squadron.*

8/JG51 Me109E-1 Wn.6293 Black 9+ Crashed at Foxhole Farm, Wadhurst, East Sussex. Ff: Fw Hermann Siemer killed. *See report of A-S/Ldr Edge, 253 Squadron.*

Stab KG1 He111H-3 Wn.5606 V4+FA Started with about thirty other bombers to bomb the Commercial Dock, London, from 21,000 feet. Hit by AA in one engine and then chased to the coast by fighters, which stopped the other engine. The pilot landed at Broomhill Farm, East Guldeford, East Sussex, and set fire to the aircraft which burnt out. Bo: Lt Otto Behm and Ff: Fw Johannes Sommer both PoWs. Bf: Uffz Paul Moeck, Bm: Uffz Gerhard Arndt, and Bs: Gefr Martin Männich all wounded PoWs.
See reports of P/O Watkinson and P/O Bodie, 66 Squadron.

1/KG1 He111H West India Docks. Returned with 10% damage by AA fire and fighters. Bm: Fw Fritz Schöwer badly wounded. Rest of crew safe.

3/KG1 He111H-3 Wn.3233 V4+KL The route taken was Clairmont - Mouth of Somme (where the fighter escort was picked up - Boulogne - London, this aircraft being in the leading Kette. Bombed West India Docks from 19,000 feet and then hit by AA fire which stopped the starboard engine due to loss of oil. Falling behind the formation the aircraft was attacked by fighters that according to the crew 'shot up everything that there was to shoot up'. The pilot belly landed at Hildenborough, Kent, due to wounded being on board, rather than bale out. The crew tried to set fire to the aircraft with an incendiary bomb, but soldiers pulled it out. Ff: Uffz Herbert Steinecke and Bo: Uffz Walter Hirsch both PoW. Bf: Uffz Erwin Kramer, Bm: Gefr Willi Pfeiffer, and Bs: Gefr Heinrich Pümpel all wounded PoWs.
See reports of F/Lt Parnall, P/O Neil and P/O Pattullo, 249 Squadron.

3/KG1 He111H-3 Wn.6852 V4+AL Landed at Amiens with 60% damage on return from bombing the West India Docks. Bm: Fw Hermann Klammer badly wounded and died following day, Bo: Obfw Hans Welscher and Bf: Uffz Willi Berg both badly wounded.

Luftwaffe Casualties

11 September 1940 - 15.30 - 17.30 hrs Combat A.

6/KG1 He111H-2 Wn.5364 V4+RW Started from a small field aerodrome twenty miles south-east of Amiens to bomb ships in the London Docks. The route was St. Pol - Cap Griz Nez - London, the fighter escort being picked up over Cap Griz Nez. About twenty-five to thirty bombers took part flying in Ketten Vic astern. This aircraft was the last of the formation. Before sighting London they were attacked by fighters that stopped both engines. The bombs were jettisoned and the pilot made a landing at Broomhill Farm, East Guldeford, East Sussex, where the crew set the aircraft on fire. Ff: Uffz Bernhard Hansen, Bo: Uffz Karl Markert, Bm: Uffz Johannes Krall, and Bs: Gefr Günter Wilhelm all PoWs. Bf: Uffz Hans Wiesehoff wounded PoW.
See reports of S/Ldr Leigh, F/O Oxspring and Sgt Hunt, 66 Squadron, and P/O Wright of 92 Squadron.

6/KG1 He111H-2 Wn.2733 V4+BW Landed with 10% damage at Boisville, France, on return from London. Bs: Gefr Quirin Steger badly wounded and died the following day. Bm: Gefr Fritz Kostka slightly wounded. Rest of crew safe.

Stab I/KG26 He111H-4 Wn.6965 1H+AB Landed with 15% damage at Wevelgem, Belgium, on return from London. Crew safe.

Stab I/KG26 He111H-3 Wn.5616 1H+BB Landed with 40% damage at Wevelgem, Belgium, on return from London. Bm: Uffz Günter Wolf badly wounded and lost his right arm. Rest of crew safe.

Stab I/KG26 He111H-3 Wn.5680 1H+CB Started from Courtrai and met their fighter escort at Dover. Before reaching London the aircraft was hit by AA fire and damaged by fighters. The bombs were jettisoned near Sevenoaks and the pilot landed at Burmarsh, Kent, where the crew set fire to the aircraft. Ff: Fw Heinz Friedrich, Bf: Uffz Kurt Hoffmann, Bm: Uffz August Dreyer, and Bs Uffz Heinz Stirnemann all PoWs. Bo: Fw Heinz George was also captured, his wounds were so severe that he was repatriated to Germany in 1943 via the Red Cross.

Below: Another Press photo of Feldwebel Heinz Friedrich after being captured on Romney Marsh.

1/KG26 He111H-4 Wn.6981 1H+KH Attacked 19,000 ft by 'fifteen Spitfires' before reaching London. The right engine was hit, so the crew fired a red Verey signal to show they were damaged and jettisoned the bombs. They were attacked a second time by three Spitfires and pilot Ff: Fw Wilhelm Jabusch baled out from 6,000 feet over Uckfield where he was captured at Ketches Farm. *See reports of F/Lt McKellar and P/O Jones, 605 Squadron.*
A complete uniform bearing the name Uffz Schilling, including a greatcoat on a clothes hangar, an Iron Cross and other decorations, a ceremonial dagger, a set of shaving tackle and a large flat iron floated down from the heavens in the Tonbridge area.

The Bo: Lt Franz Zimmerman then took control and flew the aircraft back to Dieppe, where he crash-landed with his crew. Bs: Sdfr Wilhelm Trapp slightly wounded. Bf: Fw Gerhard Schilling and Bm: Oberfw Wolfgang Hasebrink safe.

1/KG26 He111H-4 Wn.6962 1H+AH   Target Woolwich. When over the target area at 15,000 feet the crew found that the bombs would not release and on leaving the target they were hit by AA fire. The aircraft crashed at Gate Farm, Staplecross, East Sussex, where the bomb load later exploded. Hptm Wolfgang Künstler, Ff: Fw Erich Büttner and Bm: Uffz Erich Schmidt all PoWs. Bf: Fw Johannes Schäfer and Bo: Uffz Walter Schang both killed. *See report of P/O Lock, 41 Squadron.*

1/KG26 He111H-4 Wn.6977 1H+EH   Returned with 15% damage. Bf: Gefr Johannes Fritzsche slightly wounded. Rest of crew safe.

1/KG26 He111H-4 Wn.3214 1H+HH   Returned with 40% damage. Ff: Oblt Johannes Lensch badly wounded and died following night. Rest of crew safe.

2/KG26 He111H-3 Wn.3215 1H+JK   Fell into the Channel. Bf: Fw Walter Horn killed. Rest of crew rescued by Seenotdienst.

2/KG26 He111H-3 Wn.5603 1H+FK   Returned with 15% damage. Ff: Uffz Rudolf Blutharsch and Bo: Fw Richard Hilland both slightly wounded. Rest of crew safe.

3/KG26 He111H-3 Wn.6854 1H+BL   Returned with 15% damage. Crew safe.

3/KG26 He111H-3 Wn.3157 1H+ML   Target London Docks. When over the target the aircraft was hit by AA fire in one wing and fell back from the main formation. It was then attacked by Hurricanes and Spitfires that stopped both engines. The pilot and the wireless operator baled out before it crashed at New Barns Farm / Hoopers Farm, Dormansland, Surrey. Ff: Oblt Wolf Abenhausen baled out unhurt PoW. Bf: Fw Heinz Hauswald baled out wounded PoW. Bo: Fw Henry Westfalen baled out, but parachute caught on aircraft and he fell dead on the Starborough Estate. Bm: Uffz Bruno Herms and Bs: Gefr Fritz Zähle both killed.
See reports of F/Lt McGregor, F/O Molson and F/O Yuile, 1 (RCAF) Squadron. S/Ldr Blake and P/O Rozycki, 238 Squadron. P/O MacPhail of 603 Squadron. P/O Currant and P/O Glowacki of 605 Squadron and Sgt Levenson of 611 Squadron.

Stab II/KG26 He111H-3 Wn.6856 1H+AC   Returned with 25% damage. Ff: Fw Krothe, Bo: Major Eckhard Christian, and rest of crew all safe.

Stab II/KG26 He111H-5 Wn.3545 1H+BC   Fell into the Channel. Bm: Uffz Erwin Meusel killed, Ff: Lt Ernst Wesemann, Bf: Fw Heinz Gies, and Bo: Fw Hermann Gutacker all missing.

4/KG26 He111H-5 Wn.3540 1H+CM   Returned with 30% damage. Ff: safe, Bs: Flgr Walter Patzl killed, Bm: Uffz Erich Scheinert badly wounded in legs, Bm: Fw Richard Hermann slightly wounded.

5/KG26 He111H-3 Wn.6903 1H+JN   Started from Holland for a target in the Thames Estuary. They were following the Staffelkapitän, the escort being picked up over Dover at 18,000 feet. Before reaching the target, they were attacked by fighters and being damaged they turned for home, but had to make a forced landing in the sea 5 miles off Hastings. Bo: Lt Ferdinand Cramer killed, Ff: Oblt Gustav-Otto Bertram, Bf: Gefr Gustav Schröter and Bm: Gefr Rudolf Endrich rescued by fishing boat all PoW unhurt.

5/KG26 He111H-3 Wn.6936 1H+EN   Landed at Gilze-Rijen with 40% damage. Crew safe.

5/KG26 He111H-3 Wn.3935 1H+FN   Returned with 30% damage. Crew safe.

1(J)/LG2 Me109E-7 Wn.5579   Wrecked on landing at Wissant. Ff: Fhr Hans-Joachim Marseille safe.

3(J)/LG2 Me109E-7 Wn.2029   Dived into the ground by the Pilgrim's Way, Wrotham Hill, Kent. Ff: Uffz Albert Hechmeier killed. *See references to Sgt Wojtowicz, 303 Squadron, and Sgt Budzinski, 605 Squadron.*

1/ZG26 Me110C-4 Wn.2190 U8+KH   Landed at Calais-Marck with 20% damaged sustained off Dover. Bf: Uffz Josef Haschke killed, Ff: Oberlt Wilhelm Spies safe.

Stab II/ZG26 Me110C-4 Wn.3625 3U+HM   Fell into the sea three miles off Margate. Ff: Oblt Walter Henken missing, Bf: Fw Josef Radlmair killed.
See report of F/Lt Bayne and F/O Czernin, 17 Squadron.

Luftwaffe Casualties

11 September 1940 - 15.30 - 17.30 hrs Combat A.

2/ZG26 Me110C-3 Wn.1372 U8+HL   Started from St. Omer with between twenty and thirty fighters forming the escort for He111s. While flying at 13,000 feet before reaching the target an engine defect developed and while coming down this aircraft was attacked by a fighter. Pilot landed with retracted undercarriage at Cobham Farm, Charing, Kent. Ff: Fw Hermann Brinkmann and Bf: Uffz Erwin Grüschow both PoW.

4/ZG26 Me110D-2 Wn.3392 3U+DM   Fell into the sea. Ff: Oblt Randoald Birkner and Bf: Uffz Hermann Klaiber both missing.

6/ZG26 Me110D-2 Wn.3400 3U+HP   Fell into the sea. Ff: Lt Rudolf Volck missing, Bf: Obergefr Ernst Hofmann killed.
East Sussex Police reported that an aircraft landed on the sea off Winchelsea Beach. Two airmen were seen on the wings, but disappeared when the plane sank. Rescue boats were sent out, but failed to find anything. This is believed to refer to one of the lost ZG26 Me110s.

9/ZG26 Me110C-4 Wn.3231 3U+LT   Dived Into the ground at Barnes Cote, Harvel, Kent. Ff: Oblt Joachim Junghans and Bf: Gefr Paul Eckert both missing.
See report of Sgt Jennings, 19 Squadron and P/O Glowacki, 605 Squadron.

Stab II/ZG76 Me110C-4 Wn.3285 M8+KC   Ditched in the Channel. Crew both rescued by the Seenotdienst.

Above: More views of Me110 U8+HL of 2/ZG26 at Cobham Farm in Kent.

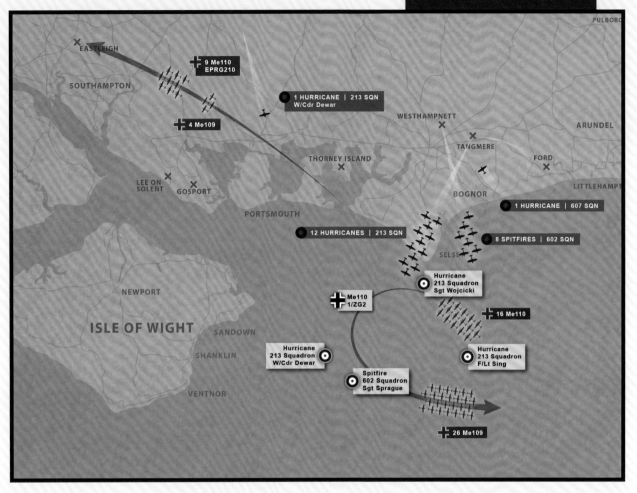

As the main attack on London was taking place, another raid approached from Cherbourg and the Seine far to the west. Three squadrons were scrambled from Tangmere to meet the raids heading for Selsey Bill. 607 Squadron stayed over Tangmere to guard against another attack, while 213 Squadron was briefed to take on the bombers and 602 Squadron the fighters that appeared, as predicted, 5 miles east south-east of Selsey Bill at 16.10 hours. The briefed target was the Supermarine works at Eastleigh, near Southampton. As the combat developed Erprobungsgruppe 210's Me110s broke away and bombed the Cunliffe Owen aircraft works, adjacent to the Supermarine works. Although the damage to the factory was not considered 'significant', 46 workers were killed immediately, 48 were seriously injured and 41 more slightly injured. The final death-toll rose to 52.

602 Sqn 8 Spitfires up from Westhampnett to intercept over Selsey Bill T.O. 15.42 Hrs
213 Sqn 12 Hurricanes up from Tangmere to intercept over Selsey Bill T.O. 15.45 hrs
607 Sqn 1 Hurricane up from Tangmere to patrol base T.O. 15.45 hrs

Luftflotte 3 Report
Frame 499

A special attack was made on the Supermarine works at Southampton at 16.15 hours by nine Me110s and four Me109s of Eprg 210 that dropped 23 x SC500 and 1 Flam 250. Escort was provided by 16 Me110s from II and III/ZG76, V(Z)/LG1 and ZG2 with 26 Me109s from I and III/JG27, JG2 and II/JG53 *. One Me110 of Eprg 210 did not attack because of the lack of cloud cover, but dropped two SC250 bombs on Littlehampton railway station. Two Me110s dropped four 500kg bombs on Portsmouth Harbour.
One Ju88 of I/KG54 bombed Banbury and one Aldershot.
Losses 1 Me110 of ZG2.

Author's note: From the Luftwaffe's own records it would appear that Luftflotte 3 struggled to get enough aircraft and pilots to form the escort and with a total of just 42 aircraft none of the units were operating at anything approaching full strength.

RAF and Luftwaffe Victory Claims

11 September 1940 - 15.45 - 16.50 hrs Combat B

RAF Victory Claims	The Southampton Raid		15.45 - 16.50 hrs
213 Sqn	F/Lt J E J Sing	Me110 damaged	Selsey Bill
213 Sqn	F/O R W Kellow	Me110 destroyed	Selsey Bill
213 Sqn	F/O M Duryasz	Me110 destroyed	Selsey Bill
213 Sqn	P/O G Cottam	Me110 damaged	Selsey Bill
213 Sqn	Sgt M E Croskell	Me110 destroyed	Selsey Bill
213 Sqn	Sgt R T Llewellyn	Me110 destroyed	Selsey Bill - north Portsmouth
213 Sqn	Sgt R T Llewellyn	Me110 destroyed	Selsey Bill - north Portsmouth
602 Sqn	F/Lt R F Boyd	Me109 destroyed	5 miles south of Selsey Bill
602 Sqn	F/Lt R F Boyd	Me109 probable	5 miles south of Selsey Bill
602 Sqn	Sgt C F Babbage	Me110 destroyed	5 miles south of Selsey Bill
602 Sqn	Sgt A McDowall	Me110 destroyed	5 miles south of Selsey Bill
602 Sqn	Sgt J Proctor	Me110 destroyed	5 miles south of Selsey Bill
602 Sqn	Sgt J Proctor	Me110 damaged	Selsey Bill

Luftwaffe Victory Claims	The Southampton Raid		15.45 - 16.50 hrs
JG2	Unknown pilot	Hurricane	
3/JG27	Oblt Gerhard Homuth	Hurricane	5km south west of Selsey Bill
15(Z)/LG1	Oblt Otto Weckeiser	Hurricane	Southampton
LG1	Unknown pilot	Hurricane	
ZG2	Unknown pilot	Hurricane	
ZG2	Unknown pilot	Hurricane	
4/ZG76	Oblt Walter Borchers	Hurricane	south of Portsmouth
6/ZG76	Oblt Wilhelm Herget	Hurricane	5-10km east of the Isle of Wight
III/ZG76	Unknown pilot	Hurricane	

Below: Devastation in the Cunliffe Owen aircraft works in Southampton after the 11 September raid. Aircraft being repaired in this photo are two Albacores, a 615 Squadron Hurricane and a Heinkel 111!

213 SQUADRON INTELLIGENCE REPORT

Combat took place at Selsey Bill at 16.05 hours 11.9.40. 12 aircraft of 213 Squadron had taken off from Tangmere at 15.45 hours to patrol base. They were vectored to Selsey Bill where about 20 Me110s were sighted and a combat took place at 15,000 feet. The enemy were flying in slight echelon, line astern, and immediately formed a circle as our aircraft approached. 213 Squadron carried out a quarter attack, attacking in the following order: Red Section, Blue Section, Yellow Section, Green Section.

Red Leader (F/Lt Sing), carried out a quarter attack on an Me110 and damaged it, but before he could attack a second time he was himself hit, and baled out. He was picked up out of the sea by a tramp steamer and landed at Shoreham.

Red 3 (Sgt Llewellyn) carried out a quarter attack on an Me110 and fired a two seconds burst at it from 100 yards, the e/a immediately dived vertically into the sea. He then turned his attention to the enemy bombers (Jaguars) which were then behind Portsmouth. He carried out a beam attack on the rear Jaguar which was flying to and fro, acting as 'Lookout'. He opened fire at 300 yards, closing to 75 yards, giving three or four bursts and saw smoke and flames coming from it, when last seen the aircraft was burning furiously.

Meanwhile Yellow 1 (F/O Kellow) had singled out an Me110 and after a quarter attack on it watched it dive into the sea.

Yellow 3 (F/O Duryasz) did precisely the same thing, and also watched his opponent dive into the sea.

Yellow 2 (Sgt Croskell) waited above the circle of e/a until they turned for home, then he attacked the rear one from above and from the beam. E/A immediately went into a steep dive into the sea. In 'A' Flight Blue 2 (P/O Cottam), Blue 1 (F/Lt Strickland) and Green 3 (Sgt Dunscombe) all carried out quarter attacks on Me110s and claim a damaged a/c each. One of our pilots is missing - Sgt Wojcicki (Polish). He was seen to make for centre of the enemy a/c and go down in flames.

COMBAT REPORT:
F/Lt J E J Sing, Red 1, A Flight, 213 Squadron

I was leading the squadron on patrol over Selsey Bill when E/A were sighted. We attacked and I carried out a quarter attack and damaged one Me110. There was some smoke coming from port engine which was idling. I was not able to see what happened to E/A. I climbed up and round into sun to make a second attack but before I could attack I was shot down. Shells hit gravity and glycol tanks. Elevators were damaged. I was unable to see anything owing to smoke and baled out. I did not see the machine which shot me down.

COMBAT REPORT:
F/O R W Kellow, Yellow 1, A Flight, 213 Squadron

As Yellow 1 I was patrolling Selsey Bill behind Red Section. 15 Me110 were sighted 10 miles south and the formation climbed up into the sun and the Me110s formed line astern and turned round to form a circle. I followed the last 110 round and the one from the end banked steeply inwards going round the circle. I gave one burst of approx. 10 secs which struck the E/A underneath. It turned upwards, stalled and fell to the sea with smoke trailing behind. I followed it down to 7,000 ft and saw it go straight into the water.

COMBAT REPORT:
F/O M Duryasz, Yellow 3, A Flight, 213 Squadron

I was No. 3 Yellow Section when we intercepted E/A over Selsey Bill. One broke away. I went below it and had a good target and gave it a short burst in a left-hand turn. Left engine started smoking. It started to dive down, I followed it down to within 1,000 ft of sea when it burst into flames and dived straight into water.

Contemporary Accounts 602 Sqn

11 September 1940 - 15.45 - 16.50 hrs Combat B

602 SQUADRON INTELLIGENCE REPORT

Combat took place 5 miles off Selsey Bill at 16.10 hours. 602 Squadron, 8 Spitfires, took off from Westhampnett at 15.42 hours. Blue 1 (F/Lt Boyd) leading, ordered to patrol base at 15,000 feet in co-operation with 213 Squadron Hurricanes 1,000 feet below. 602 Squadron was to attack enemy fighters, 213 enemy bombers. On south course at 19,000 feet over Selsey Bill, 213 being on same course in front and approximately 3,000 feet lower, there were sighted 20/30 Do17s (query Me Jaguars) escorted behind by 20/30 Me110s all at 15,000 feet on northerly course several miles east-south-east. There were also approximately 25 Me109s at 23/25,000 yards behind Do17s and Me110s but presence of these was not immediately seen. E/A were not in easily defined formations. 213 Squadron circled to port of e/a preparatory to flank attack, and 602 Squadron made wider circle to attack Me110s.

Blue 1 and Blue 2, Green 2 and Red Section in line astern dived to attack Me110s which had formed defensive circle. Blue 3 (fitted with V.P. airscrew) was unable to keep up with other Spitfires (fitted with C.S. airscrew) and accompanied 213 to attack. Blue 3 reports presence of Me Jaguars which formed defensive circle on being attacked. Green 1 was suspicious that Me109s might be present so flew full circle of e/a at 19,000 feet and was shortly attacked by Me109s, being compelled to dive to 8,000 feet to escape. Red 3 broke from Spitfire formation to attack Me110s before Squadron Leader did so. Blue 1 attacked two Me110s without result and then attacked single Me109 head-on 250 yards closing to 150 yards 2 second burst; this e/a destroyed. Then attacked second Me109 full beam from below 250 yards closing to 150 yards 2 seconds burst, seeing heavy black smoke from between radiator and leading edge of wing; this e/a claimed as probable. Blue 2 followed Blue 1 and three times attacked Me110, first full beam 250 yards closing 100 yards 3 seconds, second head-on 400 yards closing 100 yards 3 seconds (head-on attack accounts for long opening range), third full beam 250 yards closing to 100 yards 3 seconds; this e/a crashed in sea. Blue 3 selected Me Jaguar which had broken from defensive circle and was flying south, beam attack changing to a quarter astern 300 yards, closing to 50 yards 9 seconds; this e/a fell away and crashed in sea. Blue 3 climbed, saw Me Jaguars had formed line astern and were approaching Portsmouth, and attacked a straggler, beam 250 yards closing to 30 yards 5 seconds, using all ammunition. Blue 3 claiming this Jaguar damaged as whole of Perspex was shot away. Green 1 in breaking away from Me109s dived to 8,000 feet and attacked single Me110 flying south-east dead ahead opening 400 yards closing to 150 yards, 3 seconds (head-on attack accounts for long opening range) and destroyed this e/a.

7 Spitfires landed Westhampnett by 16.35 hours. Weather hazy up to 7,000 feet. Cloud negligible.

Enemy losses	Pilots	Ammunition	Stoppages
1 Me109 destroyed (sea)	Blue 1 (Leader)		
1 Me109 probable	F/Lt Boyd	600	Nil.
1 Me110 destroyed (sea)	Blue 2 S/P Babbage	1260	Nil.
1 Jaguar destroyed (sea)	Blue 3 S/P Proctor	2400	Nil.
1 Jaguar damaged			
1 Me110 destroyed (sea)	Green 1 S/P McDowall	1200	Nil.
Not known	Green 2 S/P Sprague	not known	-
Nil	Red 1 F/Lt Mount	1950	2 split cases
Nil	Red 2 P/O Payne	2000	Nil.
Nil	Red 3 P/O Rose	160	Nil.
		9570	

COMBAT REPORT:
Sgt A McDowall, Green 1, B Flight, 602 Squadron

I was Green 1 and when Villa Leader (Blue 1) climbed above and behind Me110s escorting Do17s and dived to attack, I felt that Me109s were present although I could not see them, so circled again and was then attacked by enemy Me109s. I fired at and possibly damaged 3 Me109s. I was forced to break away and dived. At 8,000 ft when on NW course up Channel Coast off Isle of Wight, I saw one Me110 approaching me in the opposite direction. I did attack 10 to 15 degrees off dead ahead (on his starboard side) and he dived vertically into the sea, making a big splash between Selsey Bill and the Isle of Wight. I then returned to Westhampnett.

COMBAT REPORT:
Sgt C F Babbage, Blue 2, B Flight, 602 Squadron

I was Blue 2 and followed Blue 1 in attack on Me110s. One Me110 before we got within range detached itself from remainder and headed south. I attacked this full beam from 500 feet above on E/A's starboard side, and broke away behind. E/A then turned into sun but I saw it again manoeuvring to attack me. I made head-on attack same altitude, swinging left to avoid return fire. I climbed into sun, and made another beam attack. E/A dived 45 degrees and I followed until it crashed into sea. I climbed back to 16,000 ft and was attacked by 2 Me110s which were on a southerly course, one of which I fired at without visible effect (head-on); after breaking away I lost sight of E/A and returned to base.

COMBAT REPORT:
Sgt J Proctor, Blue 3, B Flight, 602 Squadron

I was Blue 3 but could not maintain position with Blue 1 (fitted with VP airscrew instead of CS airscrew) and when I got tallyho saw Jaguars 1,000 ft below at 9 o'clock from me when I was flying West. I had no hope of catching Spitfires so attached to other Hurricanes and selected a Jaguar that had broken away from circle (they were circling when Hurricanes attacked). I did beam attack changing to quarter astern from slightly above using up 2/3 of my ammunition. E/A fell away close to circle of Jaguars and I followed 1,000 ft and I watched this E/A dive into sea, 7 miles south east of Isle of Wight. There were three small ships in close proximity and nearer shore.

I climbed again towards the sun. The circle by now formed into long line and was approaching Portsmouth. I selected a straggler at same altitude and did one beam attack. I saw perspex at top fuselage break up all along. All my ammunition was then expended so I dived to sea level and returned to base.

Below: A 602 Squadron Spitfire at Westhampnett during the Battle of Britain. The trolley acc is plugged in ready for a quick start. Note how the serial number has been painted out, a common early war security feature.

RAF and Luftwaffe Casualties

11 September 1940 - 15.45 - 16.50 hrs Combat B

RAF Casualties	Combat B	15.45 – 16.50 hrs

213 Sqn Hurricane W6667 AK-P   Sgt A Wojcicki - missing. Fell into the Channel one mile off Selsey when flying with Green Section. during combat with Me110s.

Antoni Wojcicki (26)
Born: Essen, Germany.
Joined the RAF in February 1940.
Joined 213 Squadron 19th August 1940 from 6 OTU.
Victory claims - none.

213 Sqn Hurricane P3780 AK-A   F/Lt J E J Sing - safe. Hit in glycol and gravity petrol tank by unseen aircraft during combat off Selsey Bill. Pilot baled out, landed in the sea and picked up by a ship.

213 Sqn Hurricane V7306   Acting W/Cdr J S Dewar DSO DFC (Station Commander Exeter flying a 213 Squadron aircraft) - killed. Failed to arrive at Tangmere on routine flight from Exeter to attend a conference the following day and pay a surprise visit to his wife. Aircraft shot down into the Solent. Body washed ashore at Kingston Gorse, Sussex on 30.9.40.

John Scatliff Dewar (33)
Born: Mussoori,Lahore Province, India.
Joined the RAF in 1926.
Joined 87 Squadron in December 1939.
Victory claims - 11.
5 in the Battle of France.

11/7/40 Me110 destroyed.   13/8/40 Ju88 destroyed.
11/7/40 Me110 destroyed.   25/8/40 Ju88 destroyed.
11/7/40 Me110 damaged.   25/8/40 Me109 probable.

Highest ranking RAF officer to be killed in the Battle.

253 Sqn Hurricane P2883 SW-R   Unknown pilot - safe. Damaged.

602 Sqn Spitfire L1027   P/O S N Rose - wounded. Landed at Westhampnett after being damaged over Selsey Bill. Pilot had gunshot wound in left elbow. Starboard mainplane, tailplane and fuselage extensively damaged by cannon shells and bullets.

602 Sqn Spitfire X4269   Sgt C F Babbage - safe. Starboard wing damaged by Me110s over Selsey Bill.

602 Sqn Spitfire N3282   Sgt M H Sprague - killed. Shot down by Me110s south of Selsey Bill. Crashed into the Channel. Pilot washed ashore at Brighton on 10.10.40.

Mervyn Herbert Sprague (30)
Born: Richmond, Surrey.
Joined the RAF in 1935.
Joined 602 Squadron 18th June 1940.
Victory claims - none.

Luftwaffe Casualties	Combat B	15.45 – 16.50 hrs

1/ZG2 Bf110C-4 Wn.3576 A2+MH Fell into the Channel while escorting Erprobungsgruppe 210 to Southampton. Ff: Gefr Erich Kling and Bf: Gefr Waldemar Sossna missing.

Note: Although Luftwaffe records record this aircraft loss as a 1 Staffel machine, the unit code of 'A2' denotes a II/ZG 2 aircraft, the fourth character 'H' denoting 4th Staffel. This could indicate that 1 Staffel borrowed a 4 Staffel machine, and then had a 2 Staffel crew to fly it. Or a clerical error could have been made and the true fuselage code was 3M+MH.

1/ZG2 Bf110C-4 Wn.3623 3M+LH Landed at St Aubin with 50% damage. Crew safe.

The loss of Johnny Dewar

11 September 1940 - 15.45 - 16.50 hrs Combat B

Casualty File

23rd October 1940

26029 A/W/Cdr J S Dewar DSO, DFC

Sir,

I have the honour to refer to No.213 Squadron's signals A.85 dated 12th September, 1940 and P.41 dated 30th September, 1940 concerning the circumstances in which the late 26029 A/W/Cdr J S Dewar DSO, DFC was reported missing and previously reported missing now killed in action.

A/W/Cdr J S Dewar on 11th September, 1940 gave orders that he would be flying to Tangmere and the normal procedure for advising Operations at this station was carried out.

This officer took off at 15.00 hours in Hurricane V.7306 and before doing so was advised of enemy activity over Selsey Bill. The route, however, to be flown was from Exeter, via Winchester, then to Tangmere, thus avoiding the balloon barrage over Southampton.

The flight was expected to take some forty minutes in duration and ETA being 16.00 hours.

At 16.00 hours intense enemy activity developed over the Southampton area and it is presumed that A/W/Cdr J S Dewar decided to engage the enemy, although there is no definite evidence to support this supposition. A pilot of the rear protective section reported later that he noticed a lone Hurricane had followed his squadron just before the enemy aircraft were engaged.

S/Ldr R S Mills, acting Station Commander at RAF Exeter, examined the Raid Tracings of Sector Station Tangmere, and formed the opinion in view of anti-aircraft gunfire over Southampton, that A/W/Cdr J S Dewar followed one of the operating squadrons and definitely sought engagements as he would have been in the operational area at about that time.

On 30th September, 1940 a body clothed in a shirt was washed up on the beach at Kingston Gorse, Sussex, and subsequently identified as A/W/Cdr J S Dewar by means of laundry marks. A tunic was also found nearby the body, marked J. S. D. and had the ribbons of DSO and DFC.

It was established that this officer was killed by machine gun fire, there being bullet wounds in the back and head, and the left leg was practically shot off.

I have the honour to be,
Sir,
Your Obedient Servant

R S Mills
Squadron Commander, Commanding,
No.87 Squadron, RAF

COMBAT C 17.45 - 18.45 hrs... Ashford and The Channel

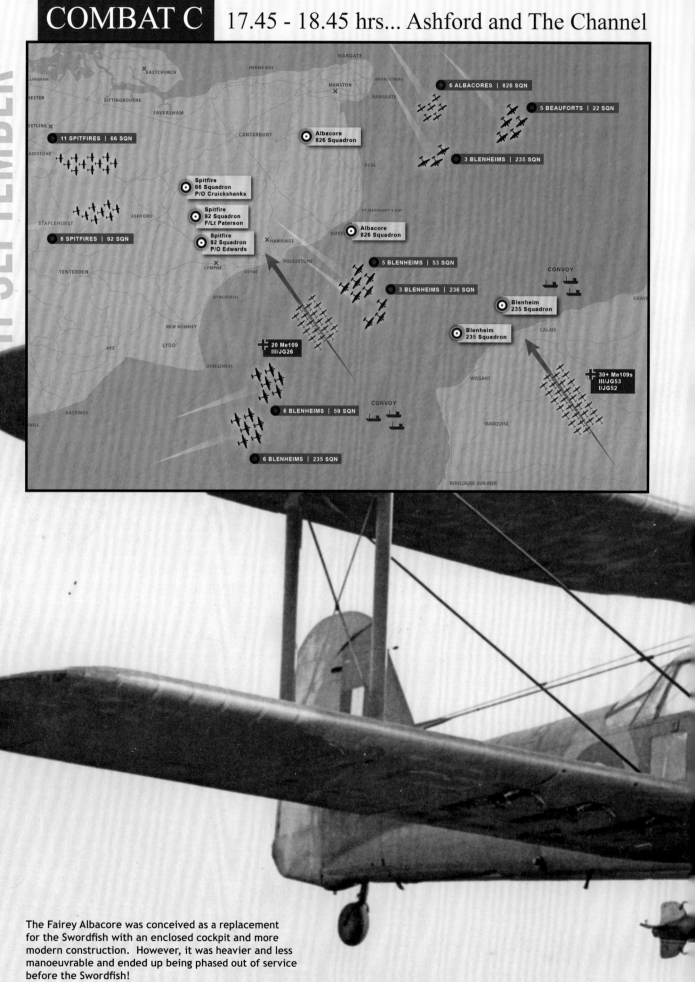

The Fairey Albacore was conceived as a replacement for the Swordfish with an enclosed cockpit and more modern construction. However, it was heavier and less manoeuvrable and ended up being phased out of service before the Swordfish!

Battle of the Albacores

11 September 1940 - 17.45 - 18.45 hrs Combat C

During the day a photographic reconnaissance Spitfire reported shipping off the Belgian coast, moving west. Two special Blenheim sorties were then dispatched by 53 Squadron Coastal Command to shadow a convoy of ten enemy vessels steaming towards Calais. It was believed that the convoy comprised ships towing barges to be used in the impending invasion and a 'Strike Force' was rapidly assembled by 16 Group.

235 Squadron Coastal Command* sent 3 'fighter Blenheims' from Bircham Newton in Norfolk to escort 6 Albacores of 826 Squadron Fleet Air Arm, also from Bircham Newton, to Calais.

236 Squadron Coastal Command* 'A' Flight sent 3 'fighter Blenheims' from St Eval to Detling to escort 5 Blenheims of 53 Squadron Coastal Command, based at Detling, to a convoy 5 miles south west of Calais.

22 Sqn sent 5 Beauforts from North Coates in Lincolnshire to rendezvous with their fighter escort over Detling.

235 Squadron Coastal Command 'B' Flight sent 6 'fighter Blenheims' from Thorney Island in West Sussex to escort 6 Blenheims of 59 Squadron Coastal Command, also from Thorney Island, to Boulogne.

These squadrons were transferred from Fighter Command to Coastal Command, but the airmen qualified for the Battle of Britain clasp.

An escort to protect the bombers from prowling Me109s whilst over Kent was to be provided by 8 Spitfires from 92 Squadron and 11 from 66 Squadron.

The planned rendezvous between the two Spitfire squadrons did not happen and 92 Squadron ran into a fighter sweep of Me109s near Ashford where two of their Spitfires were shot down.

The Albacores and Blenheim bombers carried on and made a shallow diving attack on the convoy off Calais, but no hits were observed. Heavy anti-aircraft fire was encountered from a coastal battery at Calais. In an engagement with 36 enemy fighters, three Me109s were claimed brought down and a Do18 hit.

In a second attack by 59 Squadron off Gris Nez between 17.12 and 17.20 hours, one merchant vessel was left burning amidships and another probably damaged by two near misses. An Me109 was claimed shot down into the sea and an E-Boat was seen picking up the survivor.

Two fighter Blenheims of 235 Squadron were shot down, one Albacore lost and three others damaged.

22 Squadron's 5 Beauforts from North Coates missed the rendezvous with their fighter escort over Detling and went on alone and attacked shipping off Ostend. One 6,000 ton ship was claimed as sunk by torpedo; one torpedo exploded on a sandbank and three failed to release due to electrical failures.

RAF and Luftwaffe Victory Claims

11 September 1940 - 17.45 - 18.45 hrs Combat C

RAF Victory Claims		Ashford and The Channel		17.45 - 18.45 hrs
92 Sqn	S/Ldr P J Sanders	Me109 probable	Ashford	
92 Sqn	P/O A R Wright	Me109 probable	Folkestone	

Luftwaffe Victory Claims		Ashford and The Channel		17.45 - 18.45 hrs
Stab III/JG26	Hptm Gerhard Schöpfel	Blenheim		
7/JG26	Oblt Joachim Müncheberg	Spitfire	east of Ashford	
8/JG26	Lt Heinrich Oetteking	Spitfire	West of Ashford	
8/JG26	Fw Josef Gärtner	Hurricane	south east London	
8/JG26	Lt Gustav Sprick	Hurricane	Canterbury-Ashford	
8/JG26	Fw Gerhard Grzymalla	Spitfire	south east London	
1/JG52	Lt Günter Büsgen	Albacore	north west of Calais	
1/JG52	Lt Günter Büsgen	Blenheim		
1/JG52	Lt Franz Essl	Blenheim	north west of Calais	
1/JG52	Ofw Oskar Strack	Albacore	north west of Calais	
Stab III/JG53	Hptm Wolf-Dietrich Wilcke	Albacore	Dover-Calais	
8/JG53	Oblt Walter Fiel	Blenheim	Calais	
8/JG53	Oblt Walter Fiel	Albacore	Calais	
8/JG53	Oblt Siegfried Stronk	Albacore	Calais	
9/JG53	Oblt Jakob Stoll	Blenheim	Calais	

92 SQUADRON INTELLIGENCE REPORT

Eight aircraft of 92 Squadron were ordered to take off from Biggin Hill at 17.45 hours to escort bombers to the Channel. They were to join 66 Squadron above base but did not contact. 92 Squadron was vectored towards Ramsgate and when over Ashford encountered a formation of Me109s. Squadron was split up and individual attacks were carried out with the result that two Me109s were seen to half roll and dive down with smoke coming from them.

Five aircraft landed at Biggin Hill about 19.20 hours. One aircraft landed at Gravesend to re-fuel and stayed there on account of darkness.

F/O Paterson baled out - aircraft burnt out. Pilot very slight burns and now being treated in Woolwich hospital.

P/O Edwards is missing - no news yet received.

COMBAT REPORT:
S/Ldr P J Sanders - Ganic Leader - 92 Squadron

After patrolling Ashford to Ramsgate at 16,000 feet I sighted smoke trails above me near Dover. I climbed to investigate and found several single Me109s at 20,000 feet. I gave the warning 'Snappers' and attacked one from below and slightly to the left using deflection. I could see the bullets striking the enemy aircraft and grey smoke came out. E/A half rolled very slowly to the right and dived out of sight.

COMBAT REPORT:
P/O A R Wright - Green 1, B Flight, 92 Squadron

I took off at 17.45 hours in formation of eight aircraft. We escorted bombers to the channel. At approximately 18.15 hours squadron split up and attacked some Me109s above (our height 20,000 feet). I managed to climb to same height as one Me109. I could not catch him up so fired four second burst from 500 yards. He immediately dived sharply with some smoke and I lost him going towards Folkestone. Still diving at over 500 mph at 5,000 feet.

235 SQUADRON OPERATIONS RECORD BOOK

'A' Flight (3 aircraft from Bircham Newton) escorting bombing raid by Albacores on Calais. Formations were attacked by AA and Me109s.

'G' F/Lt Flood shot down.

'D' P/O Coggins returned

'E' P/O Wickings-Smith shot down

2 Me109s were shot down, one by P/O Coggins after the E/A had shot down P/O Wickings-Smith, with him was P/O Green Observer and Sgt Watts Air Gunner. F/Lt Flood failed to return with his crew P/O Shorrocks and Sgt Sharp.

'B' Flight (6 aircraft from Thorney Island) cooperating with 6 Blenheims of 59 Sqn from Thorney Island carried out escort sighted 4 Me109s and F/Lt Fletcher shot one down, P/O Wordsworth and Sgt Hobbs concentrating on one Me109 fired remainder of ammunition. It is believed that this E/A was badly damaged. Remainder flew off. These operations were carried out after dusk. Cloudy.

'A' F/O Laughlin returned

'J' P/O Jackson Smith returned

'K' Sgt Hobbs

'Q' Sgt Sutton

'P' Sgt Nelson

'?' P/O Wordsworth

236 SQUADRON OPERATIONS RECORD BOOK

A Flight from St Eval 10.30 hrs for Detling. 3 Blenheims to escort 5 Blenheims of 53 Sqn to convoy 5 miles SW Calais. 36 E/A seen.

Below: Blenheims of 235 Squadron photographed during the Battle of Britain.

RAF and FAA Casualties

11 SEPTEMBER

RAF Casualties	Ashford and The Channel	17.45 - 18.45 hrs

66 Sqn Spitfire X4339 P/O I J A Cruickshanks - injured. Force-landed north-east of Ashford.

92 Sqn Spitfire R6613 F/Lt J A Paterson - injured. Shot down by Me109s and crashed at Zigzag Farm, Hastingleigh, Kent. 20-year-old New Zealander James Paterson baled out with his clothes on fire and landed with a badly burned face. He insisted on returning to his squadron as soon as possible and made a flight six days later, even though he could not see properly.

92 Sqn Spitfire P9464 P/O H D Edwards - killed. Shot down by Me109s and crashed into a wood at Evegate Manor Fm, Smeeth, Kent.

Casualty File

P/O H D Edwards - killed in action 11/9/40

P/O Edwards took off from Biggin Hill with 7 other aircraft to escort bombers to the Channel. The squadron was over Ashford when a large formation of Me109s was encountered.

After the combat, which was individual, P/O Edwards was missing. On the 7th October notification was received from Hawkinge that P/O Edwards' machine had been found at Evegate Farm, Smeeth, near Hawkinge.

The body was recovered from the wreck by Home Guards and buried at Hawkinge on 10/10/40.

Above: New Zealander James Paterson of 92 Squadron was shot down and badly burned in this combat, but returned to his squadron and flew just six days later. Just ten days after that, his fellow pilots saw him again struggling to get out of a blazing Spitfire after being hit by a 109. Sadly, he didn't make it, he was just 20 years old.

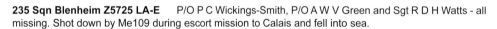

Harry Davies Edwards (24)
Born: Manchester (although said to be from Winnipeg, Canada).
Joined the RAF in January 1939.
Joined 92 Squadron in October 1939.
Victory claims - 6 in the Battle of France.

235 Sqn Blenheim Z5725 LA-E P/O P C Wickings-Smith, P/O A W V Green and Sgt R D H Watts - all missing. Shot down by Me109 during escort mission to Calais and fell into sea.

235 Sqn Blenheim L9396 LA-G F/Lt F W Flood, P/O N B Shorrocks and Sgt B R Sharp - all missing. Shot down by Me109 during escort mission to Calais and fell into sea.

826 Sqn FAA Albacore L7097 Damaged by Me109s north-west of Calais and returned to Bircham Newton. Sub-Lt A H Bacon and crew safe.

826 Sqn FAA Albacore L7098 Damaged by Me109s north-west of Calais and landed near Staple, Kent. Sub-Lt T Winstanley and crew safe.

826 Sqn FAA Albacore L7114 Damaged by Me109s north-west of Calais and returned to Bircham Newton. Sub-Lt A M Tuke (Pilot) unhurt, Sub-Lt E G Brown (Obs) and NA1 R E Matthews (Gunner) both wounded.

826 Sqn FAA Albacore L7117 Badly damaged by Me109s north-west of Calais and ditched just outside Dover Breakwater. Lt A S Downes wounded and Sub-Lt C R Mallett unhurt - both rescued by MTB and landed at Dover, NA1 J A M Stevens (Gunner) missing.

Peter Claude Wickings-Smith (22)
Born: Southend, Essex.
Joined the RAF in 1939.
Joined 235 Squadron 5th August 1940.
Victory claims - none.

Alexander William Valentine Green (21)
Born: Craigavad, County Down, Ireland.
Joined the RAF in June 1939.
Joined 235 Squadron March 1940.
Victory claims - none.

Reginald Douglas Haig Watts (23)
Born: Far Cotton. Northampton.
Joined the RAF in April 1939.
Joined 235 Squadron July 1940.
Victory claims - none.

Frederick William Flood (25)
Born: Roma, Queensland, Australia.
Joined the RAF in April 1936.
Joined 235 Squadron 1st June 1940.
Victory claims - 2.
1/6/40 He111 damaged.
21/8/40 Hs126 destroyed.

Norman Basil Shorrocks (29)
Born: Chorlton, Lancashire
Joined the RAF in June 1939.
Joined 235 Squadron 1st April 1940.

James Alexander Moffat Stevens (18)
No details known.

Bruce Robertson Sharp (27)
Born: Edinburgh, Scotland.
Joined the RAF in November 1938.
Joined 235 Squadron July 1940.

Luftwaffe Casualties	Ashford and The Channel	17.45 - 18.45 hrs

None identified.

Other Casualties

11 September 1940

46 Sqn Hurricane P3525 PO-S   Sgt S Andrew - killed. Returning from an operational patrol, broke away from formation and stalled in a very steep turn too near the ground at Stapleford Tawney. 11.10 hrs.

Stanley Andrew (21)
Born: Swanland, Yorkshire.
Joined the RAF in 1937.
Joined 46 Squadron in April 1939.
Victory claims - 2.
8/9/40 Do17 destroyed.
8/9/40 Do17 damaged.

Luftwaffe Casualty

Führungskette X Fliegerkorps Heinkel He111H-3 Wn.3253 P4+BA Damaged and port engine stopped by AA fire when attacking a convoy north of Kinnaird Head, Scotland. Landed at Stavanger-Sola - 30%.
Ff: Hptm Robert Kowalewski wounded in neck, rest of crew safe.. Aircraft P4+BA

Left: As night fell on the 11th, London's defences prepared for another busy night. This all female crew are operating a sound locator which helped to track the flightpath of incoming bombers.